UNCOMMON SENSE
THE LIFE OF
MARSHALL ERDMAN

■ ■ ■

BY DOUG MOE AND ALICE D'ALESSIO

Trails Custom Publishing

Black Earth, Wisconsin

Library of Congress Catalog Card Number: 2003105887
ISBN: 1931599319

Development Editor: Daniel Erdman
Project Manager: Becky Peck
Creative Director: Kathie Campbell
Graphic Design: Hoot Communications

All proceeds from the sale of this book benefit the Frank Lloyd Wright Foundation.

Printed in China.
08 07 06 05 04 03 6 5 4 3 1
Trails Custom Publishing, a divison of Trails Media Group, Inc.
P.O. Box 317, Black Earth, WI 53515
(800) 236-8088
e-mail: info@wistrails.com
www.trailscustompublishing.com

To Bayla, Jonas, and Nonas Erdmanas, mother, father,
and brother of Marshall Erdman who did not live
to share in the wonderful life their son
and sibling enjoyed in his adopted country.

THIS BOOK WAS BASED IN LARGE PART on interviews conducted with Marshall Erdman's friends, associates, and family. For sharing their memories and thoughts, the authors wish to thank: Fred Miller, the late Ed Hart, Gaylord Nelson, Grace Lukken, Marvin Braude, Connie Threinen, Charlotte Turyn, David Levitan, Max Levitan, Debbie Erdman, Tim Erdman, Rustin Erdman, Jean Massell, Jackie Collins, Dominick Russo, the late Phil Derse, Margaret Derse, Paul Okey, the late Collins Ferris, Bob O'Malley, Dick Garland, Jack Kammer, George Garner, Edgar Tafel, the late Bob Kassell, Howard Crook, Ingo Grebe, Roger Hauck, Ellen Johnson, Tom Rosengren, Joan Burke, Jim Bradley Sr., Jerry Sholts, Leon Stutzman, Tom Casey, Andres Duany, and Dorothy Ballantyne.

Books, newspapers, and periodicals also were helpful. The authors drew on articles about Erdman in *The Capital Times,* the *Wisconsin State Journal,* the *Milwaukee Journal, Isthmus, In Business* magazine and *Madison Magazine. The Emergence of Modern Lithuania* by Alfred Senn and *The University of Wisconsin: A Pictorial History,* by Arthur Hove were likewise helpful, and especially the book *Frank Lloyd Wright and Madison: Eight Decades of Artistic and Social Interaction,* most particularly the excellent chapter on the Unitarian Meeting House written by Mary Jane Hamilton and the chapter by Paul Sprague on prefabricated houses.

Bob Davis, architect and de facto Erdman company archivist, was an enormous help guiding us through voluminous amounts of company historical material. Tom Brock shared with us his research on Shorewood Hills history. And the Wisconsin State Historical Society was generous in assisting with photographs.

In addition, Mary Jane Hamilton deserves special thanks for her patient perseverance in finding source material and supplying the authors with invaluable information about Frank Lloyd Wright, the building of the Unitarian Meeting House, and the Wright-Erdman prefabricated houses, among other topics.

We are grateful to Gaylord Nelson for providing a foreword to this book, filled with his own reminiscences of his long friendship with Marshall. Finally, a special note of appreciation is due to Marshall's youngest son, Dan Erdman, who first contacted the authors with the idea for a book on his father. Dan persevered as the point man throughout the long period of research and writing, offering encouragement and good humor. Simply put, without Dan there would be no book.

by Gaylord Nelson

former Wisconsin state senator,
Wisconsin governor, and U.S. senator

THOUGH MARSHALL ERDMAN WAS A good friend and delightful companion for almost a half century, I wouldn't attempt to describe what he was all about. No matter what I said, it would fall short. However, all who knew him could and would agree that he was a remarkable person by any measure, by any standard. And to a rare degree, he possessed in abundance all of those qualities we most honor and cherish.

In my eighty-seven years of rattling around the world, I have been privileged to know some quite exceptional people—not just good, honorable, decent people who have contributed much to the common welfare, which is admirable in and of itself, but genuinely exceptional people who stand out because they have done far more. If I were to jot down a list of exceptional people I have known, Marshall would rest comfortably at the very top.

As friends of Marshall know, his first prestigious work as a builder was the Frank Lloyd Wright–designed Unitarian Meeting House in Madison, Wisconsin. This lucky opportunity came to him as a young fellow just getting started in the building business. Frank Lloyd Wright had sought a well-known builder out of Chicago who was much too expensive. Marshall was suggested by one of the members of the congregation, and he undertook the task because he relished the opportunity to work with the great architect. Near the end of the project, the building fund was exhausted and Marshall cashed in his life insurance policy to pay for the materials to complete the construction. Marshall considered that he was adequately rewarded by the opportunity to work with Mr. Wright and learn from him, and ultimately to become a friend.

Over the years, Marshall worked on a number of projects with Mr. Wright. One day Marshall asked Mr. Wright a profound question and forthwith received a profound answer. He said, "Mr. Wright, when you have finished a building, how do you know whether it is good?" That's a complicated question with endless ramifications. One could write a book trying to explain, and many have. But Wright had the answer ready. He said, "It's very simple. If you walk into a house that doesn't have any furniture and you feel as comfortable as you do in your best-tailored suit, it is good." Marshall already knew that, but he hadn't thought of it in Wright's descriptive way. Marshall was not a technician with a slide rule. He was an artist. He could instantly see and feel what was right and wrong with a design or a concept. Marshall didn't learn it from Wright. It came from within himself.

Marshall knew that excellence was in the details, and no detail was too small to warrant his attention. On weekends, I enjoyed traveling around with Marshall, visiting his buildings in various states of construction. On one occasion, we looked at a house he was building for a Madison doctor. It was designed by Frank Lloyd Wright. Some small detail about the design concerned him, so he had to drive directly and immediately out to Taliesin to resolve it with Mr. Wright. Incidentally, this would be my first introduction to Mr. Wright. About twenty minutes after we arrived at Taliesin, Mr. Wright materialized in the living room jauntily attired in an elegant cape and a flowing tie. Marshall introduced us, saying, "Mr. Wright, this is Senator Nelson. He's your state senator."

Mr. Wright glanced briefly in my direction and turned to Marshall, saying, "Marshall, do we really need one?"

If I were asked to describe those qualities that best characterized Marshall, a few words immediately jump out: integrity, quality, an uncompromising commitment to excellence, a love of beauty, generosity, compassion, and, despite his many recognitions and successes, modesty.

In the mid-1980s, Marshall redecorated his offices on University Avenue with a wonderful dis-play of art in the hallways, waiting rooms, and offices. The place looked like an elegant art gallery. On the day of the grand opening for public visitation, I walked around with Marshall on his final inspection. Everything was as close to perfection as it could get—but not close enough for Marshall. He opened a cabinet door, and as he closed it, he heard a little click of wood on wood. He immediately inspected the door, only to discover that someone had made the horrendous blunder of failing to affix those little fingernail-sized felt pads on the inside corners of the door. It was just one hour before the grand opening, but all activity came to a halt in that part of the building until Marshall found someone to rectify this inexcusable offense against the concept of good workmanship. Never mind that none of the visitors would ever know. Marshall knew, and that was enough. At the same time, everyone in the organization learned that excellence was in the details and that no detail was too small.

Of course, a good building is a totality, not just a collection of details. When his design department presented Marshall with the plans for the Monroe Clinic in Green County, it had a large glass entryway some fifty-six feet high. The design department explained that this was the kind of entry the clinic wanted. Marshall's view was that it did not fit the building. Furthermore, his calculations were that it would waste $2,000 more per month to heat in the winter and cool in the summer. Marshall advised the design department that he would not build the clinic with that glass front. He said, "Tell them I said you don't have enough money to pay me to do something that isn't right." He offered to redesign

Ed Hart and Marshall often shared breakfast together at Hart's house.

the front without charge. That was the bottom line. The clinic agreed. He built the clinic.

Marshall was allergic to paying attorneys' fees. He wouldn't hire an attorney until every conceivable alternative option had been exhausted. Marshall could not figure out what product lawyers had to sell for which hard cash was worth paying. He did have many lawyer friends, though. Ed Hart was one of them. For years, every morning at 6:00 a.m., Marshall walked a few feet over to Hart's house for coffee, and possibly absorbed free legal advice as well.

Some years ago Siemens Corporation, the huge German conglomerate, called Marshall to inquire as to whether he would build a structure to house its MRI equipment. When Marshall arrived at the meeting in New York, the hospital had four representatives present and Siemens had six, including three lawyers. After exchanging pleasantries, a Siemens representative asked when Marshall's lawyers would arrive. To their astonishment,

Marshall replied, "I don't use lawyers." They wanted to know how a contract could be drafted if he didn't have any lawyers. Marshall advised them to draft the contract as they saw fit with all the specs spelled out, and he would give them a firm bid and a time schedule. The meeting was brief, and Marshall constructed the building on schedule.

Marshall gave generously of his time and resources to many good causes, including the University of Wisconsin in Madison, the architectural school in Milwaukee (University of Wisconsin–Milwaukee), the Madison Art Center, the Frank Lloyd Wright Foundation, and many more. Oh yes, I should mention that one of his especially good and patriotic causes involved several contributions over the years to the election and re-election of a long forgotten former governor and U.S. senator.

I know that most of Marshall's acts of generosity and kindness I never heard about, nor did anyone else, but those I do know about would fill several pages.

Marshall was blessed with an acute sense of fairness and justice. Some forty-odd years ago, Carson Gulley, the popular and respected chef at the University of Wisconsin Union, purchased a house in Crestwood, a planned community on the west side of Madison, not far from the Erdman offices, run as a housing cooperative. Because Mr. Gulley was black, some people put up "for sale" signs on their lawns because they thought the sale to Mr. Gulley would lower their property values. A meeting of the cooperative was called to calm the situation. Because Marshall owned property in Crestwood, he was a voting member of the co-op. He showed up at the meeting and, after listening for fifteen or twenty minutes, rose to announce that he would buy each and every house in Crestwood that anyone wished to sell. That ended the meeting and the controversy.

Marshall was one of those rare persons about whom it can be said that everything and every person he touched was better for it. He set a standard that, if emulated by the key leaders in both the private and public sectors, would instill in the hearts and minds of American people an unshakable confidence in the rightness and goodness of their government and our private institutions. Marshall set the standard for all leaders in all walks of life.

Marshall Erdman looking out over the land that would become Middleton Hills.

■ ■ ■ CONTENTS

Frank Lloyd Wright and Marshall surveying the site of their first prefab house.

immigrant with an idea

IF MARSHALL ERDMAN CAME INTO YOUR life, you remembered him. He was a presence not easily ignored.

He became a pioneer in prefabrication, a prominent figure in the business world, and a visionary designer-builder and community leader in Madison, Wisconsin. But he was just a skinny immigrant from Lithuania with a shoestring construction business when the great Frank Lloyd Wright approached him in 1949. Wright was desperately searching for a contractor to build the meeting house he had designed for the Madison First Unitarian Society. With his first glance he sized up the awestruck twenty-seven-year-old. "Baby," said Wright, "how would you like to be famous?"

Marshall Erdman never forgot those words, a clear reference to Erdman's obvious youthfulness. To Erdman, the meeting with Wright and the friendship that developed between them were the genesis of his career. It was a long and colorful career that carried Erdman from Wisconsin to Washington, Africa, Europe, and Puerto Rico in the company of governors, senators, business heavyweights, artists, inventors, and even heads of state.

It was true that Wright had been unable to find any contractor to build the church for the limited budget of the Unitarians. The congregation had set 5 percent over $75,000 as its absolute limit, and when the plans were sent out to big-name companies in New York, Chicago, and other places, the lowest bid that came back was for $400,000. Still, Wright would not have entrusted his design to someone who would be unlikely to succeed. What was there about an unprepossessing Lithuanian immigrant that made such an impression on Wright and, through the decades, on everyone he met?

Just a boy of sixteen traveling alone in a foreign country when he first arrived on an uncle's doorstep in Chicago, Erdman was of medium height and as skinny as a rail. He grew heavier in later life, built like a bulldog, with broad shoulders and a barrel chest. He was ruddy complexioned and brown-eyed, with a mat of sandy curls clipped short. In dress, he preferred bow ties and often short pants. Madison journalist Marc Eisen recalled, in an article for the local weekly *Isthmus* ("A Man Who Cut His Own Path," September 22, 1995): "Bow tie, dress shirt, wing tips, knee-high dark socks and (what's this?) shorts. I never got around to asking him why he dressed so wacky-like. (How many

Bow tie, shorts, knee-high socks—it was never difficult to find Marshall Erdman in a crowd.

other people were too awestruck by Erdman to ask the obvious?) Marshall, being Marshall, dressed as he darn well pleased."

He could be impetuous, impulsive, engaging, and infuriating. He was a man of boundless curiosity and amazing energy. He had an uncanny knack for getting things done, for drawing people to him, and for binding them with an unreasoning affection and loyalty. As one of his many longtime associates said, "Everybody wanted to be where Marshall was, because that's where things were happening."

Once he had decided on a course of action, no one and nothing could sway him. In his last years he became enamored with the concept of "New Urbanism," the term coined to describe a development where office and retail use were integrated with a mixture of housing types. A 150-acre parcel of land that he owned overlooking Madison's biggest lake seemed ideal to him for this type of development, and he fought a long and frustrating battle with zoning officials and other administrators, neighbors, and scoffers to see his dream of Middleton Hills realized. Although many developers would have put their highest-priced houses on the lots with the lake view, he reserved this area as green space for the whole community to enjoy.

He was a man of many contradictions, and yet, once his contradictions were understood, he was consistent in his attitudes and passions. To his friends, clients, and associates, he was a warm and genial host who loved nothing better than to invite a big group to his family's Middleton "farm" (not a working farm, but a country retreat) for food and conversation. He was a raconteur who could be charming, in large part because he had a naiveté and sense of wonder that were completely honest.

He picked up friends everywhere—at meetings, in airports, at trade shows. "He was a real 'people' person," said his son Dan. "Papa needed people, depended on them, took care of them. And sometimes he meddled in their lives—especially his family, and often his employees as well."

And to both his family and employees, he could be a tyrant with an explosive temper. It was well known that employees tried to hide when they saw him coming. He was strongly opinionated, with a volatile streak that propelled him easily to anger. He did not tolerate what he thought were foolish or stupid mistakes, and those whose judgments fell within this category never forgot the lambasting Marshall gave them. And yet, surprisingly, he was sentimental to the point of tears, long before it was appropriate for men to cry in public. One of the longtime Erdman & Associates division managers and later board member, Roger Peterson, said, "He's like an M&M—hard on the outside and mushy on the inside."

Another of the contradictions that distinguished him had to do with money. Despite having built an enormously successful business and become one of

Marshall in his University Avenue office, 1956.

Madison's wealthiest citizens, he was, in the time-honored tradition of self-made millionaires, frugal to the point of eccentricity. Said his longtime executive secretary, Grace Lukken, "I don't think he realized right up to the end that he was wealthy. You don't know how many times I tried to get that man to fly first class. He said, 'I can't do it. My employees can't fly first class, I can't fly first class.'"

During a long and vigorous life, most of which he spent in and around his adopted city of Madison, Wisconsin, Marshall built his empire and made his mark. The company he founded on borrowed money grew to substantial proportions, ranking within the top fifty businesses in Wisconsin during his later years. Its primary success was in the design and construction of medical office buildings and clinics. In medical circles, the Erdman name was synonymous with quality, reliability, and function. At the time of his death, the firm employed more than 800 people and had designed and built in nearly every state in the country. Company records listed more than 2,500 facilities for upward of 25,000 physicians, not including additions and remodeling.

Marshall showing off a project model in 1985 from his second-floor office.

But his interests did not stop there. In fact, he was easily bored with success and constantly searched out new challenges to fire his imagination. Was there something impossible to be done? He found a way to do it. Was there a better way to build or manufacture? He would plunge in and try it. Did everyone advise against it? No matter.

There were fortunate breaks along the way. Marshall would be the first to credit Frank Lloyd Wright for getting his career off to a good start— and certainly the great architect opened many doors. But Marshall himself found the doors and, once opened, walked through them. He was no slouch, no shrinking violet.

The first big break came when Wright, possibly the world's most famous architect, trusted the struggling, unknown builder to construct the church for the First Unitarian Society.

From a business standpoint, what Erdman didn't need was a project that promised a wealth of experience but little cash. Still, he didn't hesitate. "In architectural school," Marshall said, "Wright's name was revered. To me he was an idol. Frank Lloyd Wright was the man. Any one of my instructors would have given their right arm to shake his hand."

The church was a tremendously complicated design, with a soaring glass prow. There was no money to hire adequate help. Wright had grossly underestimated the cost, and the congregation had difficulty raising adequate funds. It cost Marshall his fee, his pickup truck, the cash value of his life insurance, and many sleepless nights. But despite the fact that the project nearly ruined Marshall, Mr. Wright became his mentor and lifelong idol. Marshall carried Wright's ideas and ideals, as well as a wealth of Wrightian anecdotes, with him for the rest of his life. It was particularly indicative of his feeling that, although he insisted everyone, colleagues and employees, call him "Marshall," he never referred to Wright except as "Mister Wright," spoken with the tone of reverence usually afforded monarchs.

Some risks were worth taking. The themes that dominated the next five decades of Marshall Erdman's life: innovation, hard work, integrity, a stubborn belief in himself, and the idea that he was here for some large purpose, were presaged in his willingness to jump off the cliff for Wright.

Later in his life, when Marshall was a well-established Madison business icon, he was frequently asked his philosophy for achieving success. He loved to give talks and almost never turned down an invitation to speak. The talk frequently included the Erdman four-point plan, which he would expound on in various forms, as though he had started out his business career with the formula in hand. But even though he had the advantage of hindsight in describ-

Marshall posing in front of his University Avenue office.

ing his successes, the individual points were amazingly consistent with how he did business.

From a videotaped address to company employees, dated 1988, he described his philosophy: "I never go into something just to make money," he said. "First, I look for a void, a place where there's a need, where something isn't being fulfilled.

"Second, I think of a way to fill that void or solve that problem in a way that makes a real contribution.

"Third, I have to have the courage of my convictions and stand pat with it, because I cannot think of anything that I have ever started that I was not criticized for.

"And number four," he said, "which is the real backbone of the company, I hope, is to have real integrity. Regardless whether you're making money or losing money, you finish the job and finish it the best way you know how.

"Last comes profit—the item that most businesses put first. If you follow the four points, you get a sense of satisfaction, a sense of reward that is far greater than profit. And the thing is, it pays off. The money will follow."

And follow it did. But there were many years in his early career when he could not have imagined how the money would follow. There were years when he lay awake nights in a cold sweat, wondering how he would pay his bills; there were days when his waiting room was full of creditors, not clients.

The story of Marshall Erdman is a true American success story, paralleling the classic rags-to-riches stories that were popular in the early 1900s: a poor lad works hard and meets a great man who recognizes the lad's honesty and diligence and gives him a start; through much hard work, the poor lad achieves great wealth and goes on to do good and help others.

But the Erdman story had some additional twists, including the mystery of his origins, that raised it above the level of the typical success story and into the realm of drama—the kind of story that keeps unfolding even after the hero is gone. The basic facts that he listed in résumés only hint at the substance of a life that was rich, colorful, productive, and far-reaching.

He was born Mausas Erdmanas in Lithuania, in 1922. So that Mausas could escape the political turmoil in Eastern Europe that eventually resulted in World War II, his father sent him to the United States in 1938 when he was barely sixteen years old. He spoke no English. He lived with relatives in Chicago while completing his high school education, and then he attended the University of Illinois at Urbana-Champaign for several years. By then the United States had entered the war, and Mausas left college to join the Army Corps of Engineers.

After the war, he enrolled at the University of Wisconsin and received his bachelor of science degree in political science. At the UW, Marshall met and married Joyce Mickey, a prominent campus leader who became a distinguished Madison citizen in her own right.

Although he had toyed with a career in international relations, his interest in architecture and building led him inevitably to establish his own firm. He never earned an architectural degree himself, but he pioneered the design-and-build approach by hiring registered architects, engineers, construction managers, and workers, and eventually built his own factory where building components were prefabricated. Later, after the business was successful, he had many opportunities to involve himself in international projects.

Marshall always said there were eight milestones in the development of the company, and he listed the building of the Unitarian Meeting House with Frank Lloyd Wright first. The second came when he built a cluster of small individual doctors' offices off University Avenue in Madison, in what he called Doctors Park. They were forerunners of what would become the heart of his business. The third was when Frank Lloyd Wright either offered or (depending upon which version of the story you believe) agreed to design three models of prefabricated houses for Erdman to build. The involvement of the great architect with Erdman's prefab houses brought a huge wave of publicity that far overshadowed the eventual outcome of the collaboration.

The fourth milestone was when Frank Lloyd Wright died in 1959, and Marshall took time off from the company to go back to architecture school at the University of Illinois at Urbana-Champaign. The fifth was when he was asked to go to Puerto Rico to design and build a training camp for the first Peace Corps.

The sixth was when he was asked to go to Gabon, West Africa, in 1962, to build schools, and spent some time with Albert Schweitzer, the legendary medical missionary. The seventh was an invitation by the Agency for International Development (AID) to go to Tunisia and set up a standardized building system. In preparation for that, he toured all the major manufacturing companies in Europe that were supplying the building industry and discovered the sophisticated machinery they had developed. The high-precision machinery, designed to mill to exacting tolerances, simply wasn't available in the United States, where wood was plentiful and waste was acceptable. And so his eighth milestone came when he ordered a whole factory full of that machinery for himself, built a factory, and embarked on the furniture manufacturing business.

He added milestones after this summary, most notably the unique fine-art department that he established within the firm and the experimental urban development that would be known as Middleton

A portrait sketch of Marshall drawn by longtime Erdman employee John Caldwell.

Hills. And every one of these milestones was buttressed by its own mythology as anecdotes accumulated around them, of which friends, associates, and Marshall himself wove and rewove the details.

"The main thing that developed this company is luck, luck, and a little more luck," Marshall told his employees at one of the regularly scheduled noontime talks designed to enhance internal communication.

The luck may have been there, but it was probably quite secondary to an inner vision. It was the vision that carried him so far, and the vision that was so difficult to explain. Where did it come from? How was he able to make others accept it? To

Marshall, it was only common sense: find a void, fill it, do the best job you can.

He would add, "Frank Lloyd Wright used to say, 'Common sense is so uncommon.' And it's amazing how little competition you have when you use common sense." The commonsense quote was one of Marshall's all-time favorites, and he pulled it out and dusted it off on many occasions when it was appropriate.

Robert O'Malley, a Madison banker who knew Marshall for more than four decades, said, "You meet very few people in a lifetime who have this rare sense of vision that doesn't come from a desire to make money, but from seeing how the world is changing and moving and acting upon it."

"Besides his knack for business and commerce," wrote Madison journalist Marc Eisen, "he was a determined nonconformist the way American visionaries almost always are."

How fully Marshall realized his vision and how many lives he touched in his remarkable career were evidenced by the outpouring of affection at the memorial service following his death in September 1995. The setting for the service—the Unitarian Meeting House he built nearly a half century before—was profoundly appropriate, as was the broad range of people in attendance. Dignitaries stood beside draftsmen and listened as close friends and family recalled the intense, charming, private, restless, brusque, and immensely talented man who was Marshall Erdman.

It was only after his death that the truth about his past was revealed. In fact, just hours after Marshall's death, his children received a phone call from David Levitan, a retired lawyer living in New York, telling them he not only knew Marshall as a boy in Lithuania, but that he was a relative. This was the first the children had heard from anyone on their father's side of the family. They didn't know their father had any living relatives and that there was a generous and caring network of them in this country. And they had no clue their relatives were Jewish. A few months later, a musty old trunk belonging to Marshall was discovered in the basement of his home. Full of old photos and letters, this discovery would shed more light on Marshall's early life and the tragedies that scarred him.

Marshall had come a long way—further than many in the crowded Unitarian Meeting House realized. And the journey was a fascinating one.

Hundreds packed the Unitarian Meeting House September 21, 1995, for Marshall's memorial service.

Marshall as a young boy on the steps of a nineteenth-century Lithuanian palace in Palanga, a seaside resort his family visited near their home in Telsiai.

CHAPTER 2

Mausas Erdmanas

IT BEGAN IN LITHUANIA, A COUNTRY along the Baltic Sea of 25,000 square miles, less than half the size of Wisconsin. Bordered also by Latvia in the north, Belorussia in the east, Poland in the south, and Kaliningrad Oblast (formerly East Prussia) in the southwest, the country has a turbulent history. From the dawn of its existence, the Lithuanians had to cope with the expansionist ambitions of their neighbors.

Lithuanians were among the most ancient peoples of Europe. Legends say they are descended from the Romans, but scholars have speculated they arrived from Asia as long as 10,000 years ago.

In the thirteenth century, to protect themselves against invaders from the north and the south, the Lithuanians formed a strong unified state, one of the largest states of medieval Europe, including all of Belorussia, a large part of the Ukraine, and sections of Great Russia. Through marriage, Lithuania became allied with Poland, and the country rose to the height of its power and size. This was Lithuania's heyday.

A decline set in in the 1400s. In 1569, hard-pressed by the Russians, Lithuania fully merged with Poland; Lithuanian aristocracy and burghers became thoroughly Polonized, while the peasantry sank into servitude. By three successive partitions of Poland in the late 1700s, Lithuania disappeared as a national unit and passed to Russia.

A Lithuanian linguistic and cultural revival began in the nineteenth century, inspired largely by the Roman Catholic clergy and accompanied by frequent anti-Russian uprisings. However, Russia successfully put down revolts in 1831 and 1863. Though the Lithuanian bids for independence failed, they did bring some concessions, making it easier for the peasant classes to own land.

World War I and the consequent collapse of Russia and Germany made Lithuanian independence possible. In November 1918, Lithuania became an independent republic, with a new constitution. The new government pledged itself to seek the return of Lithuanian war prisoners from both Russia and Germany, to seek compensation from the belligerents for war damages in Lithuania, to establish economic order, to prepare the way for land reform by the constituent assembly, and to assure a fair deal for the workers.

The rhetoric and promises were noble, but unfortunately, the path to order and tranquility was

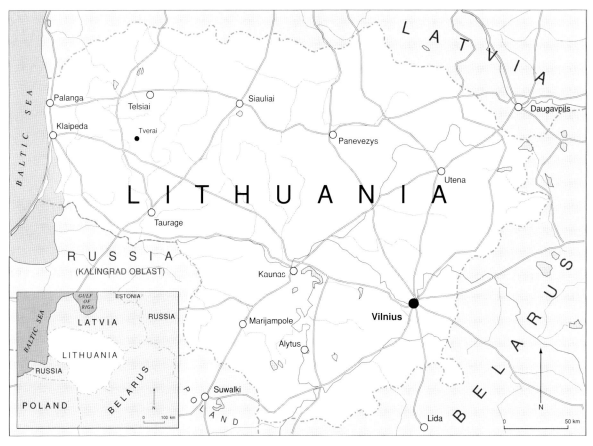

Marshall's birthplace, Tverai, is located in the upper left corner of the map.

a rocky one. Perhaps the greatest weakness of the new country was a lack of funds. Although called a republic, internal politics were unstable, and the heads of state, Augustinas Voldemaras and later Antanas Smetona, were virtual dictators.

When Marshall Erdman was born in 1922, the country of Lithuania was a place from which people were looking to escape.

In the early years of the twentieth century, Marshall's family lived in the Lithuanian town of Tverai, a small town, little more than a village, near the East Prussian border in western Lithuania.

There was a strong Jewish presence in Tverai, though Judaism was a minority religion in Lith-

uania. Lithuanian Jews constituted 7 percent of the population. Jews had lived in Lithuania for more than 500 years—since Grand Duke Vytautas invited Jewish immigrants and craftsmen to come and settle in Vilnius (the country's eventual capital and largest city).

The Jews came, but by 1900, many were looking to leave. In a 1995 letter, Max Levitan, a cousin of Marshall's who emigrated from Lithuania in 1928, recalled: "The desire to get . . . out of Lithuania arose from the usual reasons why [people] emigrated: the dire economic situation in the small towns and villages. Jews have a reputation for being good business people, but in Tverai.

. . . Jews were barely able to eke out a subsistence, a very spartan existence."

One Lithuanian boy of thirteen who emigrated from Tverai prior to 1910 was named Ben Braude. As a young boy in Lithuania, Ben entered trade school to study to be a watchmaker, but tragedy struck. Both of Ben's parents contracted tuberculosis and died. Ben was taken care of for a time by an older sister, Bayla, but there were cousins in the United States, in Chicago, who were willing to take him in.

With barely enough money for passage, thirteen-year-old Ben set out for America. He made it, and he knocked on the door of his relatives in Chicago. The reception was guarded. Nobody kissed him, something Ben would remember, and remark on, for the next seventy-three years until his death at age eighty-six.

But he was in America. "What do you do?" he was asked. Ben remembered his brief schooling at the watchmaker's trade and described himself as a watchmaker.

He wasn't, of course, but his chutzpah paid off. Ben was given a job by an importer of Swiss watches. He worked hard for the next several years, asked questions, and began to develop a sense not only of watchmaking but of the whole jewelry business. By 1915, he was buying small lots of jewelry from wholesalers, marking it up, and selling to retailers.

By 1919, Ben was in the wholesale jewelry business himself. He had also married—a working-class girl from Chicago, the daughter of a shoemaker. In 1920 they had a son, Marvin Braude.

Back in Lithuania, Ben Braude's older sister, Bayla, had also married. Her husband's name was Icikas Jankelis (called Jonas) Erdmanas. Surviving relatives remember that Bayla's marriage to Erdmanas was not altogether well received by her family.

Charlotte Levitan Turyn, a first cousin of Marshall's, remembered her mother telling her as much: "The family was kind of prejudiced against [Jonas Erdmanas]. Bayla's extended family was a very rabbinical, scholarly family, and Jonas was not. I think he was a carpenter."

Marshall rarely spoke of his family in Lithuania, and his children knew precious little of their own grandparents. However, an October 7, 1951, story in the *Milwaukee Sentinel* revealed another fragment about their father's background. In his article, Robert J. Riordan wrote that Marshall had "a legacy of skill from his father, a building and construction engineer in Lithuania who had given his son a working knowledge of building trade crafts such as carpentry, masonry, painting, and so on."

Given the deeply religious nature of Bayla's family, it does seem nearly certain that Jonas Erdmanas was Jewish. Debbie Erdman, Marshall's oldest child and granddaughter of Jonas and Bayla, says, "You couldn't marry out of the faith at that time. It was so frowned upon. Bayla would never have married out of the Jewish faith."

Charlotte Turyn concurred. In 1928, when Charlotte was four years old, she, her mother, and her two brothers, David and Max, emigrated to the United States. (Charlotte's father, an orthodox rabbi, had emigrated in 1926, and they were to join him in Rock Island, Illinois.) Charlotte remem-

As a child, Marshall was called "Goldene," which means Goldilocks, by his family

living in Tverai. Instead, they had moved to Telsiai, a town twenty miles or so from Tverai that was bigger and had more opportunities, especially when it came to education. They now had a son, Mausas Erdmanas, born in Tverai in 1922. The boy would, of course, become the man known as Marshall Erdman, and he was, by all accounts, the light of Bayla's life.

David Levitan (brother of Charlotte and Max) was twelve years old in Lithuania in 1928 when he saw the six-year-old boy, Mausas Erdmanas. "Marshall looked very much like his mother," David recalled nearly seventy years later. "His mother was a big woman, but very handsome, a blonde woman with beautiful curly hair."

Early on, David recalled, "Marshall was called 'Goldene'—Goldilocks. He had very beautiful blond locks." Young Mausas's family no doubt used the nickname in reference to his hair, and yet in translation the word also can mean someone who does good work with his hands, in a manner that everything he touches turns to gold. A Yiddish translator, interviewed for this work, asked, "Goldene? Was this person a builder?" In light of Marshall's future career, the nickname seemed prescient.

In any event, there was little doubt of Bayla's love for her firstborn. "Bayla doted on Marshall," Charlotte Turyn said. "He was the apple of her eye. Think about what she called him—Goldene. What's more precious than gold?"

In Telsiai, the intellectual center of that part of Lithuania, Mausas Erdmanas began his schooling. Max Levitan recalled: "Marshall's father enrolled him in the famous Talmudical academy of that

bered her mother telling her that on the day of their departure, that momentous day in 1928, they stopped so Charlotte's mother could say good-bye to her cousin Bayla.

Their religious convictions were such, Charlotte said "that I don't think we would have stopped to visit Bayla if her husband wasn't Jewish."

An October 1996 letter to Debbie Erdman from Charlotte's brother, Max Levitan, further confirmed the notion. Of Jonas Erdmanas, Levitan wrote, "his mother's name was Mayteh, a Yiddischization and feminization of the Hebrew 'Matisyahus.'"

By 1928, when the Levitans stopped to visit as they left Lithuania, Jonas and Bayla were no longer

town. . . . This academy was so famous that after it was destroyed in the Holocaust, at least three different institutions, two in the U.S., in Cleveland and Chicago, and one in Israel, claimed the right to use the name 'Telsiaier Yeshiva.'"

No account of Europe in the twentieth century could escape the horrific reach of the Holocaust. Marshall Erdman's family saga would not be immune. First, however, would come a less sweeping but personally devastating tragedy.

By 1930, young Mausas was eight years old. "At that time," David Levitan said, "he was viewed as the only child his mother would probably have."

But in the early 1930s Bayla became pregnant again, and a second child, another boy, was born. He was named Leizeris Notelis Erdmanas and called Nonas. The new baby, however, barely knew his mother, who died not long after, although the cause of death was not clear. The recollections of both Max Levitan and another cousin of Marshall Erdman's, Jean Massell, were that Bayla died from complications of the birth, though neither is certain.

Debbie Erdman recalled that her father, in a rare reminiscence, did elaborate on his mother's death. Marshall said that Bayla contracted stomach cancer, and despite Jonas's efforts (traveling across Europe searching for treatment), his wife died before the baby's second birthday.

What is certain was that Bayla was dead, and now Jonas Erdmanas, with two young sons to raise and the drumbeats of Hitler's rise beginning to echo, began to think of the United States. What had become of his late wife's brother, Ben Braude?

As it happened, by 1935 Ben Braude was doing

Marshall with—probably—his father, Jonas.

very well in the wholesale jewelry business. His business had grown in the 1920s, but as that decade ended, Ben actually went broke, another casualty of the economic crash. Yet someone who comes to a foreign country with no money in his pocket and succeeds once is not likely to give up. So it was with Ben. The country's economy improved, Ben reestablished his jewelry business, and in the words of his son, Marvin, today a retired city politician in Los Angeles, "became very prosperous." It meant he could move from the old ethnic neighborhood.

"Chicago," wrote Mike Royko in his classic book on the city, *Boss*, "until as late as the 1950s, was a place where people stayed put for awhile, creating tightly knit neighborhoods, as small-townish as any village in the wheat fields.

"The neighborhood towns were part of larger

Marshall and his younger brother, Nonas, shortly before he left for America in 1938.

ethnic states. To the north of the Loop was Germany. To the northwest was Poland. To the west were Italy and Israel. To the southwest were Bohemia and Lithuania." Far from home, the new immigrants retained their language, their shops, religions and holidays, and the comfort of familiar sounds and smells for as long as they could.

Braude first lived with the Jews on the west side of Chicago. (Conversely, the family of Jean Massell, another Erdman cousin, lived in the Lithuanian enclave on the south side.) But his business success meant they could move out and up and by 1935, Ben, his wife, and thirteen-year-old Marvin lived in an expensive apartment on Lake Shore Drive, an area to become known as Chicago's "Gold Coast."

As he prospered, Ben Braude became more than ever the patriarch of his extended family. First, in 1930, Ben brought his and Bayla's younger brother, Berl, to Chicago. Berl was married to a Tverai native named Rivkeh, and they were eager to come to America.

Berl Braude, however, did not share his brother Ben's work ethic. Marvin Braude recalled: "Berl was a great spender. He bought me my first bicycle. He had no money—but he was a great spender. Berl was a dreamer, not a realistic person."

Ben Braude could not have looked with approval on Berl's antics. So in 1935, when the subject of bringing one of Jonas and Bayla's two boys over to America was addressed, Ben would not want another Berl. Well, Mausas Erdmanas, Jonas's oldest, reminded everyone of Berl.

"He was the spitting image of Berl," Marvin Braude recalled. "They had the same curly, reddish-

Marshall's Lithuanian passport stated his hometown, place of birth, birth date, and other pertinent information for immigration.

blond hair. And their personalities were similar." No, Ben would not want Mausas—but rather his younger brother.

"My understanding," David Levitan said, "is that Marshall's uncle, Marvin's father, did not want Marshall to come over. He wanted the younger brother. My understanding is that Marshall's father sneaked Marshall in."

It may have been the simple fact that Marshall, while still young, was older than his brother and would fare better on the voyage. Whatever the decision, it was a momentous one. With a Lithuanian passport dated 1938, Mausas Erdmanas said goodbye to his father and brother, got on a boat by himself, and sailed for a country whose language he did not know to live with people he had never met. He was sixteen. Young Mausas didn't know it, but he would never see his father or brother again.

Lithuania fell to the Germans early during the Second World War. The number of casualties was enormous. The Germans occupied Lithuania from 1941 until 1944 and sent 160,000 Lithuanians to their deaths in concentration camps. More than 130,000 of the victims were Lithuanian Jews, whom the Germans singled out for their religious beliefs and ethnic background.

During the four years of their occupation of Lithuania, the Nazis killed as many people as the United States and Great Britain lost during five years of fighting in the Second World War. Almost one-third of its entire population perished in the slaughter.

Among the victims were Jonas Erdmanas and his younger son. Because we had no record of Marshall Erdman reacting to the deaths of his father and brother, and no later words from him on how he was affected, we could only try to imagine the impact.

In his 1995 letter, Max Levitan wrote of the village of Tverai, saying, "If it still exists." He explained: "I say 'if it still exists' [because] that area was devastated when the Germans invaded . . . in June 1941; one of my grandmother's sisters was killed in the shelling by the Germans on the first day of the invasion."

Max's sister, Charlotte, who left Lithuania with her family in 1928, recalled that her mother had many relatives still living in the Tverai and Telsiai area when the Germans invaded.

"Of all of them," Charlotte said, "one, only one, escaped. She was a socialist. The Nazis took her husband away and she and her son started walking toward Russia. They wanted to try to meet up with the Russian army. She became exhausted, but her son kept her going. They made it, and she wrote my mother." Of their hometown, friends, and family,

she wrote, "There is nothing left. Everything else is gone, gone, gone."

After her father's death, Debbie Erdman visited Telsiai, the town where her father grew up. In a letter to Max Levitan, she wrote, "I could not believe what I saw: there were two cemeteries, one where the women and children were shot, the other where the men were taken and killed in September 1941. Nonas would have been only ten years old. . . . I cried my eyes out over the thought of frightened and lonely little Nonas being shot at this massacre grounds."

Of course, the crisis was only looming when Mausas Erdmanas arrived in Chicago to begin a new life. Imagine a boy of sixteen in one of the world's greatest but most intimidating cities. He cannot speak its language. He arrives at a fabulous high-rise right on Lake Michigan. He double-checks the address on the small piece of paper he holds in his hand. Yes, this is it. The building has a doorman and an elevator operator. He is overwhelmed.

How interesting it would have been to hear Marshall tell the story of his arrival. Unfortunately, he never shared these memories with his friends and family, so we could only speculate. But it was informed speculation, for we knew the man Mausas Erdmanas later became. At that moment, standing on Lake Shore Drive, Mausas could have gone into a shell and presented himself to the Braudes as shy, deferential, a bit awed by the new circumstances in which he found himself. Or, swallowing his fear, he could have come on strong, with half-false bravado, and met the Braudes as their equal. From what we knew of Marshall Erdman's later life, we were not surprised to learn he chose the latter route.

"He was very assertive," Marvin Braude recalled in an interview sixty years later. "Marshall was very demanding. He expected a great deal, far more than his situation warranted."

It was a rocky beginning, and not what Marvin Braude had imagined it would be. "I was personally very excited about Marshall's coming," Marvin said. "I was an only child. The prospect of having a brother or something close to a brother excited me."

Mausas slept in Marvin's bedroom. There were twin beds and a master bath with access to both their room and the room of Marvin's parents. The apartment had another bath adjacent to a small servant's quarters. "We could have been very companionable," Marvin said, but it was not to be. There might have been a number of reasons.

"As an only child," Marvin said, "both my parents had always doted on me and continued to. I suspect they didn't give Marshall the attention they gave their son, and Marshall resented that." In any case, there was a problem with communication.

"Marshall couldn't speak English," Marvin recalled, "so we had trouble communicating. My father could speak a little to him in Yiddish. My father's Yiddish was very poor, but they managed."

Then, too, there could have been a reaction from the Braudes. However good their intentions, to have a stranger dropped into their home on a twenty-four-hour-a-day basis could be a challenge in the best of circumstances. A bad or careless habit that could be overlooked in a weekend visitor could begin to grate like fingernails on a chalkboard in a guest who never leaves—indeed, can't leave. If the guest was perceived as showing inadequate appreciation for the benefits

Marshall, Jean Massell, and Max Levitan on the steps of Jean's house on Chicago's South Side, where Marshall lived for a short time.

bestowed on him, the grating intensifies.

"We all extended ourselves for him," Marvin said, "but it was never enough. He always wanted more."

As the months wore on, it was clear that Mausas's biggest problem was with Marvin's mother, Rose. A simple woman, not educated, she was proud of her husband's success and thought young Mausas Erdmanas, arriving in a new, affluent culture, should have been quick to express his awe and gratitude.

But Mausas's instincts had taken him in precisely the opposite direction. He would conquer his fear by not being impressed at all.

According to Charlotte Turyn, the day Mausas arrived in Chicago, Ben Braude's wife took him to the living room window of their Lake Shore Drive high-rise and with a magisterial sweep of her arm, said, "Look, isn't this marvelous? You can see the lake."

To which Marshall replied, "Well, in Telsiai I could see the River Telsiai." Charlotte says Marshall Erdman told her that story later, and it may well be apocryphal, if for no other reason than on Marshall's first day in Chicago, the language barrier would have prevented such an exchange.

It did, however, accurately capture the confrontational nature of Marshall's relationship with the mistress of the Braude house.

"Eventually it was my mother who suggested it wasn't working out," Marvin said. "The situation had deteriorated to that point. Marshall was told he couldn't continue living with us."

Marvin is uncertain how long Marshall did stay with the Braudes—somewhere between six months and a year. Fortunately, there were other relatives in the Chicago area. Equally fortunately, and here real credit must again go to Ben Braude, it was agreed that whichever family took in the young refugee, there would be continuing financial support from Ben.

He wound up in a house on Chicago's South Side, at Essex and Seventy-ninth Street. It was the home of Rabbi Israel Meyer Levitan and his wife, Anna. They were the parents of Marshall Erdman's cousin Jean, who had just graduated as valedictorian of her high school at the precocious age of sixteen when Marshall (still Mausas at the time) arrived.

Jean Levitan Massell remembered her cousin with great fondness. The edginess of his stay with the Braudes was notably absent. "Marshall was always outgoing," Jean said, "and fun to be around." Also living in Chicago was cousin Max Levitan, who immigrated to Illinois with his parents and siblings in 1928. Max's father was the brother of Rabbi Israel Levitan. Max and Marshall became best friends during these years.

"I got to know Marshall well," wrote Max Levitan in his 1995 letter, "when he moved to the apartment of Tante Chana (Max's Aunt Anna, Jean's mother) on Chicago's South Shore. . . . At that time I was living on the west side of Chicago, attending public high school by day and the Hebrew Theological College at night. On Fridays and the eve of many holidays I would hitchhike to Tante Chana's when I needed some good food, as Tante Chana set an abundant table for the Sabbath and holidays. That's when Marshall and I became buddies. We even shared the same bed."

As with Jean Massell, Max Levitan recalled the high school-age Mausas Erdmanas with affection: "He was the epitome of restlessness, of exuberance . . . the very qualities that undoubtedly helped [him] become such a great business success."

"We were not a well-to-do family," Jean said. "But we had an enclosed porch. That's where Marshall slept."

He earned his keep by helping around the house. The man who would one day impress the world with his building innovations showed his gift early. "He was amazingly handy," Jean said. "Anything that needed repairing, he could fix."

He was finding himself, gaining confidence,

Marshall giving his cousin Jean Levitan Massell a tennis lesson.

discovering talents, growing up. His studies improved. "He was adjusting amazingly well," Jean said. "Both Max and I helped him with his English and he caught on pretty quickly."

Max Levitan concurred: "In the course of our friendship my aunt's daughter and I helped him with his high school work, and in no time at all he was fully acclimated to his new environment and picked up English quickly."

During summers there were trips to Rock Island, where Max's family, including his sister Charlotte, had settled. Rock Island is 177 miles west of Chicago, on the Mississippi River.

"They kind of considered Rock Island their

country place in the summer," Charlotte said. "People stayed with families in those days, they didn't stay in hotels. It was nice. The house would be full of people."

Of Mausas in those days, Charlotte recalled, "We'd make fun of him because he'd weigh himself constantly. He was very proud of his physique. His face wasn't particularly handsome, but he had this nice head of hair."

He seems to have been happy, according to their remembrances. "To some extent," Jean Massell said, "that really is a credit to my parents. They brought him in with open hearts."

Max's brother, David, said of Anna: "Jean

Marshall in Chicago, ready for college at the University of Illinois at Urbana-Champaign.

More sure now of himself, he got along better with others. "I think he was fond of Rivkeh," Marvin Braude said.

Because he was still in Chicago, Max Levitan would visit, and together they began their first venture into sales. Jean Massell recalled, "Even then, Marshall was an entrepreneur."

"I often stayed overnight there," Max recalled. "It was at this time that we started selling horns together every New Year's Eve. It was on the corner of State and Randolph in the theater district of downtown Chicago. The last time we did I was reluctant to do so because I had a date to take a girl to a New Year's Eve dance at a major downtown hotel, but [Marshall] was so persuasive that I had to join him in the horn business and not take my date to the dance till well after midnight."

With an eye on college, Mausas worked a number of odd jobs, though none perhaps odder than selling horns at midnight on New Year's Eve. "Both of us held many jobs," Max recalled. In a 1992 interview, Marshall remembered that his first job in the United States was painting a house.

The money helped pay for schooling. Mausas had begun to formulate a passion for building and design and was thinking of studying architecture, according to Levitan. This career direction was probably driven by his father's influence, even though it had been more than two years since he had last seen his father.

"We spent a lot of time discussing college plans," Max said, "and I advised him to attend the University of Illinois at Champaign-Urbana rather than attend the Chicago city junior colleges."

Massell's mother was sort of angelic, almost a saint. They lived in a one-bedroom apartment, but they didn't turn anyone away."

Some time after Mausas left the Braude house to live with Jean's family, Ben Braude's younger brother, Berl, died of tuberculosis, the disease that killed his parents. Berl left his widow, Rivkeh. When Mausas was in his late high school years, Jean's family moved, and it was decided that Mausas, again with Ben Braude's financial support, would move in with Rivkeh, who lived in the Albany Park section of Chicago. It worked well.

Max Levitan landed a partial scholarship to the University of Chicago, later parlaying it into a full scholarship based on his grades. His advice, Mausas thought, was worth taking.

So it was off to Urbana-Champaign and the University of Illinois, where he enrolled in the School of Architecture. It also happened to be one of the few architectural schools in the 1940s that even acknowledged the idea of prefabrication as an important building concept. Although he might not have realized it at the time, the University of Illinois was, for Mausas Erdmanas, a perfect fit.

Marshall at boot camp in Fort Lewis, near Tacoma, Washington.

from U. of I. to G.I.

MARSHALL ERDMAN ENTERED THE University of Illinois at Urbana-Champaign on September 14, 1940, two weeks before his eighteenth birthday. A transcript obtained from the university provided some information about Marshall's college and precollege years. It reported that he graduated from Von Steuben High School in Chicago (255 out of 345 students). His guardian was listed as Ben Braude of 3530 Lake Shore Drive, Chicago, and his major was architecture. The name on the transcript was Marshall Erdman, not Mausas Erdmanas. Though it seemed likely that it was updated years later by the university, there was some confusion over exactly when Mausas became Marshall, and it seemed that he used both names concurrently at least for several years.

A Social Security card dated 1939 listed the name Marshall Erdman. And yet more than once over the years, Marshall would tell friends and family that his name was changed from Mausas Erdmanas to Marshall Erdman by a gruff judge or army officer at Fort Lewis in Washington State in 1943. In fact, Jackie Collins, a friend who would meet Marshall while working near Fort Lewis for the United Service Organization, said that Marshall

Marshall strikes a collegiate pose in front of Altgeld Hall on the University of Illinois campus.

THE UNITED STATES OF AMERICA

ORIGINAL
TO BE GIVEN TO
THE PERSON NATURALIZED

No. 5815582

CERTIFICATE OF NATURALIZATION

Petition No. 8924

Personal description of holder as of date of naturalization: Age 21 *years; sex* Male *color* White *complexion* Fair *color of eyes* Blue *color of hair* Lt. brown *height* 5 *feet* 10 *inches; weight* 165 *pounds; visible distinctive marks* Several small moles on face *Marital status* Single *former nationality* Lithuanian

I certify that the description above given is true, and that the photograph affixed hereto is a likeness of me.

(Complete and true signature of holder)

UNITED STATES OF AMERICA } ss:
WESTERN DIST. OF WASHINGTON }

Be it known that at a term of the U. S. District *Court of* Western District of Washington *held pursuant to law at* Tacoma , Washington *on* September 4, 1943 *the Court having found that* Marshall Erdman *then residing at* Fort Lewis , Washington *intends to reside permanently in the United States (when so required by the Naturalization Laws of the United States), had in all other respects complied with the applicable provisions of such naturalization laws, and was entitled to be admitted to citizenship, thereupon ordered that such person be and (s)he was admitted as a citizen of the United States of America.*

In testimony whereof the seal of the court is hereunto affixed this 4th *day of* September *in the year of our Lord nineteen hundred and* Forty-Three *and of our Independence the one hundred and* Sixty-Eighth

JUDSON W. SHORETT
Clerk of the U. S. DISTRICT *Court.*
By _____ *Deputy Clerk.*

It is a violation of the U.S. Code (and punishable as such) to copy, print, photograph, or otherwise illegally use this certificate.

DEPARTMENT OF JUSTICE

Inscription into the army in 1943 gained Marshall immediate American citizenship.

told her, "The judge out there who was giving him his citizenship said, 'Why don't you take a name more fitting to this country?'"

Debbie Erdman said her father related a similar story: "An officer said, 'Mausas Erdmanas? What kind of name is that? If you want to be a soldier and get along in this country, that won't work. I'm going to call you Marshall Erdman.'" As with many of Marshall's stories, the details could change depending upon his mood or audience.

A Certificate of Naturalization confirmed at least the date. "By decree of the court, as part of naturalization proceedings held September 4, 1943," Mausas Erdmanas officially became Marshall Erdman. For the purposes of receiving Social Security, it seemed, he had decided on the name Marshall Erdman at least four years earlier.

Also of interest in the University of Illinois transcript: When asked to name a parent, he wrote, "Issac Erdman, Telsiai, Lithuania."

Apparently Marshall took the opportunity to Americanize his father's name as well. When his daughter visited Lithuania after Marshall's death, she learned the official names of the father and brother that Marshall lost. In Lithuania as in many Slavic countries, people were known commonly by nicknames that bore little resemblance to their real names. Thus Icikas Jankelis became Jonas, and Leizeris Notelis became Nonas.

The campus that was home to Marshall Erdman in the early 1940s had a small-town feel. The pocket-sized University of Illinois students' handbook for 1941–42 included a page of "Illinois Social Customs." It presumed a complete absence of sophistication in the fledgling students, and in the case of Marshall Erdman, it may have been right.

"Informality, naturalness, and friendliness are the most valuable keys to success at Illinois," the handbook counseled. "Ordinary dates are usually made a few days to a week beforehand. Special occasions like large dances are reserved by a boy at least two weeks in advance. Since few cars are permitted, students walk everywhere, and like it. Nickel busses are used for entertainment away from campus town. It is still polite for men to stand on crowded busses. . . .

"It is an unwritten rule that a girl dates only one boy at a time from the same fraternity or house. Likewise a boy can see the propriety of following similar procedure. . . .

"Needless to say, promptness on dates for both boys and girls is still correct. Breaking dates is risky business and an embarrassment to all parties concerned. Boys usually walk on the street side of dates. Girls sit on the right of men at tables."

The University of Illinois did not encourage students to work while attending school. "Do not seek work unless you absolutely must have it," the handbook advised. "There are always more men than jobs.

Marshall's University of Illinois student handbook.

. . . One who takes a job and does not need it is lessening his chances of academic success."

Marshall Erdman needed to work. His friend Max Levitan said Marshall's interest in architecture and engineering "plus the low tuition costs for Illinois residents" were the main reasons for choosing the University of Illinois.

Levitan continued: "I believe his allowance from Mr. Braude stopped upon finishing high school, so he had many, generally rather menial, jobs in Champaign-Urbana . . . the only one of his I can recall is that he was a part-time night watchman at a bank."

The realities of the academic rigors at Illinois must have hit Marshall and his self-confidence hard. So much so that after failing rhetoric and composition and getting a D in both college algebra and architecture projections his first semester, he transferred out of the School of Architecture and into general studies. His grades improved slightly after that first semester, but whether it was because he had to work, or more likely, had difficulty reading English, Marshall's academic career at Illinois was not particularly distinguished.

It was also interesting to note that Marshall took only one architecture class while at Illinois. Yet that class may have been enough exposure to cultivate in the young student a lasting general interest in architecture and construction, if not an academic one.

Summers he attended summer school at the

Marshall as a soldier at Fort Lewis, an army base in Washington.

university and spent what vacation there was back in Rivkeh's apartment in Albany Park, according to Max Levitan.

Marshall's father and brother were shot by the Nazis when he was just beginning his second year at Illinois. When did he learn of the horrific news? What was his reaction? To date, no letters have been found and no specific memories provided by those who knew him touch on either of these questions. However, it is safe to assume that, faced with such heartrending tragedy, Marshall concealed his feelings and put them behind him as best he could to focus on the prospect of his future.

However, the beginning of Marshall's junior year at Urbana-Champaign provided a clue that college life had undergone a major change. For in that first semester, along with courses called "public administration," "American constitutional system," and a philosophy course on Hume, Darwin, Marx, and Freud, Marshall's class list included courses titled "infantry drill" and "infantry theory."

The war in Europe was requiring more young men all the time. On January 28, 1943, Marshall Erdman withdrew from the University of Illinois and joined the military service.

This was a major crossroad in Marshall's life. By enlisting in the army, foreigners like Marshall were granted immediate U.S. citizenship. America was now his home, and no longer could there be thoughts of returning to Lithuania.

His first stop in a uniform of the United States Army was a base outside of Tacoma, Washington, called Fort Lewis. A man named John Zabel recalled meeting Marshall at Fort Lewis in the fall of 1943.

"I was in a different platoon and didn't see a lot of him," Zabel said. "But he was a nice fellow with curly blond hair. I remember he liked to repair watches. When one broke, he could fix it" a skill doubtless learned at the elbow of Ben Braude in Chicago.

Private Erdman's closest friend at Fort Lewis was a fellow soldier named Dick Cannon. Jackie Collins, who worked at the enlisted men's club run by the USO in Tacoma, dated Cannon and through him met Marshall Erdman.

"I don't think Marshall fit very well into the army," Collins said. "He looked nice, but with all his curly hair his cap didn't fit right and he just didn't look like a soldier. He was alone quite a bit. But he and Dick hit it off and were friends."

Jackie Collins remembered Marshall as "a very good dancer." When Dick Cannon gave the OK, Marshall would ask Jackie to dance. She recalled: "They'd be playing fast music, but Marshall would go to the orchestra and request a Viennese waltz. Everyone else would leave the floor, but that didn't seem to bother him. We'd be the only ones. But he was an individual and it didn't bother him."

Marshall Erdman during those years always had a girlfriend. Whether it was his shock of curly blond hair, his accent, his shyness that was somehow not at odds with his vitality, or whatever it was, women were attracted to the young Marshall Erdman, and he to them. In fact, throughout his life, he was a great admirer of women, particularly smart and lively women. He sought their company and craved their friendship. And they reciprocated.

During his stay at Fort Lewis the woman's name was Julia Anne. A sad circumstance produced that information. Marshall, in Europe with the 44th Infantry Division, received a letter in May 1945, mailed from Seattle.

"Dearest Mausas," the letter began (which showed that Marshall still wasn't entirely comfortable in his new persona) "On February 12th I wrote a letter to Dick Cannon. Well, today it came back, marked on the envelope, 'Deceased.' Had you heard about it? I don't know when I have felt so badly about the death of someone I knew so slightly—partially because I know what a loss it will be to you, and partially because I had taken a great liking to him myself, and was looking forward to having him as a friend after the war, and now that can never be. It is hard to be philosophical about such things, or to accept them as happening for the best. It isn't the best—it isn't even logical. I suppose he must have been killed in Europe. . . .

"I'm terribly sorry, darling, and you know that too.

"All my love, Julia Anne."

Additional letters from Julia Anne as late as fall of 1945, when the war was over and Marshall was back in the states, indicated that the relationship had continued and that they were much more than just friends. There was more than one mention of marriage. However, in October of 1945, she wrote the proverbial "Dear John" letter. We have no way of knowing the reaction of the young Mausas, awaiting his mustering out in Arkansas.

But all that came later, after his tour of duty in Europe. From Fort Lewis he was sent to Camp Phillips, Kansas, before going overseas. Dominick

Russo, now a retired certified public accountant living in Florida, met Marshall Erdman at Camp Phillips in the summer of 1944.

"We were in the ASTP program together—Army Specialized Training Program," Russo said. "It was for guys who had been to college and we sort of banded together." The stop at Camp Phillips was for two months. The time was spent, Russo said, "rehashing basic training. We were training to go overseas."

Overseas meant the real possibility of combat. The shared strain of that knowledge helped develop camaraderie, though Russo remembered Marshall as something of a loner. "I recall him as skinny, with curly blond hair and a fast determined walk," Russo said. "It was almost a swagger. He didn't suffer fools gladly and he kept to himself. He was intelligent. The people he did gravitate toward were quality people, people who were going places."

On first meeting Marshall, Russo noticed his strong accent and asked Marshall where he was from. "He said Lithuania, but he wasn't anxious to elaborate," Russo said. "He was a bit secretive."

Still, as the days passed and they got to know one another, Marshall relaxed his guard. Russo recalled: "Marshall said, 'When this war is over, I'm going to do some things to better myself. I'm going to take engineering and architecture. And I'm going to marry a rich girl!'"

In Kansas, female companionship again was not a problem. During the weeks at Camp Phillips, Marshall grew close to a girl named Maxine. She was a college girl who lived with her parents in nearby McPheron. When Marshall could leave the base, he and Maxine would play Ping-Pong at the USO or go to Ken's, a local eatery, for the culinary specialty known as the "biffburger."

Maxine would later write, "I feel closer to you after three weeks than I feel toward most of my friends after years and years of acquaintance."

Marshall's unit was to leave for the East Coast, as a prelude to Europe, on August 20, 1944. The night before, a Saturday, he had a final date with Maxine. He brought her home before midnight and stayed a bit; when he left, Maxine sat down and expressed some thoughts she perhaps had wanted to say out loud, but couldn't.

"Marshall, old dear," she began. "Fifteen minutes ago you walked out of my front door and probably—at least tangibly—out of my young life. . . . Following your departure this evening I felt quite pensive and rather more depressed than I anticipated . . . my mind wandered from thought to thought and I decided I might try to transmit a few of them to you. . . . In brief I was considering how much you had challenged my often traditional viewpoints, how much I had enjoyed just talking and being with you, and how I shall miss you. . . . I feel that my 'love' for you is something I shan't soon forget.

"Maxine."

On September 4, 1944, the 44th Infantry Division sailed for Europe on the *USS Monticello*, with Marshall Erdman aboard. According to Dominick Russo, who was also on the ship, they docked outside Southampton, England, then proceeded on to France. They landed in Cherbourg on September 15.

Once in Europe, Russo did not see much of Marshall, as they were in separate units. Further, while Russo was on the front lines, helping liberate towns from the retreating Germans and finally crossing the Rhine into Germany, his buddy Marshall Erdman had experienced a different war.

The first Russo knew of it was one quiet day in a small town in France early in 1945. He was relaxing and daydreaming of home when someone called his name.

It was Marshall Erdman, alone in a jeep with a big grin on his face. Russo walked over and surveyed the jeep. "What's all this?"

"I'm Colonel Alvord's orderly," Marshall replied. "Look, why don't you ask for a few hours' leave? We'll go for a ride."

Recalling the day after more than fifty years, Russo laughed. "We met up with some girls Marshall knew and had some fun. Marshall was leading a pretty sheltered life. He had an important position with the colonel."

"Colonel Alvord" was in fact Lt. Col. Charles B. Alvord, who had assumed command of the 63rd Engineer Combat Battalion (Marshall's unit) in June of 1944. His job as Alvord's orderly likely kept Marshall out of the significant fighting engaged in by the 63rd Battalion. A book written about the 44th Infantry Division had this to say:

"The Battalion was in combat . . . from October 22, 1944, until the war ended on 5 May, performing such tasks as clearing mines, constructing bridges, repairing roads, laying mine fields and barbed wire, and executing demolitions in facilitating the rapid advance of the division." Of course, the top aide to the leader of the battalion probably didn't lay too much barbed wire.

A lighter moment with the 44th Infantry Division, somewhere in France.

Did Russo, or the other soldiers, resent Marshall for his favored treatment? "Heck, I admired him," Russo said. "He was surviving. And he was performing a job. He had the brains to do it. Let him do it."

It's interesting to note that although many people pass through their lives without leaving a ripple, Marshall always made waves. He made strong impressions on people who remembered him well even fifty years later.

Another admirer, albeit now from a distance, was his cousin Jean Levitan Massell, the young

9932

Honorable Discharge

This is to certify that

MARSHALL ERDMAN

36 447 466 Private First Class
Battery B 217th Field Artillery Battalion

Army of the United States

is hereby Honorably Discharged from the military service of the United States of America.

This certificate is awarded as a testimonial of Honest and Faithful Service to this country.

Given at   SEPARATION POINT
Camp Joseph T Robinson Arkansas

Date   15 November 1945

OFFICE OF REGISTER OF DEEDS
DANE COUNTY, WISCONSIN
Received for Record Jan 28
A. D. 1947 at 4:00 o'clock P. M
and recorded in vol. 37
of Discharges on page 119
A. O. Paton Register

H E WRIGHT LT COL MC
Executive Officer

Marshall's discharge papers from the Army.

woman with whose family Marshall had stayed after leaving the Braude home in Chicago. Jean had married a young man named Ric Massell. Ric, too, had entered the service and gone overseas. Jean had wondered if there was a chance that he and Marshall might connect. There was. In late March of 1945, about the time Marshall and Russo were traversing the French countryside in Colonel Alvord's jeep, Jean Massell sat down and wrote Marshall a letter.

"Dear Marshall," she began. "How wonderful that you and Ric were able to meet and spend some time together! Leave it to Marshall to do the impossible, I thought when I found out about it. Only generals of the armies and Marshall can do such things, Ric remarked in his letter.

"By the way, I first knew of your meeting from V-Mail from Ric, then came your letter the following day and the day after that Ben Braude phoned me about it. Thanks for the report on my husband's health and spirits. We were glad to get a similarly favorable report on yours from Ric."

Apparently Jean's husband was impressed with how well Marshall had ingratiated himself with the French people, particularly the young women. "Ric writes you have made many friends among the population," Jean wrote Marshall, "as I well knew you would if you got the chance. By the way, how do European women compare with American women?

Now you can compare them with a more mature outlook than when you first came to America. . . ."

Everyone was upbeat, and why not? The war was almost over. Jean said as much at the end of her March 1945 letter:

"The news is wonderful from the Western Front these days and maybe V.E. day will actually happen next month as Drew Pearson suggests or predicts. I guess he, like others, are saying there won't be formal surrender at once of all fighting Germans but he feels that sometime in April, those Germans who remain fighting will be insignificant in number and strength."

The 44th Infantry Division came home from Europe in July of 1945. According to Dominick Russo, they were lucky. "We were to be one of the first divisions on the beach in Japan," Russo said, "and instead we were one of the first divisions home."

Russo didn't see his buddy Marshall Erdman when they got off the boat in New York. He wouldn't see him for several years, not until the mid-1950s, when Marshall was again visiting New York City.

"He called me and told me to come over," Russo said. "He was staying at the Waldorf Astoria, and he'd put on about thirty pounds!"

Marshall Erdman, landing with his fellow soldiers on the New York docks in the summer of 1945, was now on the verge of making his mark on the world.

Marshall and Joyce prior to their marriage in 1946.

Marshall's choice

THE WAR DEPARTMENT ISSUED A pamphlet to returning soldiers called "Going Back to Civilian Life." The chapter germane to Marshall was called "Education and Training." It stated that as a World War II vet he was entitled to a year of school paid for by the government under the G.I. Bill of Rights. In addition, Marshall qualified for extra free school equal to the amount of time he was in the service. Totaled, it was enough paid schooling to get him a degree.

Not surprisingly, Marshall enrolled as soon as possible: the spring semester of the 1945–46 school year. But he did not go back to Urbana-Champaign. Instead, on January 23, 1946, Marshall enrolled at the University of Wisconsin–Madison. There are differing opinions on why he chose the UW.

"He came to Madison because he wanted to study political science," said longtime Erdman employee Paul Okey, and indeed, Marshall eventually ended up with a degree in political science.

Paul Sprague wrote in his book *Frank Lloyd Wright and Madison: Eight Decades of Artistic and Social Interaction*, that Marshall Erdman "entered the University of Wisconsin to study for the foreign service under [political science] Professor John Gaus."

Gaus was a huge figure at Wisconsin, and his contribution to political science has been compared to Frederick Jackson Turner's contribution to history. Ironically, Gaus was better known for his theories on American urbanism than anything foreign related.

"As people move out to cleaner air and nearer open country and streets with less traffic," Gaus was quoted in his 1944 obituary (*Wisconsin State Journal,* May 30, 1969) ". . . as express highways lead traffic out more swiftly, as super-markets and neighborhood shopping centers move out, the inner core faces declining values, blight, and competition with the suburbs, despite its equipment of public services which have to be duplicated in the new areas."

Could this have been an early genesis for Marshall's Middleton Hills project late in his career? In any event, Marshall somehow did hear about Gaus and enrolled in political science at Wisconsin.

"He talked about going back to Lithuania," Okey said, "and he thought an understanding of government would help him make a difference back there."

Marshall would go back to Lithuania only once, many years later, and one wonders if that's truly what

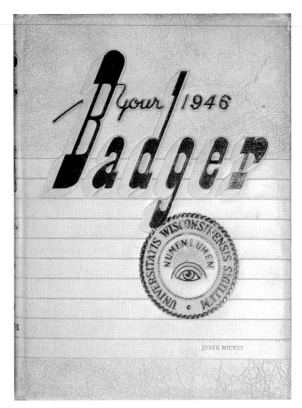

Joyce's 1946 yearbook from UW.

led him to the UW. Another possibility is the explanation offered by his boyhood friend Max Levitan. "His fascination with Frank Lloyd Wright [born in Wisconsin, the famous architect had built his home and school near Spring Green] was the reason for his moving to Madison," Levitan wrote in a letter.

At that stage in his life—indeed as in most lives—there could have been a number of motives, and probably an interest in foreign service was one of them. Marshall was not above telling a story about the circumstances and motives of his early years if it sounded good. He once related yet another version of why he came to Madison to his youngest son, Dan.

In the early '40s, Marshall said, a friend of his at the University of Illinois had received a "Dear John" letter from his girlfriend, who was attending

UW–Madison. The boy chose to argue his case in person and asked his friend Marshall to accompany him on the drive to Madison. Once there, Marshall fell in love with the beauty and ambience of the campus. After the war, with the G.I. Bill money in his pocket, he remembered Madison and the university and decided to enroll.

The story might well be true. The UW–Madison campus was beautiful, and it was surely serene in the early '40s, when Marshall said he'd visited. The war had dropped UW enrollment from 11,376 in 1940 to 6,615 by 1944. But Marshall Erdman was not the only returning vet with an eye on Madison. The campus Marshall found in January 1946 was bustling.

In his book, *The University of Wisconsin: A Pictorial History*, Arthur Hove wrote, "The G.I. Bill gave veterans access to higher education in overwhelming numbers, and enrollment more than doubled in 1946–47, reaching 18,598. . . .

"A major housing shortage—for both students and faculty—accompanied the return of the veterans. . . . On campus, trailers appeared on the grounds of Camp Randall, the former Civil War encampment. Virtually all available housing facilities in the greater Madison area became potential student quarters. . . . Quonset huts were constructed on the Lower Campus. Temporary buildings scattered throughout the campus provided classroom and office space. . . ."

It would not be long before Marshall Erdman would use the housing shortage, which existed not just on campus but all over Madison, to his advantage: It would allow his fledgling building company a start. But that was still a year or two away. First he had an education to finish—a task, Hove noted in his book on the UW, the returning vets took seriously:

"They were not interested in the customary sophomoric antics that periodically characterized undergraduate campus life. They had to make up for lost time, to get through the university and into the work force as quickly as possible. As a result, they concentrated on their studies and got better grades."

Certainly this was true of Marshall Erdman. His grades were decidedly better at Madison than they were at Urbana-Champaign. That may have been due in part to the reasons Hove mentioned, but it was also true that Marshall's English skills, confidence, and overall sense of self must have benefited from surviving the rigors of basic training, traveling overseas, and returning victorious.

He lived in a rooming house off Wisconsin Avenue, at the far eastern end of campus, past the fraternities and sororities on Langdon Street. That first semester, Marshall took classes in geography, botany, English, and political science. When he wanted to relax, he went ice skating.

During the fall prior to Marshall's arrival in Madison, a young woman named Connie Fuller enrolled at the UW. Fifty years later, still in Madison, she recalled those days—those distant days when she was eighteen, away from home for the first time, and living in Ann Emery Hall on campus.

One night during the second semester, in February of 1946, Fuller and a friend decided to go ice skating. A field on the lower campus had been flooded to make a rink. Fuller couldn't skate very

Marshall and his skating partner, Ann Durr, showing off at the Hoofers' 1946 Winter Carnival on the UW campus.

well, and neither, for that matter, could most of the other skaters. One problem was the skates, which were poorly made compared with today's versions.

"But we saw this one guy skating around the rink," Fuller said, "who was a beautiful skater. He was definitely noticeable, and after a while he came over to talk to us. He was very blond, and had an accent, but he spoke very good English."

It was Marshall Erdman. Fuller recalled that he seemed more taken at first with her friend, but eventually he called and asked Fuller for a date. She wasn't sure. At twenty-three, Marshall was five years her senior. But he was nice, and Fuller said yes.

They began seeing each other. It was not a

Marshall with his new fiancée, Joyce Mickey, in front of the Tri Delt House on Langdon Street on her graduation day in May 1946.

He agreed, but asked why. She said she was seeing someone else, although she wasn't. They'd be friends, and that was fine. But Fuller was surprised, a couple of weeks later, when she saw Marshall at the Memorial Union in the company of a young woman who was, in Fuller's words, "well known on campus"—a doer, an achiever, and, in fact, president of the Wisconsin Student Association.

Her name was Joyce Mickey. How she and Marshall met is not in dispute, though there are at least two accounts of the precise circumstances.

Joyce was a member of Delta Delta Delta, known as the Tri Delts, living in the sorority's beautiful home on Langdon Street. By the spring of 1946, Joyce was in her last semester of a distinguished undergraduate career.

On Saturday, March 2, the Tri Delts gave a party to which they invited the boys from Delta Kappa Epsilon, or Dekes, as they were known. Marshall Erdman attended that party.

According to their daughter, Debbie, Marshall had a job in the sorority house, sweeping and cleaning up. But in a 1982 taped interview with his son Dan, Marshall said, "I met Joyce at the Tri Delta house. I was at the Deke house and they invited us over to go dancing."

In any event, the meeting almost didn't take place. Joyce was upstairs and didn't really want to attend the party. A friend, however, persuaded her, and she began to dress. Downstairs, Marshall was getting ready to leave, and his making his way to the door coincided with Joyce's descent of the stairs in a stunning gown. "I saw somebody coming down the stairs in a black dress," Marshall told his son Dan,

serious romance, but Marshall would take her to lunch on State Street, or to a movie. He talked of being Lithuanian and of his days in the army, but he didn't really open up. Fuller began to feel uncomfortable about accepting lunch dates when her lunch was paid for at Ann Emery, and the spark necessary to lift a relationship to the next level was missing. One spring evening, after they'd been to a movie, she told Marshall she thought they should stop seeing each other.

and the rest was history.

"The chemistry," said Debbie, "must have been unbelievable."

It must have been. Joyce jotted down in her calendar that they had their first date the next night. After just a few more dates, on March 16, Marshall proposed to Joyce Mickey and presented her with a ring.

The campus paper, the *Daily Cardinal*, carried the news on March 19, "The campus got a mighty surprise when Tri Delt Joyce Mickey announced her engagement and ensuing marriage to Marshall Erdman after a whirlwind courtship of nine days . . . talk about love at first sight." Marshall liked to joke later that the paper said "Joyce Mickey engaged" and barely mentioned his name.

Anything Joyce Mickey did on campus in 1946 was big news. In that year she became the first female president of the Wisconsin Student Association. She was a young woman of distinction—attractive, ambitious, serious, someone who was going places.

Her journey began in Washington, D.C., where she was born in 1924. Joyce's father, William Mickey, had attended Harvard Business School and was a top salesman with the National Cash Register Company; her mother, Louise, taught high school English. The family home was on 29th Street N.W. Joyce attended Woodrow Wilson High School in Washington and received excellent grades.

After high school, Joyce went first to the Women's College of Middlebury in Vermont, and then, in May of 1944, she arrived in Madison to enroll in the summer session at the UW and stayed to complete her education. She chose Madison

Joyce Mickey became the first woman president of the Wisconsin Student Association while attending the UW.

because of the reputation of the economics department. In particular, Joyce wanted to study under a brilliant and somewhat controversial professor named Max Otto, who was part economist, part philosopher, and much in demand when students chose their courses.

Not surprisingly, Joyce's academic career at the UW was outstanding. She made As and Bs almost exclusively and graduated in the spring of 1946. By then her whirlwind courtship by Marshall Erdman had resulted in wedding plans. Joyce was not deterred by the fact that she had been seriously involved with someone back East. She wrote him a "Dear John" letter, or more precisely, "Dear Bill," for the young man's name was William MacPhail. Years later he would become president of CBS Sports. Joyce Mickey was not attracted to milquetoasts.

Marshall and Joyce wanted to get married sooner rather than later, but circumstances forced them apart, at least for the summer of 1946. Joyce was committed to attending a summer school session back home in Washington on "forming and effectively utilizing political action committees." Marshall was enrolled for the summer session at the UW.

They stayed in touch by mail. There was no money for more than a weekly phone call, but they could write. Letters found in a musty old trunk in the basement of the family home by Marshall's children after his death, provided a glimpse of the couple's feelings and thoughts in the summer before their marriage. Joyce proved to be exceptionally prolific, sending Marshall daily dispatches in which she discussed her political action classes and fussed over plans for the pending union. They were tentatively looking at a date in August.

On June 27, Joyce wrote: "Dearest Marsh—Two days without writing—I'm mucho apologetic. . . . This PAC school is really an experience. Wednesday night Senator Morse and several other more or less well known political figures spoke to us. . . .

"Glad you like the proposed wedding plans. . . . Are you getting nervous? I don't think I'll be a bit nervous when the time comes, but right now I'm still somewhat excited."

Money was a constant concern. Joyce wrote Marshall suggesting that she send one of her father's lightweight suits to Madison. Marshall could have it altered and wear it for the wedding. Marshall, for his part, found a basement apartment at 514 North Carroll Street for the couple to live in rent free for the first five months, and thereafter for the bargain price of $35 per month. However, the lease was contingent on Marshall installing a gas stove, a kitchen sink, an icebox, and a bathroom shower. He also showed his resourcefulness by building much of the furniture for the apartment.

How serious was their need for money? On July 3, Joyce wrote Marshall: "I got an idea the other night on methods of getting more money. Some of the pre-med boys I used to know would get $25 for donating a pint of blood every month or two. Why don't you find out about it at Wisconsin General [Hospital] and sign us both up? Since it isn't wartime anymore I wouldn't feel bad about donating blood for money. . . ."

Joyce worried that her letters weren't romantic enough. It wasn't her style to get mushy by mail. In a letter dated July 4, she asked, "Are my letters too business-like? I never was much good at verbal smooching in letters. Anyway, I do love you, Marsh."

Another time, she explained that her life had been uneventful, giving her nothing of substance to write, so she'd take the opportunity to help Marshall with his English. He had been writing almost daily so Joyce had a fund of his prose to critique.

"Now's a good time to let you know some of the words you misspell," Joyce wrote, "so the graduate assistant doesn't make the same mistakes later on." There are eleven words: lonly (lonely), preffer (prefer), brodcast (broadcast), and eight others.

Plans for the wedding dominated her thoughts as the summer rolled on. A date was set: August 17. On July 10, Joyce wrote: "Hey, Marsh, are you going to get the gold wedding rings? I think you should see about that immediately. Probably that place on the Square [most likely E. W. Parker]. Don't get mine too wide, but for your own, wider bands are nice. Also see about the engraving on the inside. 'Joyce Mickey to Marshall Erdman. August 17, 1946' is what they usually put, I believe, or something like that. . . .

"Cheeze," Joyce concluded, "maybe I'm planning too much. If you have any objections, say so."

Wrapping herself in details allowed Joyce to avoid the larger implications. In a month, she would be married to a man she had known fewer than five months. It was July, but Joyce's feet were growing cold.

In a letter written July 23, three weeks prior to the wedding date, Joyce wrote: "Wedding plans are sort of going ahead. Mom had a good suggestion—have a very small wedding; then we would go away to the beach for several days. When we came back we would have a good-sized reception here at the house [in Washington] and then we could leave for Madison. That sounds nice and also fairly inexpensive. Any further suggestion or comments?" It was not the letter of a woman trembling with excitement over what may be the greatest day of her life. Later in the same letter, Joyce spelled it out:

"Naturally you're in my thoughts most of the time. What I don't want to have happen is to just go on planning our marriage and to let that dominate my thinking about you. Do you know what I mean? In other words, I don't want the wedding plans to cause me to just accept the fact that I must love you so that I wouldn't question whether or not I actual-

The basement apartment at 514 North Carroll Street that Marshall fixed up for the couple.

ly do. I think I do, Marsh. Certainly I know that logically we have everything that would make for a successful marriage. Yet there must be something more and there I'm not sure."

As for Marshall, he had no doubts about the pending marriage, and in his July 24 letter to Joyce he lobbied his case very diplomatically:

"I could perfectly see how those doubts would arise at such a time, and that they are no true indication of anything, except that marriage is an important step in life and that any rational person should be careful in taking such a step. Darling, I feel so sure about us that I can not doubt any more, except in moments when things don't go well, and then everything looks 'blue.' Joyce I love you."

According to Debbie Erdman, Joyce's doubts intensified as the date grew closer. At one point she said to her father that maybe they should call the wedding off. William Mickey had stood quietly by when his daughter had abruptly dropped her boyfriend Bill MacPhail for someone she'd just met at college. Now, however, he had something to say. Joyce could cancel her marriage plans, if she felt she must, but she wouldn't do it in a letter or over the telephone. If she was going to do it, she'd tell Marshall in person.

So she went to Madison. Ed Hart, the Erdmans' great friend who lived next door to them for decades, heard the story of what transpired. "Joyce had decided not to marry him," Hart said. "Marshall was desperate. But he'd worked very hard fixing up the basement room in the house on North Carroll Street where they were going to live. When she came out here he showed it to her and she was really impressed."

Debbie recalled being told, "Papa said, 'Look what I've done!'" Joyce was impressed enough, the story goes, to reconsider, and not stop the wedding.

While that was almost certainly an oversimplification of what happened, Joyce's Madison visit, by simply allowing them to spend some time together again, allayed her fears. She did love him, and she was doubtless deeply moved by the measure of his love for her.

There was one more potential stumbling block. It is not clear precisely when, but at some point that summer Marshall had finally confided to Joyce that he was Jewish—part Jewish, he said. Perhaps it was when she was pestering him in her letters to make up a list of the people he wanted to invite to the ceremony. "In your next letter," Joyce asked, more than once, "can you send me a list of your friends you want the invitations to go to? The thing is we've got to know how many to order."

Marshall's July 24 letter (only two of his letters survived, and the other one, undated, dealt almost entirely with details and sketches of his apartment fix-up project) indicated that he may not yet have confided in Joyce about his background.

"How are the wedding plans coming? Have you sent out the invitations already? Remember to keep out all the invitations going to Chicago till I write you about it."

One does well to remember that this was more than fifty years ago. Even today, in strongly religious families, marriages between Jews and Protestants or Jews and Catholics can be a delicate matter. In 1946, prejudice was in full flower. Jews were routinely turned down for membership in many private clubs. The Nazis had recently sought to exterminate them. For many on both sides, it was "us versus them." And Marshall Erdman, coming not from just any Jewish family but one that included rabbis and others with deeply held beliefs, had to wonder not only how his new in-laws out in Washington would react to his Jewishness but also what his own relatives in Chicago would make make of his marriage to a Gentile.

If Marshall invited his friends and relatives to his wedding, he would have to start with Max Levitan, Rivkeh, and perhaps Marvin Braude. All Jewish. So sometime that summer, Marshall told Joyce, who, much to her credit, was unfazed. But they agreed that it was probably best not to publicize it, which, as a practical matter, meant not inviting any of Marshall's relations to the wedding.

Joyce and her father, William Mickey.

In an undated letter that summer, Joyce wrote Marshall of breaking the news to her parents. "I told them about your being part Jewish," Joyce wrote, "and they were really very full of common sense about it. They said it didn't make any difference to them if it didn't to me. They thought the best thing would be to say nothing about it and go on living as if the problem never existed. What do you think?"

Marshall agreed, and it became one of the defining moments of his life. The implications were profound. Keeping silent about his Jewishness meant not seeing the people—mostly in Chicago—who had been his family, indeed his lifeline, in America over the past decade. And he would not see them, any of them, for nearly fifty years, when David Levitan, visiting his son, Stuart, coincidently living in Madison, telephoned Marshall and they met for lunch.

Along with dropping a curtain on his past, Marshall's decision was bound to affect his future. It meant not being wholly truthful with his four children, who didn't learn of their father's Jewish background until after his death.

How sensitive this issue was can be seen in Debbie Erdman's comments in an early interview for this work before the letters were discovered. "I'm sure my father never told my mother, either," Debbie said. "She shared everything with me."

Not quite everything, as it turns out. For Joyce's letter to Marshall was proof that she indeed knew of his background.

The abrupt and secretive nature of Marshall Erdman's rejection of his Jewish heritage led to much speculation about his motives. Perhaps it was as simple as taking his future in-laws' advice: to "go on living as if the problem never existed."

Debbie thought this theory had as much validity as any. "I think that he didn't like religious families," she said. "The Jewish family he came from was very religious. It had a lot of rabbis in it. He probably hated all that. He might have thought, 'I don't have to admit to any of this.' He met my mother, fell in love, and that was the end of that."

Some speculated that Marshall blocked out his past to help erase painful memories of his family left behind in Lithuania. Debbie also agreed with that suggestion. After visiting the cemetery where her grandfather and uncle had been shot by Nazis, she wrote, "Now I understand a bit better why Papa, in sheer defense, negated the very fact of his first sixteen years of existence. The shame, the anger, all the emotions that were too powerful to acknowledge."

"He came to America on the eve of the Holocaust," David Levitan said. My understanding is that his uncle [Ben Braude] did not want Marshall to come over. He wanted his younger brother. We've always wondered in our family, whether Marshall had some guilt that he survived and his brother died in the Holocaust. That was something

he had to overcome."

Even his close friend Ed Hart never parted the curtain, though independent of David Levitan he formed a similar theory.

"Nobody ever really knew about his family and where he came from," Hart said. Hart, Marshall's neighbor in Madison, shared a breakfast table with Marshall for almost forty years. "He was very close-mouthed about it. He successfully avoided any detailed discussion of his family, more or less implying that a terrible tragedy had overtaken them. Everybody just assumed he had gotten over here to escape the Germans. And that's all we ever knew. It was a real mystery. "

Once again, it may be that the truth was a composite of the theories. Marshall must have felt real pain over the deaths of his father and brother at the hands of the Nazis, and maybe some "survivor's guilt" as well. Then, too, while he was fond of and appreciated the Levitans, Marvin Braude, Jean Massell, and Rivkeh, their religious zeal was not what he liked best about them.

There may well have been days when he regarded his heritage as a burden. Meeting and falling in love with a non-Jewish girl gave him the chance to rewrite part of his personal history, and he took it.

Let no one assume it was easy. His Jewish relatives had been kind to Marshall; they were good-hearted people, to the extent that most would have forgiven his marriage outside of the Jewish faith. Jean Massell said, "He may not have realized that they would have been much more lenient than he imagined."

Charlotte Turyn, sister of David and Max Levitan, concurred. "Ben Braude wanted to go to

Joyce and Marshall were married August 17, 1946, in Washington, D.C.

the wedding, even though it was going to be in a church. He was going to overlook all that and go. But Marshall said, no, he didn't want him there." Nor Rivkeh, nor anyone in his family. According to Charlotte, just days before the ceremony, Marshall telephoned Rivkeh in Chicago.

"He called on the eve of his wedding, crying. He was very prone to tears. He cried and said he didn't know if he was doing the right thing."

The one hurt the most may have been Max Levitan, who went on to become a distinguished professor in cell biology, anatomy, and human genetics at Mount Sinai Medical Center in New York. Max

had last seen his cousin before Marshall went overseas in the army. Marshall had visited Chicago to see his relatives and was headed back to his unit, most likely to Camp Phillips in Kansas.

"The last time I saw him," Max wrote, "I was keeping him company for several hours one day in the vicinity of Chicago's Union Station while he was waiting for a train to take him back to camp."

Max continued: "There is no question in my mind that his break with his relatives was related to his marriage. Rivkeh told me that he called her just before the wedding, tearfully, if I recall correctly, to tell her of the impending event (and perhaps apolo-

CHAPTER 4—Marshall's choice

45

gize for not being able to invite her). I believe this was the last time he had any contact with any of his relatives until the early '90s.

"Although he knew that such a marriage would not be looked on with approval by most of our family, many would not have discontinued their relationship with him on that account."

Max went on to wrongly theorize that Marshall hid his Jewishness from his in-laws. "I can only conclude that the major factor for his estrangement from us was that he was afraid of the disapproval of his wife's family if they knew he was Jewish."

Max concluded, "His break with us was particularly hurtful to me." The pain in those words echoes over half a century. Could the hurt have been avoided? Perhaps. Marshall and Joyce had their reasons. The life they led subsequently, the depth revealed in their characters, was testimony to that.

In hindsight, much remains uncertain. What was certain in 1946 was that one part of Marshall Erdman's life was over and another vastly different phase was set to begin.

Marshall and Joyce as newlyweds.

Interior of the Unitarian Meeting House.

baby, how would you like to be famous?

MARSHALL AND JOYCE DIDN'T HAVE A LOT of time or money to spend on a honeymoon, but they made the most of what they had. Joyce knew the Pocono Mountains from family vacations, and after the summer heat of Washington, an opportunity to enjoy the fresh mountain breezes of northeastern Pennsylvania was appealing.

The honeymoon had been choreographed by Joyce's father, and it would not be the last time William Mickey helped the newlyweds. Earlier that summer, Mickey called a favored hotel, the Pocono Manor Inn, and was told it was booked during the third week in August.

"Well," Mickey replied, "my daughter and her husband were planning on having their honeymoon at your place. Of course, I wouldn't forget you when I send an envelope."

In a July letter, Joyce related the story to Marshall and added, "Isn't that subtle?" But it must have worked, for later Joyce laid out the details. "I think if we had about a week for the honeymoon that will be just about right. Mom and Dad will give us about $300 for that and I believe we would be well justified

in having a good time of it that week."

Joyce continued: "After the reception, we'll take the train up to New York (as that is the only place we can get the train to Pocono Manor—it would take all day if we took the car . . .) and we'll spend the night there, taking the train up to the Poconos early Sunday morning."

After the honeymoon, Joyce wrote, they'd "go back to Madison right away and have about two or three weeks to get settled before school begins."

The newlyweds began their life together in the basement apartment Marshall fixed up at 514 North Carroll Street, on the eastern edge of the UW campus, not far from the state capitol. Marshall had a year of undergraduate study to earn a degree in political science, while Joyce began work on a master's degree in economics. Although Joyce's parents helped with her tuition costs and the G.I. Bill paid for Marshall's, money was tight for the couple. They took on odd jobs, including painting, washing windows, and shoveling snow for anybody who needed the help.

Joyce, inspired by Marshall's ability to fix up

Joyce and Marshall in their basement apartment near the UW–Madison campus.

their apartment on a shoestring budget, saw an opportunity and sent an article and photographs to *House & Garden* magazine in the fall of 1946 describing the cost-cutting measures they had used to make a little home out of their basement apartment. *House & Garden*, reflecting the postwar times, was filled with stories about creative ways to add to and improve living spaces in homes for do-it-yourselfers. Although the editor wrote back to Joyce that he "liked the story very much . . . and will probably be able to use the story . . . and will be able to pay you $50 for it," there was no record of the article ever being published.

Before the spring semester began, Joyce and Marshall decided to build their own house. They used Joyce's savings of $3,000 and a considerable amount of their own sweat equity. City records showed that on January 24, 1947, they purchased a lot in Sunset Village on what was then Madison's far west side at 509 North Meadow Lane for $1,000. A week later they obtained a building permit for the relatively modest 1,200-square-foot house Joyce

Marshall working on his first house at 509 North Meadow Lane, which originally was intended for himself and Joyce.

had designed. Although both were still going to school full time, life was just beginning to get interesting for the Erdmans.

A former classmate and friend of Marshall's, Leon Stutzman, remembered his first introduction to the Erdman entrepreneurial spirit.

"We were all in a two-semester course together in the fall of '46 and spring of '47—my wife Mary Lou and I, and Marshall and Joyce. It was political science. Mary Lou had known Joyce from when they were in the same UW dormitory. (The course was Advanced Comparative Government with Professor Llewellyn Pfankuchen. Because no political science classes appear on Joyce's transcripts, it seems likely that she attended the class for Marshall's benefit. He was still having trouble with grades, judging from his GPA of 2.17 from the pre-

vious semester, but received a B in both semesters for this class.)

"We got to chatting and it turned out we'd all been married about the same time that summer. One day both Marshall and Joyce came to class in overalls—which was unusual in those days. We asked them what was going on and they said, 'We're building our own house.' So three times a week they'd show up in overalls. Then they told us they sold the house before it was even completed, for more than they'd put into it, and bought three lots in Shorewood Hills."

In fact, it was sometime that spring when a woman named Elsie Fansler, a widow, saw the house the Erdmans were building and made an offer to buy it from them. It's hard to know what went through the young couple's minds at this fate-

Joyce was a major contributor in both design and construction work in the early days of Marshall Erdman & Associates.

That he should plunge into home building as his first venture was not surprising. Madison during those years was suffering from an acute housing shortage, as was much of the country. Veterans returned to hometowns and universities in huge numbers and found it nearly impossible to locate a place to live. Articles in the Madison newspapers at the time outlined the crisis. A January 11, 1946, article in *The Capital Times* by Cedric Parker placed some of the blame on the Madison City Council for vetoing a federal housing plan in 1939. "After rejecting a federally financed million-dollar housing project six years ago, Madison city officials today are scrambling frantically hither and yon looking for temporary houses of any kind—straw or otherwise—to take care of a vastly increased population."

A six-part series by Joseph T. Capossela (who incidentally would later live in an early Erdman house in Indian Hills) in the *Wisconsin State Journal* in January of 1946 proclaimed that the United States was "faced with a major problem as important and necessary to defeat as were the infamous roads of Fascism. This new 'war' is the acute housing shortage gripping the nation." The series proceeded to explore the causes, including the surge of returning veterans and the reluctance of home builders to initiate new starts, due to government red tape and uncertainty over costs and availability of materials. "Home builders are faced with such a headache in constructing new houses that they have decided to sit back and wait. What happens is that home construction just creeps, while a nation hungry for homes is demanding action."

"Look for a void, a place where there's a need,

ful moment and when the lightbulb went on for Marshall: that he could make a living out of building. It is even more difficult to imagine how this inexperienced twenty-four-year-old would, in fewer than two years, be building an acclaimed structure for the world's most famous architect.

In any event, what was to be the couple's first home was sold for $14,000. The deal closed on July 23, and the next day they purchased two more lots on Meadow Lane. This was in addition to the three lots Stutzman mentioned that they bought on Cornell Court in Shorewood Hills a couple of months earlier. At this point there was no doubt: Marshall Erdman was now in the house-building business.

Marshall did much of the labor on the early houses he built.

where something isn't being fulfilled," said Marshall Erdman years later in describing the first key in his business philosophy. He clearly found that void here and seized the opportunity.

The summer of '47 was a busy one for the Erdmans. Joyce was finishing her last three courses to earn her master's degree. Marshall was still short a couple of courses to get his bachelor's degree and took one class in botany. They also, amazingly, had under construction or just completed six houses that Joyce designed and Marshall built.

One of the houses, at 910 Cornell Court in the Village of Shorewood Hills, became their home for the next five years. They moved into it that fall. Located just west of the campus area, the village was established in the 1920s and principally developed by Jack McKenna Sr. as an upscale, lakefront neighborhood of winding, wooded streets and expensive houses. The houses the Erdmans built on Cornell Court, however, were very modest and all less than 1,000 square feet.

In June 1947, Marshall Erdman & Associates was established as a sole proprietorship. Those very early associates were not the typical construction professionals one would expect. Marshall pooled his talent with the unskilled muscles of a squad of uni-

Joyce and Marshall relaxing with friends Jenny and Albi Houghton.

versity friends and got the houses built. Leon Stutzman was one of those associates. "That summer I worked for Marshall, doing landscaping, painting, light construction," he recalled. "My major was physical therapy, but I could do a lot of things, and needed the money."

Stutzman graduated in 1949 and left Madison for Portland, Oregon. Now a retired physical therapist and former member of the county planning commission in Monterrey County, California, Stutzman recalled, "I really liked working for Marshall. He was always trying something new—something better, quicker, more efficient. I learned ethical principles from Marshall as well. We kept in touch and visited back and forth for years."

By the beginning of 1948, the Erdmans were going full bore in their new business. Joyce had finished school and was able to devote more time to helping her husband manage their burgeoning enterprise. (Marshall still had a two-credit astronomy survey course left to satisfy requirements for the degree he received that spring.) They had built or had under construction at least nine houses.

In a bold move that revealed some of Marshall's early leadership skills, he initiated a local grassroots program that aimed to provide quality low-cost housing for qualifying war veterans who had children and household incomes of less than $3,000. This got the community's attention. A front-page story in the *Wisconsin State Journal* on Sunday, February 8, 1948, included two large photos of Joyce and Marshall working at their drafting board and one of the houses they had built. The headline read: "Builder Cuts Rates for Vets' Home."

The article noted: "Countless words have been uttered and written about veterans' housing in

Joyce and Marshall's first home at 910 Cornell Court in Shorewood Hills.

Madison. Committee meetings have been held, almost without number. But the first project to get under way, the groundwork for which has been laid quietly and with no fuss and feathers, will be that of a young Madison builder. By cutting his own profits and working with suppliers who have pledged themselves to furnish materials on which they will take a lesser profit, he will pass on savings to veterans in need of housing.

"The builder is Marshall Erdman, World War II veteran and former University of Wisconsin student. This spring, as soon as the frost leaves the ground, he will start digging the basements for 11 houses on Midvale Blvd. in Sunset Village.

"The houses will be completed in six months, and if the project proves a success, he will build another 10 before the end of the year."

What was remarkable about Marshall's plan was not only the ambitious timetable and his assurance that it could be done, but also the coalition of well-established building contractors and suppliers he had managed to pull on board his project, including the Marling Lumber Company; Hyland Hall Electric; and Wolf, Kubly, and Hirsig hardware suppliers. The project was financed through the

Bank of Madison. Jack McKenna Jr., one of the city's major developers and owner of a number of lots on Midvale Boulevard, sold lots in a block at a discount on the proviso that the builder and other contractors and suppliers would join in the project and pass along the savings to the veterans.

Considering that he had been in the construction business less than a year, and with few credits to his name, the cooperation of contractors and suppliers seems noteworthy and speaks to Marshall's ability to command attention and attract believers, even at this early age.

In describing the project, the article noted: "Each house will be individually designed and they will not be 'in-line' with one another. . . . The houses are to be designed by Erdman and his wife, who have designed and built some of the more attractive small homes in the city. Mrs. Erdman is the former Joyce Mickey, onetime president of the student board at the University of Wisconsin.

"The veterans will get a cost sheet showing exactly what was paid for what. Erdman will limit his profit to 5 percent.

"By efficient design and cutting of profits, the Erdmans hope to build a house which will sell for about $8,000. Because of the lower price made possible through profit cutting, veterans should be able to borrow the full amount under G.I. loan, Erdman estimates."

Marshall purchased four lots from McKenna on Midvale Boulevard just south of Regent Street and built houses on each that year. However, those were apparently the only houses built under the Erdman plan. For whatever reason, the collaboration collapsed.

Phil Derse, who with his wife, Margaret, bought one of the Midvale houses, said Marshall had an arrangement with the federal government to provide housing for the veterans. "Vets were going to buy those houses from Marshall. But then something happened and the deal fell through and the homes became available to us."

What had happened was, in 1948, the Wisconsin Supreme Court made a decision that invalidated a 1947 law providing for a doubling of that state's liquor tax, with one half of the revenues assigned to veterans' housing. The provision was reinstated by an amendment to the Wisconsin Constitution later in 1948, but since the funds were channeled into the general fund, money was not readily available for housing.

Derse remembered meeting Joyce and Marshall in the summer of 1948, as well as Joyce's parents, William and Louise Mickey, who had come to visit and to help Marshall get his business off the ground. "Her folks were delightful," Derse recalled. "They drove us around in a big convertible and helped Marshall show us the house."

The house, at 5 South Midvale, was modest by any standard—thirty feet by twenty-four feet.

Margaret Derse, however, remembered that even with its severe size limitations, it was clear the home's builder had talent. The finished product was undoubtedly a collaboration on the part of Marshall and his wife, with neither of them having architectural credentials, and both having strong opinions on what they liked.

"These houses [the four on Midvale] were very minimalist," Margaret said. "They had the same dimensions but were different architecturally. We had a coal furnace, and there was a fireplace with a mantel. There were some nice architectural touches. There was indirect lighting, and an L shape separating the living and dining rooms. Those things were unique, given that the house was really a strawberry box house."

The Derses moved into the house on October 1, 1948. They paid $9,850 with $100 down. The other three houses sold in the same price range, more than what Marshall had hoped but still about $1,000 under the going price at the time.

Ed Hart, who had just gotten out of the service, along with his wife, Martha, were neighbors of Joyce and Marshall's in Shorewood Hills. He remembered his first meeting with Marshall. "Marshall came over one day to ask for something and we got to know him. The next time he brought Joyce along. In those days they lived in a very small house on Cornell Court. Marshall's garage was his workshop. That's how he got started."

The Harts and the Erdmans hit it off from the start and began lifelong friendships. "He seemed like a nice guy," Ed Hart said, "and Joyce was always well dressed. Marshall was pretty quiet, didn't talk much. He never talked much when Joyce was around."

Hart recalled that for Marshall, money was a concern. It was always a concern in those days. Starting a business, particularly a building business, which is capital intensive and notorious for budgeting problems, was a daunting proposition. Joyce assisted with the business (at least until daughter Debbie was born in 1950), but times were hard. The backdrop for everything in the early years of Marshall Erdman & Associates was that there was plenty of work but never enough money.

Friends helped find him work. One day late in 1948, Hart spoke with a friend, Fred Miller, who would later become publisher of Madison's *The Capital Times* newspaper. Miller had just paid $3,600 for a lot on Arbor Drive, off Monroe Street on Madison's west side, close to Lake Wingra and the University Arboretum. He wanted to build a three-unit apartment on the land. Miller told Hart that the well-known Madison contractors couldn't do the job for what Miller had to spend. Hart said, "I have a young client who probably could." It was Marshall Erdman. Miller recalled: "He rang our bell one day and introduced himself. He came in dressed in a sports jacket, gray flannels, and a bow tie. I thought this was a guy after my own heart."

They did, in fact, become close friends. But in 1948 they were wary young men about to enter a business relationship. Miller showed Marshall the plans for the building and told him how much he had to spend. Marshall thought for a moment. "Let me take the plans home," he said, and did that, where he presumably talked them over with Joyce.

Joyce designed many of the homes that Marshall built in the early days.

He came back to Miller the next day and said, "Yeah, I can build it for that price."

Miller proposed a fee. "I told Marshall we'd pay him a thousand dollars when he broke ground, a thousand when he put the roof on, and another thousand dollars when it was done. Three thousand dollars." Marshall replied, "That sounds good to me."

Miller, however, asked the young builder to get a performance bond that would in effect ensure Miller that all the subcontractors on the project were paid. Marshall came back a few days later and said he couldn't secure the performance bond. "They want collateral," he said. "I don't have any assets."

In the end, Ed Hart drew up a second mortgage on the Cornell Court home, which Marshall gave to Miller for security. It proved unnecessary. Marshall built the building, on time and on budget.

"He did exactly what he said he'd do," Miller recalled. "That was always true of Marshall. If he said he'd do something, he did it." Miller added

Paul Okey had many duties, including babysitting the Erdmans' youngest child, Dan, left, while the family vacationed in Florida. (Paul's daughter Paula is on the right.)

tight, because he had no money. He wanted somebody to work for him, but he couldn't pay much."

The position didn't sound overly attractive, but Okey sensed something about Marshall that made him say yes. More than a half-century later, Okey reflected on his decision:

"I actually had another job offer that paid three times what Marshall could pay, a job I thought I would like, but I knew that if I could stay with this guy, if he made it, I would make it. You just knew he was going places. He was a human dynamo. He never stopped."

Demanding? Yes. "After my second interview," Okey said, "Marshall said, 'You're hired. Show up in the morning.' I said, 'I can't do that. I'm right in the middle of final exams.' He said, 'You don't need that anymore. You're working for me now.'" Okey laughed. "That was Marshall."

Okey started to work in early 1950. He can't say he didn't see it coming. The work was hard, the hours exhausting, even outrageous. "I would be there at 5:30 in the morning and sometimes we worked until midnight. He was building about six custom homes a year. Although Joyce was not a trained designer, she would create the plans. The first ones were on Midvale Boulevard (near a tract of land owned by the University of Wisconsin that would later become Hilldale Shopping Center), then some in Crestwood, further west, as well as Shorewood and Orchard Ridge, on the far southwest corner of the city.

"Of course," Okey said, "one of my first jobs when I started was the church." The church was the Unitarian Meeting House—the project that simulta-

that Marshall's fundamental integrity may have contributed to his lifelong enmity toward lawyers and contracts. A man does what he says he'll do—period. Why would anyone need a contract? Despite Marshall's antipathy toward lawyers, Ed Hart was one of his closest friends, and he didn't hesitate to use Hart's expertise when he needed it.

By late 1949, Marshall was getting enough work to think about adding a full-time management position to the business. He called the placement bureau at the University of Wisconsin–Madison and asked them to post a notice.

A young man named Paul Okey saw it. "It said he was looking for young people interested in construction," Okey said, and he called for an interview. Of that first meeting, Okey recalled, "He was a tiger. You knew that the minute you saw him. He was

neously put Marshall Erdman on the map and nearly ruined him. The saga began in the fall of 1945, when the First Unitarian Society, consisting at that time of seventy-five "voting units," either individuals or families, decided to accept an offer by the city's largest department store, Manchester's, to purchase their church near the Capitol Square for $105,000. Their decision meant that the Unitarians would have to build a new church at another location.

Frank Lloyd Wright was chosen as architect for the project, though not without some controversy. In an essay included in the book *Frank Lloyd Wright and Madison*, writer Mary Jane Hamilton noted that one local Unitarian, opposed to Wright, called him "unendurable, arrogant, artificial, brazen, cruel, recklessly extravagant, a publicity seeker, an exhibitionist, egotist, sensationalist, impatient, unscrupulous, untrustworthy, erratic and capricious." But Pastor Kenneth Patton supported Wright, as did others, and in January of 1946 he was hired. Hamilton wrote:

"While the selection of Wright as architect solved one side of the building equation, the question of where to build remained. Initially several downtown Madison locations were considered, but all were rejected due to the high cost of the land and the scarcity of parking space. . . . The Unitarians . . . turned their attention to other properties in the area and in 1947 purchased four acres on University Bay Drive in Shorewood Hills, north of University Avenue for $21,500.

"Wright was pleased with the idyllic site, and envisioned a design that would open outward into nature instead of turning inward upon itself. . . .

Marshall (left) watches as Rev. Fred Cairns breaks ground August 12, 1949, for the Unitarian Meeting House. Looking on are Frank Lloyd Wright (center), Harold Groves, and Erdman employees Frank Tetzlaff and Dan Weber.

Society members first saw Wright's drawings for the building he would later call the 'Meeting House' at a parish meeting held in May of 1947."

Later that month, Wright sent the society a bill for his early work, and Hamilton noted that the congregation was startled that the architect's projected cost for the church was $75,000—up from a $60,000 estimate three months before. If the Unitarians hadn't known before that Wright could occasionally be loose with other people's money, they did now.

According to Hamilton, Wright completed the first set of working drawings in the fall of 1948 and again billed the society (close to $4,000). That almost squelched the deal, but Wright's supporters, most notably Harold Groves, secretary of the church and a member of the building committee, convinced the society to pay.

Aerial view of the Unitarian Meeting House project site. The VA Hospital, also under construction, is located in the upper right.

While Wright was in Arizona in early 1949, Groves, plans in hand, talked to building firms both in and out of Madison. They all projected the cost of building Wright's design at a figure considerably higher than Wright's latest estimate of $75,000 (though the architect conceded he hadn't included landscaping, furnishings, or his own fee in that figure).

Groves, an economics professor at the University of Wisconsin, had a thought. He and his wife, Helen, had become friendly with a young—and undeniably inexperienced—Madison builder named Marshall Erdman through his wife, Joyce, who was a former student.

Another important link to the Unitarians was a house that Marshall had built for Joseph Mire. Mire had been elected to the governing board of the First Unitarian Society, and because of his firsthand building experience with Marshall, supported the idea of hiring him to do the church. In his memoirs, Mire wrote: "In 1949, we had our first house, built at 40 Glenway. The builder was Marshall Erdman. . . . Erdman was generous and let us do a few things ourselves. . . . Our house was the first semi-modern house he had built. We had no hesitancy in recommending him when Professor Harold Groves, the head of the building committee for the Unitarian Church, asked us about him."

In the interview with his son, Dan, in 1982,

Frame of the prow of the Unitarian Meeting House, as viewed from University Bay Drive.

Marshall said, "At the time we were starting to build houses in Madison we got to know the Groveses. Apparently we impressed them, or Joyce did. And one day Harold Groves came over and asked if we'd be interested in building the Unitarian Church."

Marshall was twenty-seven years old, and according to him and to those who knew him at the time, he held the name Frank Lloyd Wright in awe. Of course he was interested. And he was further charmed a short time later when Wright, returning from Arizona in the spring of 1949, uttered the memorable salutation: "Baby, how would you like to be famous?" The details of this preposterous invitation, one of Marshall's favorite stories, changed depending on his whim, but regardless, the words are undoubtedly accurate. Calling Marshall "Baby," which Wright often did, revealed the closeness of their relationship as well as the obvious disparity in their ages.

In an interview that Marshall gave to a panel of architects at the Unitarian Meeting House in 1993, the details of the story seem to have a ring of authenticity.

He recounted that Harold Groves suggested to Mr. Wright, "There's this young architect that's doing building, and he would be very willing to talk to you about it." And that Wright's comment was, "Oh, we're not interested in amateurs, we're going

Erdman's crew taking a break at the Unitarian Meeting House construction site. Members of the congregation volunteered labor and prepared picnics for the workers.

to go to the professionals and get it built." Marshall continued, "And he got his plans out and he sent them out to some of the major [firms], Fuller, and some of the companies in Chicago, New York, and also these people that were building the Veterans' Hospital over here. . . . And the bids came back, and to the best of my recollection, the lowest bid was about half a million dollars and the highest bid was about a million-two.

"So he called up Harold Groves and said, 'who is this young fellow you were talking about? . . .

Have him come out to see me.'

"So Harold called me, and said, 'Mr. Wright would like to see you.' For me it was just like going to Mecca, so it didn't take me long to get out there. . . . I got there about 12:30 or 1:00 and Mr. Wright was still taking a nap . . . finally Mr. Wright came out about 2:00, with his cane, and the proper setup. And he looked at me and said, 'Baby, how would you like to be famous?' And that was the beginning."

On July 31, 1949 a number of society members met with Marshall Erdman at the farm of society board member Howard King.

In 1982, Marshall stated that he never made a cost estimate prior to building the Unitarian Meeting House: "I never did give a bid. I couldn't even estimate the cost. All I knew was that I would give anything to work with Frank Lloyd Wright."

But according to Mary Jane Hamilton, who had access to the society's minutes from that July 31 meeting for her chapter on the Unitarian Meeting House in *Frank Lloyd Wright and Madison*, Marshall's memory in the '82 interview was not doing its best work.

"[Marshall Erdman] told those assembled that he could not build Wright's design for less than $102,000," Hamilton wrote.

A few of those present blanched at the figure. Howard King suggested getting further bids. But they seemed predisposed toward Marshall. Remember, it was around this time that Paul Okey described Marshall as a "dynamo." According to Hamilton, when one of the members moved that "we authorize building immediately"—with Marshall as contractor—the motion carried. The contract was signed at a meeting of the board a few days later.

The official ground breaking was August 12, 1949. *The Capital Times* the next day noted the event and reported that the congregation hoped to be using the new meeting house by that coming January.

As a timetable, that was wildly optimistic. Wright's drawings, according to Marshall in the 1982 interview, "were very vague." When Wright gave Marshall the plans, the builder was dismayed. What there were of the drawings were beautiful—breathtaking—but they were vague and undefined.

Wright would indicate a window but not say what size the jamb should be, what material should be used, or how it should be finished. The plans showed plate glass attaching directly into stone.

"It was beautiful," Marshall recalled. "But I didn't know how to do it and neither did anyone else."

He knew how to work hard, so that's what he did. But there were constant budget concerns that limited the number of people he could hire. Paul Okey was his most notable assistant on the ambitious project. Other concerns would surface later, including a demand by the Wisconsin Industrial Commission that Wright prove the stability of his design for a sloping, copper-clad roof.

The most pressing early problem, the lack of bodies to help build, was solved in two ways. One way was through the use of volunteers. Helen Groves came up with the sensible idea that one way of holding down construction costs would be to get members of the congregation to help Marshall. Hamilton wrote:

"Men, women, teenagers, and youngsters assembled almost every weekend from the fall of 1949 through the spring of 1950 for the thirty-mile trip to a quarry near Prairie du Sac where they spent the day loading rock onto trucks destined for the construction site. . . . Those too old or too young to haul stone served refreshments, either at the quarry or the church site. To the amazement of Marshall, who had encouraged the project by offering the use of his truck for the stone hauling expeditions, the volunteers transported fifty tons the first weekend and by May 1950 had loaded and unloaded some 1,000 tons of stone to be used in the meeting house walls."

While it may have been fun at times for the volunteers, the project took a toll on Marshall and Okey. Marshall later reported that the strain of hauling tons of sandstone ruined his only company truck.

One lucky break for Marshall was that, just by coincidence, the construction site was adjacent to the backyard of his and Joyce's house at 910 Cornell Court. It was particularly convenient because Marshall was still working out of their house up until the fall of 1949.

Paul Okey said one of his tasks was convincing professional stone masons to help out for free—or nominal pay—on weekends. A September 1950 *Wisconsin State Journal* article, quoted by Hamilton, noted: "On two occasions [Marshall and Okey] managed to convince about thirty skilled craftsmen to donate a day's worth of labor as their personal contribution to the project."

"My job was to get the masons and all the guys to put in extra hours for free," said Okey. It wasn't easy. That it was a Frank Lloyd Wright project helped with some people. But crusty old stone masons aren't impressed by that. "Some of them we had to pay. Maybe I'd get two days' work out of them and I'd pay them for one." By necessity, it was a haphazard approach.

Okey recalled the most primitive working conditions imaginable. "We worked right through the middle of winter. We heated with smoke pots. Put a big tarp over the whole thing and burned kerosene. It was horrible. There just wasn't any money. But Marshall wanted to do this job for Wright."

Inch by inch, stone by stone, they got it done.

"He [Mr. Wright] was such an inspirational guy," Marshall recalled in 1982. "When he wanted to be nice he could get you to do anything. He'd come in—very rarely, but once in a while—and say, 'Marshall, you're doing such a good job.' And you just fell apart. He stretched you to the very limit, but every time he smiled at you, you felt greatly rewarded."

He could be charming, but some of his design detailing was simply not practical. This problem, along with the lack of funds, made things tough on his builder. In a talk he gave at a 1980 tribute to Wright in New York City, a talk reprinted in Edgar Tafel's book *About Wright*, Marshall recalled that Wright wanted light materials used for the trusses. The architect said he didn't want anything bigger than two-by-fours used for the entire building. Marshall replied that he didn't think that was possible. "What do you know, baby?" Wright said. When Wright wasn't around, Marshall substituted some two-by-sixes.

Another serious issue entailed the angled prow of the auditorium. Wright's original drawings called for patterned concrete blocks with inserts of stained glass, but in the summer of 1950, he instead decided to use horizontal panes of plate glass that would be inserted into two-by-twelve-inch sloping wood louvers. Not only did this change transform what had been virtually solid walls into transparent ones, but also from supportive to nonsupportive ones, a factor not considered when preparing the structural drawings for the roof.

Without Wright's knowledge, Taliesin architect Wes Peters designed and Marshall installed several steel beams over the north end of the auditorium.

Another apprentice designed thin steel supports that were then added to the interior and exterior to support the quarter-inch plate glass. Wright initially approved of this belated change, but the following summer he decided that the supports obscured the view and demanded that they be removed. Some of the supports on the interior were removed, but most of the exterior ones remained in place.

Another time, Marshall suggested the entrance to the Meeting House, designed to be less than six feet high, was too low. "Could we lower the step, Mr. Wright?" Marshall asked. "People will hit their heads."

According to Marshall, Wright, who was rather small in stature, replied, "Let people bow when they enter my church." Wes Peters did attempt to fix this problem by tearing out the old steps and replacing them with shallower ones to give more head room.

Marshall said Wright stretched you to the very limit. In fact, everyone was being stretched—Marshall, Okey, the society congregation, the Taliesin apprentices, even Wright himself. In February of 1951, eighteen months after the Meeting House's official groundbreaking, UW philosophy professor Max Otto gave a dedicatory sermon that was by any measure premature.

In a 1976 letter to longtime First Unitarian Society minister Max Gaebler, one parishioner, Herb Jacobs, noted that the congregation was exhausted: "They were worn out from hauling stone and aiding in the construction, and could not bring themselves to face the debt that would be involved in a big push to finish the building."

Marshall's fee for building the church was to have been $7,500, which he never collected in full.

As they neared completion, the Unitarians' budget of $75,000 was gone and the church had no roof. Jacobs also wrote that Wright himself was upset, "distressed because his own church . . . was an uncompleted eyesore, rather than a showplace."

Marshall borrowed, mortgaged, and cashed in his life insurance policy to raise the several thousand dollars needed to put on a copper roof.

Still, the ceiling and walls needed plastering, and now the money was really gone. Frank Lloyd Wright had stopped by a few times during construction to offer praise and encouragement, but now the call came summoning Marshall back out to Taliesin to meet with the architect. It was spring of 1951.

"I knew he was mad," Marshall recalled in a 1982 interview. Marshall arrived about 3:00 one afternoon and found Peters, Wright's son-in-law, standing outside with Taliesin Fellowship secretary Eugene Masselink. They were nervous. The mood was tense.

Marshall recalled: "I walked in and said, 'Hello, Mr. Wright.' He said, 'Sit down, Marshall. I want to talk to you.'"

Wright proceeded to vent his anger. "He knew I had done all I could," Marshall said, "but this was the way he was. He went on about what he had done for me, how he had been teaching me, how nice he'd been and on and on."

Finally, Wright said, "How are we going to finish it?"

Marshall, fighting back tears, promised to raise more funds somehow. As Marshall left the house, Gene Masselink, who had felt the lash of Wright's

Young Man With an Idea

Old Success Saga Finds New Hero

Wisconsin and Upper

**SUNDAY
OCTOBER 7, 1951**

The pride and joy of Marshall Erdman's building career was his part in the erection of this unusual Unitarian church in Madison. Erdman (left) is proud of the opportunity this job gave him to work with Frank Lloyd Wright, who designed the building. The project was a co-operative venture by Erdman, his workmen, and volunteer workers from the church.

Sentinel photo

Builder Erdman Practices Housing With a Heart

By ROBERT J. RIORDAN

NOW, YOU TAKE MARSHALL ERD-MAN . . . a Lithuanian high school boy . . . transplanted to America without a word of English to his name . . .

Thirteen years later, at 29, he is one of the leading builders of modern structures in Madison . . . has an organization of 60 to 90 workmen . . . had a proud part in the building of the now famous Unitarian church designed by Frank Lloyd Wright . . . and did three quarters of a million dollars worth of business during 1950.

It's a little difficult to get this story out of Erdman himself because he's been busy building houses and other structures —70 of them—since 1946.

But piecing together what you can get from him as well as friends who have watched his progress, you get a story with more interesting twists than a Hitchcock movie.

Erdman came to Chicago in 1938 as an exchange student, intent on studying architecture at the University of Illinois. There was one slight drawback—he knew not one word of English. Eight months of high school and special classes in Chicago fixed this up, however, and he made his

age forced him to take on a slight full time job besides.

He set out to build himself a house.

He had a legacy of skill from his father, a building and construction engineer in Lithuania who had given his son a working knowledge of building trade crafts such as carpentry, masonry, painting, and so on.

Marshall now pooled this capital of skill with Joyce's savings of $3,000 and the good will and unskilled muscles of a squad of university friends, and went to work.

He built one of the first houses in what is now Sunset Village, on the west side of Madison—but he was to build two more houses before actually living in any of them.

OPPORTUNITY KNOCKS

It seems that just as Marshall was straightening up from the first job, a total stranger rushed up and offered him a "startling" price for the place.

Lights began to flash, bells rang, and Marshall said to himself:

"I can build houses! What am I doing majoring in political science?"

So Joyce began briefing Marshall's college reading for him, "helped" him with term papers and coached him for tests so that between them, he was able to get his

(Please Turn to Page 4, Column 3)

PROFILE Section

Joyce Erdman helped design some of Marshall Erdman's first houses. But Joyce hasn't any time for the building business now, and two of the reasons are shown above with her—Debbie and Timmie. Joyce, who was the first elected woman president of the University of Wisconsin Student Board, still maintains outside interests as vice president of the Madison League of Women Voters.

The completion of the Unitarian Meeting House brought Marshall immediate publicity, including this *Milwaukee Sentinel* article.

tongue himself, put his arm around the young builder and said, "Marshall, welcome to the club."

Somehow, in August of 1951, a burst of new energy brought the church close to completion. Everyone pitched in, even Wright. The architect waived any more fees and offered to give two fund-raising lectures. Congregation members helped again as volunteers. Wright brought in a crew of apprentices during the early weeks of August so that the building would be ready for the lectures. Marshall Erdman, already mortgaged to the hilt, found a banker willing to lend him $8,500 for plastering the ceiling. (The final cost of the project, according to society records, was slightly more than $213,000.)

The Meeting House was, and remains today, an extraordinary structure, a triumph of engineering that "won international acclaim," according to the *Wisconsin State Journal.*

The first Wright-Erdman collaboration continued to draw visitors and praise more than half a century after its completion. In 1957 the Museum of Modern Art included the Unitarian Meeting House in an exhibition of outstanding contemporary religious buildings. In 1973, it was included in the National Register of Historic Places. For the more than 3,500 people who visit annually, either as drop-ins or on guided tours, it continues to hold a fascination. The soaring interior, the raised rostrum area of rough sandstone, and the amazing prow of glass windows inspire awe, both architectural and spiritual.

In the end, the financial and emotional turmoil during construction of the Unitarian Meeting House was undoubtedly worth it. Certainly Marshall Erdman thought so, and said so, for the rest of his life.

According to Mary Jane Hamilton, the talk Wright gave at the Meeting House in late August 1951 was a fund-raiser entitled "Architecture as Religion." In it, Wright said, "Religion is not something you profess, but what you do, and that means what you are, and how you do it."

Did Marshall Erdman hear that lecture? He may have, and if he did, he would have agreed with the sentiments. They were already an integral part of his business ethic, as clients such as Fred Miller had discovered. Now he had built the Unitarian Meeting House in Madison, against all odds and at great personal sacrifice. He did it for the man who was his idol, but forever after Marshall insisted that Wright "did ten times more for me than I did for him. He was almost like a father to me. He opened doors that never would have been open to me without his association."

Wright and Marshall outside the first prefab house on which they collaborated, at 5717 Anchorage Avenue in Madison.

prefabrication the Wright way

IF MARSHALL ERDMAN HAD WANTED AND likely deserved a rest after the tumult surrounding the building of the Unitarian Meeting House, it didn't happen. The years immediately following were hectic both personally and professionally.

The company was becoming known—the publicity associated with Wright and the Meeting House had seen to that. The problem was that you couldn't take good press to the bank, and the Unitarians' project had dug Marshall a financial hole out of which he now had to climb.

At least there was work. If Marshall Erdman & Associates wasn't profitable, it certainly was busy. A four-page mimeo "history" of the company, titled "History of Organization—Products, Peace Time and War Time" dated 1951 reported that in 1949 the firm did $175,000 of business and that jumped to $675,000 in 1950. In addition to home construction, it listed apartment buildings, stores, warehouses, and a church as some of the company projects with construction jobs in Madison, Milwaukee, and Sheboygan.

The operation also had a fully equipped mill-work shop that manufactured "sash and doors, cabinets, desks, patterns, and moldings of all kinds for other Madison contractors as well as for the needs of the firm's own construction business," according to the history document.

The origins of the company's first office and shop dated back to April 1949 when Joyce and Marshall purchased from the Robert Merrill Company a 100-foot-wide lot along University Avenue (formerly called Middleton Road) when it was still outside the city limits of Madison. Joyce's father, William Mickey, again stepped in to help the young couple by making a major cash investment of $5,000 into the business for the construction of their office and shop. That investment was later converted into stock when Marshall Erdman & Associates was incorporated in 1951. It proved to be a good investment, to say the least—of which Mickey's four grandchildren were the beneficiaries.

By the fall of 1949, Marshall was able to move out of his garage workshop on Cornell Court and into the new office at 5117 University Avenue, an address the company still had more than fifty years

The Erdman & Associates office on University Avenue in the early 1950s.

later. (The address was originally listed as 4065 University Avenue and was changed in 1951 when the land was incorporated into the city of Madison.)

The front of the office along University Avenue has remained largely unchanged from its original design. Architect William Kaeser, a neighbor of Erdman's in Shorewood Hills, designed the distinctive building. Marshall was proud of the fact that he was able to reuse trusses from postwar student housing barracks being dismantled at Truax Field (the air force base in Madison) to support the roof and frame the windows in his second-floor office.

Early in 1950, the company moved into the new 8,000-square-foot millwork shop located behind the office. The company history document stated that ten men worked in the shop, including eight cabinetmakers and millwrights. They were paid $1.65 per hour. There were another "thirty-seven men, well trained and experienced" in the field, including two

superintendents, five foremen, and thirty carpenters, masons, and laborers who were paid between $1.65 and $2.10 per hour.

A year later, Marshall, exhibiting his instincts to buy real estate before he really knew what to do with it, purchased nearly ten acres directly behind the University Avenue property. Another three years would pass before the company would begin to expand onto that land, but it provided the company with breathing room for many more years to come.

It is of interest to note that, at the time the company history document was written, the Korean War was raging and Marshall was clearly trying to position his company to take advantage if the war effort expanded:

"The recent purchase of nailing machines and a resaw will enable the millwork shop to turn out skids, crates, pallets, shooks, ammunition boxes, footlocks—in fact, anything out of wood for the defense effort. The firm is ready to begin manufacturing boxes immediately. It has the facilities and man power to produce 500 boxes per hour if necessary."

"The experienced construction force could, of course, shift from the usual peacetime residential and commercial work to building barracks, hangars, airstrips, defense housing projects, etc. for the defense effort."

Despite its capabilities, however, Marshall Erdman & Associates would never need work from the nation's war effort.

In 1951 Marshall approached Henry Peiss, a talented woodworker who had been a partner at Nelson-Peiss Products Manufacturing Company, which manufactured ammunition boxes for the army under government contract.

Paul Okey recalled, "They formed Erdman-Peiss Lumber. Marshall wanted Henry's expertise in lumber and millworking. And they could buy lumber wholesale."

Ed Hart remembered Peiss as a "wonderful cabinetmaker, very loyal to Marshall. They had a pretty good little shop going." But there were other opinions as well.

Collins Ferris, another longtime Erdman friend and later a board member, said, "Peiss was an expert finish carpenter. But he was an old German with a terrible accent, and you could see it probably wasn't going to last. Marshall was going places, while Peiss was a workman. A good workman, but a workman."

The partnership lasted until 1956. At times it was tempestuous. "They argued a lot," Okey said, and thought perhaps it was about money.

Despite the impressive number of $675,000 in 1950 business, which was published in the 1951 mimeo "history," Marshall was having trouble paying his bills.

"We used to have a monthly meeting," Okey said, "where we'd decide who we had to pay and who we could put off. We had three piles of bills: thirty days, sixty days, ninety days, and beyond." In addition, Okey recalled having to make weekly trips to collect the Erdman company's receivables in order to make that week's payroll. This meshed with Collins Ferris's recollection of his discovery that the people he saw in the waiting room in Erdman's office in 1953 weren't customers—they were creditors.

Bob O'Malley started at Madison Bank and Trust in the early 1950s. "There were many days," O'Malley recalled, "when he was overdrawn and we were fighting to get it covered."

There was just something about Marshall Erdman that made believers out of many of the bankers. O'Malley was one of them. Ed Hart recalled that there was another banker in town "who would give him 100 percent loans on all his structures."

The banker's name was Emmet Hampton who was president of Home Savings & Loan of Madison throughout most of the 1950s and '60s. Jim Bradley Sr., who joined Home Savings in 1956 and eventually succeeded Hampton as president, remembered that when he started with the bank, the Erdman company was already a significant customer. "Emmet liked Marshall and believed in his abilities and hard work ethic. When Marshall said he'd do something, Emmet could count on it. Marshall would come in to the bank to ask for a loan for a house and Emmet would always say 'you got it.'"

Marshall with his family in front of the Erdman office.

There were other people who put their neck out because they believed in Marshall. One was a young insurance broker by the name of Bob Kassel. "In the course of [Marshall's] house building, he needed a $22,000 bond," recalled Kassel. "I guess he'd called every other bonding man in Madison and they were either unavailable or didn't want to be available, and being typical Marshall style, he just kept going until he found me. I remember coming to [my wife] and telling her that I thought I was gonna be fired for signing the bond. I wasn't."

Not everyone believed in Marshall. Hart remembered one Madison bank executive advising Marshall to file for bankruptcy. Marshall wouldn't have it. "Marshall said, 'I will not ride on the backs of my creditors,'" said Hart.

Meanwhile, at home, there were mouths to feed. Marshall and Joyce's first child, Debbie, was born in 1950. Timothy followed in March of 1951 and Rustin a year later. By then, 1952, the Erdmans had left Cornell Court and moved to 3408 Circle Close, also in Shorewood Hills, into a home designed by Kaeser and built by Marshall. A modest, flat-roofed structure of cement block and wood, painted gray-blue, it was the house the Erdmans would live in for the rest of their lives. Dan, the last child, arrived in 1956.

The Erdman children, when asked to relate their earliest memories, told of a loving mother and a father who was rarely home. They remembered that while they never felt deprived, money was undeniably tight.

Debbie Erdman recalled her childhood: "The early years . . . memories of my father are nil. He wasn't around. I don't remember him; he wasn't there. Papa was building the company." Tim Erdman agreed: "There's no question Mother raised us."

In later years, Debbie would grow particularly close to her father, traveling with him around the world. But not at first. "He was a terrible father!" Debbie said emphatically. "He didn't like kids. He felt they should be seen and not heard. He never did things with us kids. We were always poor. Well, not poor. But we certainly weren't rich. We used to vacation to Florida, once a winter, with a little hammock in the back of the station wagon. All three kids (Debbie, Tim, and Rusty) would be in the hammock."

Ed Hart observed, "He was awfully tough on the kids—unusually bad." Indeed, the four children found him to be demanding as a parent, distant at times. "No question he was the authoritarian," said Rusty. "He treated his kids worse that his employees. Tim bore the brunt of it. I was the sickly one, always suffering from asthma. Maybe that protected me."

Perhaps it was Marshall's own sad childhood that generated a fear of getting too close, because if you get too close, you can get hurt. Or was it memories of his own little brother—the interloper he felt was responsible for the loss of his adored mother—that caused this unnatural distaste for small children? He was a harsh disciplinarian, expecting much from his children, and was often critical. His uncompromising nature and the very real need for him to be away for long stretches—building his business, making money—contrived to distance Marshall from establishing a positive relationship with his children as they grew up.

Times were hard. Many times Joyce told stories

of how she would awaken in the middle of the night to hear her husband throwing up in the bathroom, worrying over the company's finances in the early years. Tim Erdman recalled, "I remember Mom using double-edged razor blades to slice off the collars and cuffs of my dad's shirts and turning them to get double duty out of them."

Small wonder that the kids gravitated toward their mother. Joyce coped as she always did, with remarkable energy, immersing herself in her children while simultaneously launching herself in all kinds of political and civic directions. It was in these years that Joyce became president of the local League of Women Voters. She developed friendships with up-and-coming Democrats like Gaylord Nelson and Miles McMillin; in the late '50s she worked on a project with Wisconsin Indians for the Governor's Commission on Human Rights.

"Joyce was president of everything she got into," Ed Hart recalled fondly. "President of the village, president of the art association. She wouldn't

Joyce with (from left) Timothy, Debbie, and Rustin.

Joyce was politically active in the community while raising four children. Here she appears on television while president of the League of Women Voters.

take no for an answer." Both Marshall and Joyce had a knack for making friends with influential people even before they became influential. They sought out interesting, ambitious people, people with ideas. And inevitably these friendships lasted and proved valuable.

Marshall Erdman's financial affairs took a modest upturn in 1953 with the introduction of the U-Form-IT home. When he and Henry Peiss formed their partnership two years earlier, one idea they had kicked around hearkened back to exposure Marshall got before the war at the University of Illinois. The one architectural course he took, architecture projections, was taught by Professor James Lendrum, who became the first director of the Small Homes Council at the University of Illinois.

Prefabrication, as Marshall came to know it at the University of Illinois, was a relatively new con-

cept in the classroom of the 1940s, although the idea of a prefabricated home had a venerable history. In the early 1900s, Sears Roebuck offered a whole catalog of numerous models of prefabricated houses and options.

Generally speaking, prefabrication entailed production and assembly of standardized building components at a location other than the building site. The units to be prefabricated could include doors, stairs, window walls, wall panels, floor panels, roof trusses, room-size components, and even entire buildings. Prefabrication required the cooperation of architects, suppliers, and builders regarding the size of basic modular units. In the U.S. building industry, the four-by-eight foot (1.2-by-2.4 meter) panel was a standard unit; the architect's drafted building plans and the supplier's prefabricated wall units are based on multiples of that module.

In 1944, at the request of the president of the University of Illinois, a group of architects and professors founded what became the Small Homes Council. The purpose was to consider the role of the university in meeting the demand for housing in the United States. Returning veterans would need good low-cost housing.

The council's program of research, publication, public service, and education was designed to help not only prospective homeowners but all in the building industry who were interested in improved house design and construction: architects, engineers, contractors, builders, manufacturers, and building material dealers.

The council, which later became known as the Building Research Council, researched many critical questions that would affect the quality of the nation's housing stock.

- How could homes be designed and built more efficiently?
- What kinds of construction and production techniques worked well, and which did not?
- How did people use different kinds of spaces in their homes?
- What roles did community planning, zoning, and interior design play in how neighborhoods worked?

It seemed likely that Marshall became aware of Professor Lendrum's interest in housing from his course. From this first exposure, prefabrication apparently caught Marshall Erdman's imagination, and he maintained a commitment to its advantages for the rest of his life.

Those advantages included the cost savings of mass production, the opportunity to use specialized equipment to produce components, and standardization of parts for quick assembly and erection. The major drawback was in assigning responsibility for quality control.

Again in his 1982 interview, Marshall recalled, "The University of Illinois was one of the first [architectural] schools that believed in prefabrication. They had something called the Small Homes Council and I was involved in that." Of himself and Peiss, Marshall said, "We introduced prefabrication."

Of course that was a bit of an exaggeration. Various prototypes of the prefabricated home had

Joyce and Marshall were good friends of the Nelsons, Bardwells, and Houghtons. Shown here are Gaylord Nelson, Joyce, and Liza Bardwell vacationing in northern Wisconsin in the early 1950s.

been introduced in magazines, advertisements, and books over the previous decade, to bursts of publicity. A prefabricated house dubbed the Motohome, by American Houses, Inc., was introduced at the Chicago World's Fair in 1933 and at a Wanamaker's store in 1935. As the war wound to an end, many builders hoped there would be a mass market for this type of housing and an opportunity to use existing plant capacity to start churning out components.

A 1942 article in *Architectural Record* entitled "Prefabrication Gets Its Chance" stated: "To supply those [houses] most urgently needed in the shortest possible time, at reasonable cost, and with the greatest degree of post-war demountability, defense officials are turning to prefabrication: mass production

This article in *Life* magazine produced thousands of inquiries to the Erdman company. At top, Marshall stands with partner Henry Peiss.

of floor, wall and roof panels at the site or in the factory in quantities sufficient to complete 42,000 demountable houses by July 1."

House & Garden magazine published articles on prefabricated housing in May, August, and October of 1946. It seemed probable that the Erdmans would have been aware of these, because Joyce had submitted an article to the magazine during that time. In the October issue, *House & Garden* listed seventy-five companies then active in the prefabricating industry and showed pictures of representative houses. "Many other companies are organized and hope to enter full production soon," said the article.

Nevertheless, Marshall was convinced of the superiority of his approach. Paul Okey recalls: "National Homes were the forerunners, out of Indiana. They got it going. But they were cheap builders. They cut corners. Marshall said, 'I'm not going to do that. I'm going to do it right and with quality.'" In 1953, Erdman and Peiss introduced a line of prefabricated houses that they called "U-Form-IT."

When *Life* magazine took notice, on October 26, 1953, it called the Erdman-Peiss prefab offering "neither the first nor cheapest . . . but probably the best-designed."

It was Marshall's first real opportunity to combine design and construction as one entity, using technology to replicate those portions of buildings where it made sense to do so. He never wavered in his belief, despite detractors, including an Illinois professor of architecture who sneered at the idea. "Why would you want to dirty your hands with construction?" he said, according to Marshall.

The *Life* article was a bonanza, the 1953 equivalent of getting on network television today. "Bill Proxmire [later U.S. Senator William Proxmire] got me the *Life* article," Marshall said. Proxmire, who had a radio show in Chicago and was already making the connections he would need for a political career, worked for Marshall for a time in sales. He did some writing, specifically the instructions for the houses.

The headline on the *Life* article read: "Efficient package plan saves $5,000 on a well-designed homemade house." The spread in *Life* covered six pages, though most of that was photographs. What text there was read as if Marshall himself had written it. Clearly, *Life* was smitten with Marshall Erdman, or at least with his prefab homes.

"Of all the experts who have tackled the big idea that Americans can build their own houses," *Life* wrote, "the most promising is a 32-year-old Lithuanian immigrant named Marshall Erdman. In the U.S. since 1938, he studied architecture at the University of Illinois.

"Two years ago," *Life* continued, "Erdman joined woodworker Henry Peiss of Madison, Wis. to produce an ingenious you-build-it house. Based on the formula that the amateur can save at least $1 an hour by doing all carpentry and finishing, the Erdman-Peiss package uses many shortcuts to make the work foolproof. The amateur uses precut, premarked lumber, cabinets of building block flexibility, a new paper which both seals and finishes inside walls, a simplified heating-duct system. Plumbing and digging the basement," *Life* concluded, "are done by professionals as part of the package."

Marshall elaborated on that point in a 1954 interview with Madison's *The Capital Times* ("Erdman Firm to Build $250,000 Factory Here," March 18, 1954): "The jobs obviously not intended for laymen are done by professionals and included in the package price of $9,000. These include excavation, concrete foundations, and technical work such as plumbing, heating and electrical wiring."

The cost savings on labor estimated by Erdman and Peiss was $5,000. Their promotional material suggested that a person could build a $14,000 home in his spare time for $9,000.

In 1953, the company offered basically two models of one-story, three-bedroom homes. The design was by the Madison architectural firm of

Model B5

U-FORM-IT
Homes

If you have been dreaming of owning a modern home of your own . . . if cost has been too much for your budget, then read about U-Form-It Homes. Erdman-Peiss assembly-line custom-cutting and partial forming means that you can own a conventionally constructed home at great savings. You can save as much as $3,000 to $5,000 more by doing part of the work yourself. Choose from several models. Notice how each affords the utmost in convenience and attractiveness. All models have three bedrooms located well away from the spacious living area—an excellent traffic arrangement for children.

ERDMAN-PEISS LUMBER CO.
5117 University Avenue   Madison, Wisconsin

A company brochure for Erdman's prefab houses.

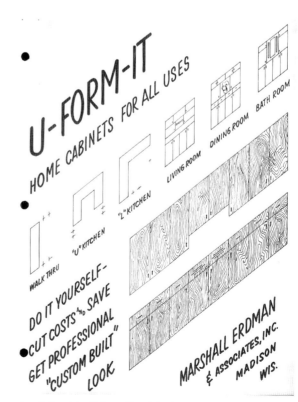

U-FORM-IT HOME CABINETS FOR ALL USES

WALK THRU   "U" KITCHEN   "L" KITCHEN   LIVING ROOM   DINING ROOM   BATH ROOM

DO IT YOURSELF—
CUT COSTS AND SAVE
GET PROFESSIONAL "CUSTOM BUILT" LOOK

MARSHALL ERDMAN & ASSOCIATES, INC. MADISON WIS.

A sell sheet for U-Form-IT cabinets.

This 1955 U-Form-IT house at 5710 Arbor Vitae in Crestwood is model C-4 and is 1,750 square feet.

Weiler and Strang, because at the time there were no architects on the Erdman staff. Each model offered a choice of two plans and included various roof and garage options. "Though kits are now available only within 75 miles of Madison," *Life* wrote, "Erdman and Peiss are already planning to expand deliveries to a 400-mile radius." The publication of the article itself would precipitate that expansion.

The response was tremendous. Collins Ferris, who would become one of Marshall Erdman's closest friends and associates, remembered meeting Marshall at the Madison Club one day after the *Life* article appeared. Ferris had recently returned to Madison from Japan, where he had been vice commander of an air force base responsible for moving troops back and forth to Korea. Ferris at the time was weighing his prospects, thinking what to do with his life, when he was introduced to "a helluva nice guy with a pretty strong accent"—Marshall Erdman. That day at the Madison Club, Marshall was shaking his head and

marveling at the response he'd been getting to the piece on U-Form-IT.

Ferris recalled, "He said he had 10,000 unopened letters sitting in his office, all in response to the magazine article." Marshall raved to Ferris about the concept. "He said the idea was that a guy who was going to own his own home ought to have a part in building it."

But with the pressing time demands, exemplified by the stacks of unopened mail, Marshall needed help. In an approach to hiring that would become typical throughout his life, he asked Ferris to come on board, to help him run the company.

"Well, Marshall," Ferris asked, "what are you going to pay me?"

"I'll pay you what I pay myself," Marshall replied.

The figure was $2,000 a year less than Ferris had made with the air force, but so infectious was Marshall's enthusiasm that Ferris signed on. He stayed only a year before moving to Madison Bank and Trust, but Ferris was one of many individuals who did time in the Erdman camp and went on to distinguish themselves in a wide variety of fields.

"Marshall had a fabulous ability," Ferris said, "to attract people to his cause who later became quite successful"—people like Bill Proxmire, Bob Froehlke (who later became secretary of the army); businessmen David Carley, Sheldon Lubar, and Reed Coleman; hospital administrator Gordon Derzon; and attorneys Jack DeWitt and Jack Pelisek. Most of them served on the company board of directors at one time or another.

In the early 1950s, in addition to houses, the company built a variety of different buildings,

The Erdman 23,000-square-foot factory behind the University Avenue office, designed by William Kaeser, was built in 1954.

mostly in the Madison area and southeastern Wisconsin. Projects ranged from apartment buildings, warehouses, and gas stations to a Howard Johnson's restaurant and a furniture store. The company built what became a campus institution, the Brat House on State Street in 1951. They did work for the University of Wisconsin at the Charmany Farms west of Madison and for the internationally known Forest Products Laboratories on the university campus. In 1954 they landed a $400,000 contract to build the Weiler and Strang–designed Queen of Peace Catholic Church in the Westmorland neighborhood of Madison, a $250,000 job to build an infirmary at the Truax Air Force Base, and a $150,000 job for the erection of the Immaculate Heart of Mary Church in Monona.

But the highest priority at this time was keeping up with the demand for the prefabricated U-Form-IT houses. To that end, in March of 1954, Marshall decided to expand. *The Capital Times* carried the news in a March 18 story: "The Erdman-Peiss Lumber Company, 5117 University Avenue, announced today it is starting immediate construc-

tion of a $250,000 plant for the construction of five U-Form-IT houses daily.

"The factory will be located on the 11 acre plot of the company on University Avenue and will cover 22,000 square feet. It will be served by a 1,000 foot railroad siding from the Milwaukee Road. More than 50 men will be employed to keep production up to five houses a day. The company decided to expand because it is convinced the 'Build it yourself' and the 'Do it yourself' movement is here to stay, Marshall Erdman, president, said." William Kaeser, who designed the adjacent company office a few years earlier, designed this factory as well.

By the time of that story, the U-Form-IT options had increased to ten designs. "All houses have three bedrooms, hot air baseboard heating, large windows [and] full basements for either garages or storage space. . . ."

A Madison Chamber of Commerce publication took notice of the expansion as well: "Materials for the first forty houses were pre-cut and marked under cover of two circus tents, the only available space on the Erdman property. . . . Early in the spring of 1954

Employees working at the Erdman factory prefabricate walls, complete with windows and sashes.

construction began on a new manufacturing plant containing 23,000 square feet. . . . Due to unexpected demand from people of higher incomes, the company is developing a deluxe 4-bedroom model which will be regularly available in 1955. . . ."

One interested and perhaps slightly amused observer of the flurry of attention being paid to Marshall Erdman was Frank Lloyd Wright. The two had stayed in touch since their difficult but exhilarating experience with the Unitarian Meeting House. Marshall spent time at Taliesin—"one of the few nonpermanent apprentices that got all the benefits without paying a lot of dues," he told *In Business* magazine in 1990.

In 1953, he was able to be of service to one of Wright's clients, Russell Kraus and his wife, who were building a Wright-designed home on their large sub-

urban site in Kirkwood, Missouri. Wright had specified cypress for the major building material. However, early in 1953, the supply of cypress ran out, according to an article in the fall 2001 *Gateway Heritage* (the quarterly magazine of the Missouri Historical Society), which detailed many of the daunting difficulties the Krauses met during the building of their home. The article continued: "After several months' delay, the Krauses contacted Marshall Erdman, the young Madison, Wisconsin, contractor who had introduced Wright's prefab house designs. Erdman supplied the lumber from his own company, Erdman-Peiss Lumber, and he visited St. Louis himself at the beginning of 1954." The article, although correct in substance, reversed the time sequence. Marshall's assistance to the Krauses illustrated his ongoing association with Mr. Wright but

Wright and Erdman surveying one of their prefab house models.

actually predated the Wright-Erdman prefab collaboration that was about to emerge.

Marshall Erdman related at least two versions of how he and Wright came to work on a prefabricated home, an event of surpassing importance in Marshall's professional life. Often, Wright dropped in at Erdman's University Avenue office. Sometimes it would be to use the telephone (the only phone at Taliesin in Spring Green in those days was a pay phone, at the phone company's insistence, because Wright rarely paid a bill).

"He'd drive up in his red Lincoln," Marshall recalled in a 1982 interview, "and knock with his cane on the outside of his car. It was always unannounced. Occasionally he'd come into my office, sit in my chair, and start bossing everybody around."

The Frank Lloyd Wright Prefabricated House
By Marshall Erdman and Associates, Inc.

This Erdman brochure promoted the Wright prefab houses. Pictured is the Jackson house, later known as "Skyview."

FRANK LLOYD WRIGHT
PREFABRICATED HOUSES

MANUFACTURED BY ▪ MARSHALL ERDMAN & ASSOCIATES, INC.

The cover of a brochure showing Prefab I Model on Anchorage Avenue (top) and Prefab II Model at 110 Marinette Trail.

In a 1987 interview with Paul Sprague, for an essay Sprague contributed to the book *Frank Lloyd Wright and Madison,* Marshall said the collaboration was Wright's idea. Sprague related the story: "One day [in Marshall's office, in 1954], after Wright had completed his calls, he turned to Marshall and said, 'I hear you're building prefabricated houses in the tent in back of your office. Let's go out and see them.'"

According to Sprague, Marshall dutifully showed the architect the U-Form-IT designs. Wright was unimpressed. Sprague writes that the architect scoffed: "Why Marshall, I thought you had more talent than that. I'm afraid you're going to go broke if you keep on with such poor design. Why don't you let me design a prefabricated house for you?" Marshall, of course, readily agreed, or so he told Sprague.

In his 1982 interview with his son, Dan, Marshall recalled the events a little differently: "Mr. Wright heard about me doing it [prefabricated homes]," Marshall said. "One day he drove up. We had a big tent in back of our factory. We were working there, making the components for the do-it-yourself houses. Mr. Wright just came out one day and said, 'Marshall, I heard you're doing prefabricated houses. Let's see what you're doing.'"

Marshall gave the architect a brief tour. "We walked through the tent and I showed him what we were doing. He said, 'Marshall, you're going to go broke. This is terrible. You're doing it all wrong.'"

When you have a lemon, make lemonade. Marshall said he saw a chance and took it:

"Just off the top of my head, I said, 'Mr. Wright, you could save me. Why don't you design a prefabricated house? I'll build it the way you design it since my designs aren't any good.'" According to Marshall, Wright replied, "Well, I guess I'll have to."

This version of events, with Marshall spontaneously asking Wright for assistance with his design, was also the way Marshall recalled it during a 1980 talk in New York City at a Wright symposium coordinated by Wright apprentice Edgar Tafel.

In his New York talk, Marshall said Wright looked at his prefabricated designs and shook his head. "He looked them over very carefully, walked back twirling his cane in the usual way, and said, 'Marshall, I think you'll really go broke this time.'"

Wright inspecting kitchen of his first prefab house built by Erdman on Anchorage Avenue.

Marshall told the audience, "I thought quickly and said, 'Mr. Wright, you could save me by designing one.' He said he'd have a go at it, and that's how I got to build the first Frank Lloyd Wright prefabricated house."

So, was it Marshall's idea, or Wright's? In any case, the seed had been planted. How quickly the famed architect moved on the project is also the subject of some debate.

Marshall said the plans came quickly. "About two weeks later," Marshall said in 1982, "I got a call from Davy Davison and Jack Howe, two of his top apprentices. They said, 'Mr. Wright wants to see you. He's got something for you.' Mr. Wright had his drawings for the first prefabricated house. It wasn't finished, there were plenty of problems, but the mere idea that he would do it was overwhelming. . . ."

According to Sprague in *Frank Lloyd Wright and Madison*, however, it didn't develop quite that quickly. Sprague wrote that after Marshall and Wright's meeting, when the architect first saw the prefabricated homes and made his disparaging comments, the first

Marshall in New York City with *House & Home* editor Carl Norgrove discuss the magazine's cover story on Wright's prefab houses.

I can think of at the moment."

Wright had produced designs for low-cost and worker housing even before 1900, and in the teens he had provided multiple designs for a Milwaukee firm headed by Arthur Richards. There are some 900 drawings for the American System Built series (also precut units) at the archives at Taliesin West, and six still extant examples of these designs. Some single family and some duplexes, built in 1916–17, were located in Milwaukee. Others were constructed in Iowa, Indiana, and other states.

A house he designed for Herbert and Katherine Jacobs of Madison in 1936 became the prototype for the development of a long line of economy houses, according to Donald G. Kalec in the book *Frank Lloyd Wright and Madison*. During the next twenty-three years, according to Kalec, Wright designed 308 of these modest-cost homes and saw 140 of them built all across the United States. He labeled these houses "Usonian," a term he coined from the words United States of North America, meaning that they were designed specifically to relate to the character and landscape of the United States. Usonian also referred to how the houses were built —no basements, usually flat roofs, and single story. They had radiant heating, small kitchens, often built-in cabinets for furniture, and dining areas instead of dining rooms. In short—homes for families of modest incomes and informal lifestyles. So it was not far-fetched to think that Wright would be interested in collaborating with Marshall on his project.

Paul Sprague wrote: "Though Wright's assistants made a fact-finding visit to Marshall's office, Wright did not get around to making a sketch for over a

thing Wright did was send the two apprentices over to get more information. He had also, Sprague noted, told Marshall in typical cavalier fashion that while the Erdman-Peiss prefab home was inferior, he—Wright—could "design a truly artistic small house . . . that could be marketed for $15,000."

That was 1954 and Wright, it should be noted, was eighty-six years old. It appeared to have taken the famed architect more than a year to get to the promised design, not the two weeks remembered by Marshall in the interview with his son.

In truth, Wright had been interested for many years in building houses of modest cost. During the Great Depression he wrote: "The house of moderate cost is not only America's major architectural problem, but the problem most difficult for her major architects. . . . I would rather solve it with satisfaction to myself . . . than build anything

Marshall Erdman & Associates, Inc.
Madison, Wisconsin

Dealer Price List

Frank Lloyd Wright Designed Homes

Model

1300	3 Bedrooms	2,130 sq. ft.	Basement with carport	$16,400
1310	3 Bedrooms	2,130 sq. ft.	Basement with carport	$16,800
1300 EB	3 Bedrooms	2,130 sq. ft.	Exposed basement with carport	$17,500
1310 EB	3 Bedrooms	2,130 sq. ft.	Exposed basement with carport	$17,900
1400	4 Bedrooms	2,830 sq. ft.	Basement with carport	$17,600
1410	4 Bedrooms	2,830 sq. ft.	Basement with garage	$18,000
1400 EB	4 Bedrooms	2,830 sq. ft.	Exposed basement with carport	$18,700
1410 EB	4 Bedrooms	2,830 sq. ft.	Exposed basement with garage	$19,100

Additions

1. Utility room vs. garage breezeway
2. Powder room in family room, back to fireplace
3. 4-foot extension to master bedroom only — $400
4. Cedar shakes vs. asphalt shingles (1300 series) — $569
5. Cedar shakes vs. asphalt shingles (1400 series) — $640
6. Cedar shakes vs. asphalt shingles with 4-foot master bedroom addition (1300 & 1400 series) — $35
7. Built-in Preway Oven #382
   - A. For builder installation in masonry wall — $150
   - B. Factory built-in cabinet — $250
8. Built-in Preway Surface Unit #386 (in kitchen center island) — $100
9. Dishwasher (unit not supplied)
   Standard opening provided unless otherwise specified
   (Width 24 inches, height 34 inches, depth 23 inches)
10. Mr. Wright's architectural fee — $750

The Wright prefab with many options.

year." Marshall first received a design from Wright in the fall of 1955. That is known because on December 29, 1955, Marshall wrote to Wright, who was at his winter home in Arizona.

Marshall wrote that he had "looked over the plans for the house and they look good. There are some changes I would like to make so I thought it would be best if I would come down to see you. . . . A great deal of interest has arisen here regarding your house which you designed for us and I sincerely hope that we can start construction of the original model within the next few months. . . ."

According to Sprague, the first 1955 designs by Wright had not survived. Marshall flew to Taliesin West in early January of 1956 to confer with Wright. Back in Madison in February, Marshall wrote Wright to say how much he enjoyed the visit and to thank him for his hospitality. He also gently urged the architect not to dally on his design.

On March 3, Wright wrote from Taliesin West.

His perspective was done. Sprague noted, "Wright sent plans for a one-story 'Usonian' house with living wing, bedroom wing, and carport controlled by a square module. As was typical for his preliminary drawings, there were three sheets: a perspective, a plan, and elevations. Although no correspondence survived to document Marshall's reaction, he must have liked the design since working drawings, incorporating only minor changes, were made in August of 1956."

"There were still budget problems," Marshall confided. "Anything he did was so expensive. He wanted to build a $5,000 house—a house for the common man. But his idea was to leave the casings off. When you do that you have to match everything so perfectly it would cost 10 times as much as putting on casings that would cover mistakes."

Word began to leak out, to the astonishment of many, that the world's most famous architect was designing a prefabricated home. Marshall began to get calls from builders across the country, including one from Jim Price, president of National Homes in Lafayette, Indiana, the country's leading company in prefabrication.

"How much did you pay Mr. Wright for designing a prefabricated house?" Price asked. "I went to Mr. Wright and offered him $100,000 to do a house for me and he wouldn't do it."

Marshall replied, "I didn't offer him anything. I didn't have anything to offer."

Recalling that phone conversation years later, Marshall laughed. "This guy couldn't believe it. The truth is neither could I. I was flabbergasted."

One thing Marshall didn't have with Wright was a contract. "Everyone told him he was nuts," said Ed Hart. Hart finally convinced Marshall that he needed some kind of financial agreement with Wright, and he drafted a contract. The two drove to Wright's Taliesin home near Spring Green. As they were ushered into the living room, Wright, imperial, was sitting at the piano playing Chopin. Five minutes passed. Ten. Finally, the architect stood. He shook hands with Marshall. Indicating Hart, Wright said, "Who is this?"

"Mr. Wright," Marshall said, "this is my attorney."

"Get that scrivener out of here!" roared Wright. Hart went out and sat in the car. An hour later, Marshall joined him—without a contract. Eventually, Marshall paid Wright $750 for each home built on one of his designs.

Plans for the first house were revised in September 1956, and Marshall began to build it on Madison's west side, in the area now known as Faircrest. The street was Anchorage Avenue, and the site was within a few blocks of the Erdman offices and factory.

Again, because of the Wright association, the world was watching. That month, Marshall received a call from Carl Norgrove, editor of the highly popular *House & Home* magazine. "Could you come to New York and meet with us?" Norgrove asked.

Marshall later recalled, "I went out to New York and they wanted the exclusive first story on the Frank Lloyd Wright house." Marshall agreed, but there was a hitch. The magazine wanted the piece for its December 1956 cover story, which, given the long lead time of national magazines, meant the home had to be finished in October. *House & Home* sent photographers to capture the construction of the home's exteriors. "All was going well," Marshall recalled. But the magazine needed interior shots as well, and Wright, who had been traveling, hadn't finished his interior design.

Finally the *House & Home* editor cabled Marshall: "We're coming in two weeks. The inside must be finished. We're going to press."

Marshall drove immediately to Spring Green and found Wright at Taliesin. "I gave the telegram to Mr. Wright. He looked at it and looked at me. He said, 'Marshall, here's what you do. Send them a telegram and tell them to do one story on the outside of the house and one story on the inside of the house.'"

Marshall could only laugh. "Nothing fazed him," he later recalled. The piece [just one] did appear as the cover story in the December 1956 issue. The publicity it generated actually helped Marshall in other areas of his business that were beginning to take off: prefabricated schools and, most important, prefabricated medical buildings.

It appears that from the first, Marshall continually pressed Wright to make his design as cost-efficient as possible, a lesson Marshall had certainly learned the hard way while working previously with the great architect. A *Christian Science Monitor* story from 1957 noted: "A condition set for the master by Marshall Erdman, prefabricator, was that Mr. Wright must use stock materials to save him from bankruptcy. 'Anyone can make a shake roof look good,' Erdman said, 'but it takes a master to make something really look new using asphalt shingles.'"

But the *Monitor* story was laudatory, conclud-

AMERICA'S BIGGEST INDUSTRY MONTHLY FOR AMERICA'S BIGGEST INDUSTRY

DECEMBER 1956

House & Home

FRANK LLOYD WRIGHT designs a prefabricated house—page 117

Prefabrication's Year: the models, the men, the market—page 130

What's new in components for 1957—page 160

How to choose and use the right outside paint—page 170

Listen to Washington's best known housing secret—page 155

NEWS BEGINS ON PAGE 33   FOR COMPLETE CONTENTS SEE PAGE 116

The December 1956 issue of *House & Home* showed the rear of Wright's Prefab I Model on Anchorage Avenue.

ing: "The Wright design and prestige in the design for the Madison prefab are expected to give further impetus to the trend of preconstructing houses either in factories or lumber yards. Experts in the building field point out that the Wright-Erdman model proves conclusively that first-class design and production-line economies can go hand in hand to the advantage of the ultimate purchaser."

Another project with Wright was also under way during these years. In 1957, Marshall wrote Wright in Arizona with an estimate to build the Wyoming Valley School, in the neighborhood of Taliesin, for $53,000. The design was a recycled version of a design Wright produced in 1926. Herb

Wright's Wyoming Valley School near Spring Green, Wisconsin.

Fritz was involved with the school building and produced the working drawings. Marshall built it, his first school but a forerunner of more to come.

Wright was planning to donate the cost of the school assembly room in his mother's name. Marshall suggested giving the school district a firm bid of $45,000 and billing Wright for the remainder. He further suggested crediting this amount toward the commissions Wright would have coming from the prefabricated houses. They also corresponded about the design for a motel on University Avenue in Madison.

The truth was the Wright-designed prefabricated home—or homes, because the architect eventually did three designs for Marshall—were not a great success, economically. A 1958 *Milwaukee Journal* article noted that a year after the *House & Home* cover story, Erdman had sold only nine of the houses. However, despite the modest number of houses, the public relations value to Marshall was tremendous. From the associated publicity, he suddenly got the kind of broad exposure and free advertising he could not have afforded.

Marshall tried to kick start the enterprise in January of 1958 by convincing Wright to attend the weeklong National Association of Home Builders convention in Chicago that month. According to an article in *The Capital Times* on January 9, 1958 ("Wright, Erdman to Hold Chicago Prefab Showing"), "The event is intended basically to set off plans for a national distribution system for the Wright-designed prefabricated units, according to Marshall Erdman." Marshall and *Look* magazine cosponsored a reception for Wright at the Chicago Athletic Club on January 21. The next day Wright delivered a lecture on prefabrication and his prefab design in the Crystal Ballroom of Chicago's Blackstone Hotel,

"In preparation for the promotion," *The Capital Times* article continued, "a Wright prefabricated home is being erected in a new, 450-acre subdivision at Barrington Hills, northwest of Chicago.

"Madison already has two of the Wright-designed prefabs. The Erdman firm erected a pilot model in Faircrest, which still may be seen by the public by appointment. The second home was built here for Dr. Arnold Jackson." The latter house, known as "Skyview," was a deluxe version of the

Marshall (center) listens while Wright (left) answers questions at the 1958 National Association of Home Builders convention in Chicago.

Prefab I design with more bedrooms.

At the convention, Marshall predicted fifty of the homes would be sold in 1958. "They will be built by fifty different builders," Marshall said. "After the builders have signed up to erect the homes, it will still be up to Mr. Wright to approve each site before a start can be made. If the site does not meet Mr. Wright's approval, we have the right to cancel the agreement to build the model home."

But it was not to be. Paul Sprague noted: "Erdman's expectations proved grossly overoptimistic." At the time of the convention, nine of the Prefab I homes had been built, according to Marshall, with ten more applications awaiting site approval. A second Wright design, which premiered at the 1959 Madison Parade of Homes in Hill Farms, sold only two houses, and his third design, which would have been the smallest and least expensive of the three, was never built. In all, Erdman built only eleven Wright Prefab homes, five in Wisconsin, two each in New York, Minnesota, and Illinois.

The genesis of this design was of interest. Taliesin Archivist Bruce Pfeiffer wrote in *Frank Lloyd Wright Monograph Series, 1951–1959* (volume eight of a large-format monograph series): "In early 1959, Erdman and Associates sent out a brochure depicting a small, one-story prefabricated house that they were about to market. It was not one of the two that Frank Lloyd Wright had designed for them, but something of their invention. Mr. Wright received a copy of the brochure, brought it into the studio and said, 'You see this plan, Boys? They are getting more and more like ours every day!' He then sat down and proceeded to make sketches directly on the Erdman brochure, and turned them over to us saying, 'Work it out, develop it, and we'll send it to Marshall to show him another custom-built prefabricated house to add to the two we have already done.'

"Using the standard component construction materials found in the other Erdman prefabricated houses, the plan for this one is simple in the extreme. Living, dining, kitchen and three bedrooms are closely grouped together in a simple rectangular form, with a curved terrace out front, the carport optional."

Wright's continued interest in the prefabrication collaboration, so close to the end of his life, was convincing evidence of his abiding interest in providing economical homes "for the common man."

Discussing the reasons why the first Wright-designed prefab home was not the huge sales success that Marshall had anticipated, Sprague wrote: "Exactly why the house did not sell is difficult to assess. It was probably a combination of its high cost and the stigma of low quality associated with prefabricated housing. . . . The high cost of the house was partly due to the amount of site work necessary."

Sprague noted that Marshall was leery of using the word prefabricated. Preengineered or precut might be better, he once told Wright. Erdman & Associates stationery from this time described the firm as "Manufacturers of Pre-Cut Buildings." The architect wouldn't have it: "What are we trying to do?" he said to Marshall. "If it is prefabrication, then call it what it is."

Erdman produced and built more than 600 prefab houses in the 1950s and early '60s, a majority in the Madison and southeastern Wisconsin area. But it was the handful of Wright houses, though not a financial success, that put Erdman & Associates on the map. Wright's death shortly after the design of Prefab III could have affected the momentum of the

marketing effort. For Marshall, the venture proved to his satisfaction the validity of prefabrication. And even before the first one was built he was already thinking in other directions. As his old friend Ed Hart later put it, "Marshall had an intuitive ability for original thinking."

In what other areas could prefabrication be applied? Before the first drawing for a prefab home was completed, Wright and Marshall tossed around the idea of a motel designed and built with prefabrication techniques. Wright eventually designed a circular motel, which Marshall considered building, first behind the Madison restaurant known as the Cuba Club at 3416 University Avenue, officially part of the Village of Shorewood Hills, then on the new Beltline highway that was built in the '50s to the south of Madison. The motel was first mentioned in the Wright-Erdman correspondence in 1955, and Wright brought it up again in a March 1959 letter to Marshall. When Wright died the following month, however, "Erdman shelved the project," according to author Paul Sprague.

Maybe not entirely. According to Dick Garland, chief accountant who joined the Erdman firm in 1961, Marshall was still toying with the motel idea in the early 1960s. An article in *The Capital Times* of August 29, 1961, reported that Marshall had gone before the Shorewood Hills village board to request a change in the village zoning ordinance to allow construction of a motel behind the Cuba Club. The motel was to have thirty units, in three, two-story buildings around a central court, and was undoubtedly the Wright-designed motel or a version of it.

Later, Marshall purchased a restaurant, Frenchy's, on University Avenue with the idea of tearing it down and putting up a motel. He was immersed in other projects, however, and the motel kept getting put off. Then something happened that probably got Marshall out of the restaurant and motel business for good.

"Marshall never really believed in insurance," Garland said. "He owned Frenchy's, but didn't have it insured. One night I got a call. Frenchy's was burning to the ground. I had to call Marshall and tell him." Marshall's response astounded Garland. "Good," Marshall said. "We can forget the restaurant and get back to what we should be doing."

By then, what Marshall Erdman was doing, with amazing success, was putting up medical facilities and, to a lesser extent, schools, using the techniques he'd been mastering during the previous decade. He had discovered the arena where he would earn his fortune.

Dentist Jack Kammer bought Erdman's sixth building in Doctors Park. He later painted his building white, much to Marshall's dismay.

just what the doctor ordered

DURING THE SAME YEARS THAT THE U-Form-IT house was being introduced and built, the firm was quietly exploring other avenues for the application of prefabricated construction. In 1954, in addition to the houses and the larger church and school projects under construction, Erdman & Associates built a relatively small building for two dentists at the corner of Monroe Street and Glenway in Madison. No one knew at the time that this modest medical clinic would serve as the launching pad for the company's eventual empire as the nation's leader in providing health care facilities for doctors throughout the country, which by the 1990s included more than 2,500 buildings.

It was later in that same year, however, that Marshall would really showcase his foresight and entrepreneurial instincts. On a five-acre plot of land immediately south of the Unitarian Meeting House, Marshall unveiled a project he called "Doctors Park."

Marshall's connection with the property went back to 1950 when he along with lumberman Larry Fitzpatrick, his neighbor Ed Hart, attorney Bob Parina, and Charles Thompson formed the Farley Land Company and purchased 6 1/2 acres of land in the Village of Shorewood Hills along University Avenue.

"We were going to build FHA [Federal Housing Administration] apartments," Hart recalled. "These apartments were to be two story, and we also talked about an idea for a high-rise medical building on the property."

The *Wisconsin State Journal* on February 6, 1950, carried a front-page story with an architect's sketch of the plan. The project consisted of fifteen buildings totaling sixty rental units at a cost of $500,000. The two-story buildings were to have gable roofs and be clad in red brick and natural wood trim. The newspaper article said that construction was tentatively set to begin April 1, contingent on approval of the Village of Shorewood Hills board of trustees rezoning the land for apartment use. It never happened.

Ed Hart went in front of the Shorewood village board to present the plan. The board was not impressed. "More than 400 people came out," Hart

Architect's sketch of proposed sixty-unit apartment complex that the Village of Shorewood Hills did not approve. Later site of Doctors Park.

recalled. "I think someone said, 'Let's hang him.'" Hart escaped the noose, but the plan was torpedoed. Shorewood Hills did not want any apartments along University Avenue.

Marshall's second in command, Paul Okey, recalled what happened next. "Marshall was friends with Larry Fitzpatrick and Ed Hart, and when Shorewood wouldn't buy their idea, they dumped their property on Marshall. They thought it was a white elephant."

Hart said, "Marshall bought it from us on a land contract." At the time Marshall acquired the land, some thought it was a mistake. However, with advice from Madison developer Jack McKenna Jr., who also worked for Erdman & Associates for a short period, Marshall came up with a new plan.

Marshall's idea was simple. Provide doctors and dentists with easily accessible offices by building small and horizontal. "Marshall decided that if he couldn't beat them, he'd divide and conquer," Okey said. "He said, 'I'll build small buildings and I'll call it a Doctors Park.'"

In an article in the *Wisconsin State Journal* on October 17, 1954 ("West Side Center for Doctors Planned"), Marshall explained his concept. "The growth of shopping centers in outlying areas has shown that people prefer to shop where they can park," Erdman said. "We are simply taking the idea one step farther in believing that people visiting physicians and dentists prefer to visit offices where they can find parking."

Marshall hired architect and neighbor William Kaeser to design the first three buildings and the company completed them by the following year.

The pharmacy in Doctors Park featured one of the first drive-up windows in the country.

Erdman & Associates would eventually build ten buildings in Doctors Park, selling some and renting the others.

Madison dentist Jack Kammer, who began practicing in the sixth Doctors Park building in 1957, leased his office until Marshall eventually allowed him to buy it.

"He had the idea to build a number of medical facilities near one another and call it a Doctors Park," Kammer said. "I found out about it, talked to Marshall, and we came to a meeting of the minds on the rest. He agreed to put in space for an aquarium for me. Eventually, over time, Marshall sold me the building. But he did all the additions on the building even after I bought it."

It was a brilliant concept on a number of levels. Marshall quickly learned what works when designing and building offices for doctors and what doesn't.

The doctors liked the "park" concept because it provided a professional yet neighborly atmosphere that facilitated referrals. Yet it was in scale with the adjacent residential neighborhood. For patients, the park could allow them to take care of multiple medical needs in one trip, particularly after a pharmacy became the eighth building to open in June of 1958. Prior to this time doctors and dentists typically had offices above a bank building, perhaps on a busy downtown street with difficult parking.

"For a group of doctors interested in maintaining independent practices and yet remaining in close touch with the doctors who are specialists in other fields," Marshall told *The Capital Times* ("Drive-In Pharmacy at Doctors Park," June 19, 1958), 'Doctors Parks' are the answer."

The new pharmacy, like all the other buildings in the development, was manufactured of components prefabricated in the Erdman factory and erected by the Erdman company. The "Drive-In Pharmacy" included a drive-up window for patients to pick up their prescriptions, standard fare in today's pharmacies but a revolutionary concept for the 1950s.

Marshall said in *The Capital Times* article that his company had sold about sixty medical buildings in Illinois, Michigan, Iowa, Minnesota, and Wisconsin. The story stated:

"Erdman attributes his success in promoting the Doctors Park plan to the low cost of the units (from $16,000 to $80,000); there are no steps for patients to climb in the one-story units. They look as much like houses as like office buildings, and therefore fit well into residential areas; they provide ample parking and additional rooms can be added economically.

"The basic unit for one doctor is a 24 by 40 foot structure," the paper continued, "with a waiting room across one end of the building and a reception room, four examining rooms, a utility room, a laboratory and a dark room located on either side of a center hallway.

"The units come with redwood, cedar or composition siding. Components are constructed at the Erdman plant (in Madison) and are shipped by van to locations within 600 miles."

To top off the success of Doctors Park, Marshall even received a letter of commendation from Shorewood Hills Village Clerk George T. Burrill dated May 1, 1959, that read, "This is to advise that the Village of Shorewood Hills Village Board has expressed to Mr. Erdman its appreciation of its devel-

opment of Doctors Park in our village. . . . There was an initial hostility toward diverting from strictly residential use of this area. The excellent appearance of the area harmonizes excellently with the areas to which it adjoins, and we feel that our village residents today enthusiastically support the Doctors Park development."

By the next year, 1959, the Erdman firm had designed and built more than 200 medical offices from the Midwest to the East Coast and Marshall was an acknowledged enough expert in the field that the trade journal *Medical Economics* asked him to write an article offering ideas for doctors thinking about new office space. Reading the piece today, more than forty years after it was written, what is fascinating is how firm a grasp Marshall had on what a doctor's practice entails—almost as if he were schooled in medicine rather than in architecture and political science.

Calling for doctors always to include more space than they think they will need, including extra examining rooms, Marshall noted: "It can improve your patient-relations. Instead of keeping patients waiting in your reception area, you can route them into your extra examining room and tell them to start getting undressed. Perhaps your aide can come in and get their medical histories. What if you don't follow for another ten or twenty minutes? Even so, the patient who's in an examining room either feels treatment has started or, at least, that he's next on your list."

That approach is standard in virtually every medical facility in the country today. Other tips Marshall offered back in 1959 included building in

Construction of the Faith Baptist Church in Monona in 1958 was the first prefab church project for Erdman & Associates. Here, Marshall discusses the job with Pastor Warren Steward (right).

a residential area if at all possible, "because that's where the patients are." He also counseled against building an office where patients have to climb steps or a slope, and he suggested a minimum of five parking spaces per doctor.

While the medical facilities were taking off in the late 1950s, Marshall was also exploring another area that held promise for the application of prefabricated components: schools. The first Erdman prefab school was in Germantown, Wisconsin, outside of Milwaukee. This school district had a one-room country school built in the 1890s, but from 1954 to 1957, the school's population jumped from nineteen to eighty-eight, with still more new homes being built in the district.

The school district clerk, William Coffin, told the *Milwaukee Journal* in May 1957 that a prelimi-

nary architect's drawing had been commissioned with cost estimates of $120,000 for this conventionally built school.

"We then heard about the prefabricated school plan of Marshall Erdman and Associates of Madison," Coffin said. "We checked on it. It was a question of how much we could afford to pay. The result we are getting is really something."

The Erdman design, using prefabricated components, was a four-classroom model that could be built for $75,000, a savings of some 40 percent compared to the conventionally built school Germantown had been planning.

According to the *Milwaukee Journal*, this first Erdman school included "a principal's office, teachers' room, restrooms and room to accommodate two additional classrooms, sinks and cabinets in each classroom, a complete kitchen to serve a lunch program and community dinners and a 28 by 40 foot room that can be used for community or kindergarten purposes."

Marshall told the *Journal* that he had worked closely with state educational officials in coming up with his design, and also said the Madison architectural firm of Kaeser & McLeod had assisted him.

"The savings achieved are the same as in the case of prefabricated houses," Marshall said. "The work is done under one roof (at the Erdman Madison plant) with no time lost during poor weather. A production line adds to the cost savings. Then, after we have worked out the first building, there isn't the constant problem of working out details on the job. It's just a matter of erection. We can erect such a school in from 10 to 12 weeks."

"In an emergency, it could be done in eight weeks. In other words, we could take orders up to June 15 for September delivery. . . . This school is not intended for high schools or real large grade schools. We aren't ready for that right now. But this is intended for the smaller community which needs a small, sound school quickly and it can't afford a high price. . . . We saw the problem of school districts trying to meet their low cost needs. With prefabrication, they could be given a flat cost in advance and actually see what they would be getting for their money by inspecting a model."

The first impact of the baby boom was hitting the schools in the last half of the 1950s, and it was apparent that there would be a need for many new buildings over the next few years. Marshall hoped

that he could turn this need into an advantage, using his methods of construction and offering lower costs. By 1958, however, it became clear that building schools or, more precisely, working with school districts and education bureaucrats, was not going to be a smooth ride. There would be controversy and criticism over the schools which never surfaced in the medical clinic area.

In July of 1958, Marshall Erdman participated in what the *Milwaukee Sentinel* called "a vigorous but friendly" debate before the state legislature's Subcommittee on School Building Economics. Marshall's opposition was Madison architect Allen J. Strang. The subcommittee was studying possible ways of helping cities and towns meet the rising costs of building new schools.

Marshall spoke first: "I would say a minimum of 30 percent and in some cases as high as 50 percent savings can be achieved by the use of standardized, prefabricated grade schools."

"That's completely without substance," fired back Strang, who had served as chair of a Wisconsin school-building committee of the American Institute of Architects in Wisconsin. The 30 to 50 percent savings, Strang said, "couldn't possibly be substantiated."

"Well, maybe it could," Marshall said. He pointed to a school his firm had done shortly after the Germantown grade school. This was the Woodside School in nearby Brookfield. The school board had wanted to add four rooms to an existing school but had to pay off its architect and discard its plan when projected costs reached $120,000.

They hired Erdman for the job, and the firm eventually built a four-room school with an all-pur-

Erdman & Associates built nine prefabricated apartment buildings for the University of Wisconsin's married-student housing complex, Eagle Heights, in 1958.

pose assembly room, kitchen, and restrooms for a cost of $90,000, which was higher than it would have been because the corridor linking the new facility with the existing school had to have brick and interior paneling that matched. Still, the district's savings were considerable.

"We gave them about 20 percent more space for about 30 percent less money, making an overall savings of about 40 percent," Marshall said.

The vice principal of the school, Robert Gull, testified before the committee and praised Erdman, saying the school cost one-third less to build than

the original school and that the building was popular with teachers and students.

A. L. Buechner of Madison, of the Wisconsin Department of Public Instruction, said the heating system used by Erdman could not be compared to that in the more costly, architect-designed school.

Marshall was incredulous. "I agree that they certainly are not comparable—as to cost," Marshall told the legislators. "The question is, how do you judge a heating system? By cost, or by whether it keeps people warm?"

It's worth quoting at some length from this

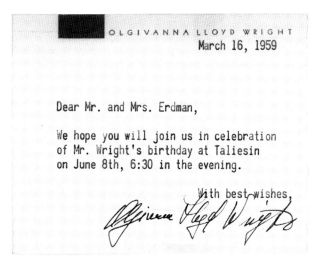

OLGIVANNA LLOYD WRIGHT
March 16, 1959

Dear Mr. and Mrs. Erdman,

We hope you will join us in celebration
of Mr. Wright's birthday at Taliesin
on June 8th, 6:30 in the evening.

With best wishes,

The Erdmans were invited to Wright's ninety-first birthday party, however, Wright died April 9.

debate because it spoke to the passionate belief Marshall Erdman had, and would always have, in the concepts of prefabrication and design-and-build. Perhaps the best example of that abiding belief came years later when Marshall, highly successful and established, was on the State of Wisconsin Building Commission and found himself aghast at how much the taxpayers were paying for state office buildings.

Schools, however, were the current uphill battle. More would be built: Glenn Stephens in Madison in 1960 and some in the state of Indiana, beginning with one in the town of Dale in 1968. A short time later, an ambitious Erdman school was built in Wheeler, Indiana—a $1.6 million facility that included a gymnasium with seating for 800 people.

Marshall himself admitted in an in-house memorandum prepared sometime in the middle 1960s that building schools was problematic. "School boards are more difficult to convince," Marshall said. "Because they bear a community responsibility, they are more hesitant to deviate from traditional methods and concepts."

Paul Okey, Marshall's employee of more than forty years, said of the school experience: "We'd have a situation where we thought we were ready to go and then the school board couldn't get bonding. Marshall would have done the drawings and the preparation for free, and the bond issue would fall through. We'd do two schools in one year and then not do another for three years. You can't build a program on that kind of hit-or-miss basis. So eventually we gave it up."

Dick Garland concurred. "We were doing schools in Wisconsin and Indiana," he said, "where they were somewhat receptive to design-and-build. The program was successful, but in the end we realized we were going upstream. We were not accepted like we were with a group of physicians."

The Erdman firm occasionally applied its prefabrication system on other building types as well. In 1957 the company won a competitive bid for 100 apartment units from Marshall's alma mater, the University of Wisconsin. The project called for nine separate buildings in the married-student housing complex of Eagle Heights, on the west end of campus. This was the second phase of a development that by the mid-1960s provided more than 1,000 apartments for students and their families.

The earlier apartments were built with some prefabricated components, but Marshall's prefabricated process clearly impressed witnesses of the construction as reported in a 1958 front-page story in the *Milwaukee Journal:*

"Three men with hammers stood on a snow covered hill in Eagle Heights out past Picnic Point on the University of Wisconsin campus. Then a semitrailer truck and a crane drove up. The three men began wielding their hammers. Ninety minutes later, the walls of a 250 foot long, two story apartment building stood on the snowy site.

"'There are good and bad kinds of prefabrication,' said Newell J. Smith, UW residence halls director. 'Some prefabricators use different materials, fastened together with gimmicks. This project is simply conventional construction . . . and is just as good as any.'"

In the spring of 1959, Marshall's ten-year relationship with Frank Lloyd Wright was drawing to a close, although there certainly wasn't any indication of it at the time. Wright was just a couple months from his ninety-first birthday. Joyce and Marshall, now part of the close circle of friends of Mr. and Mrs. Wright and the Fellowship, had received their invitation to his June 8 birthday celebration to be held at Spring Green.

Wright had a pile of work on his drafting board. Several of his projects had either just been completed or were under construction, most notably the Guggenheim Museum in New York City. Marshall, meanwhile, was working with Wright on their third prefab house design.

"I had just left him in Arizona where we were working on prefab house number three," said Marshall in the 1982 interview. "We worked three or four hours together in his air-conditioned studio discussing the design. Then we went to lunch, took a little nap, came back, worked a little more before I left to go back to Madison."

Marshall said he received a telegram two weeks later from Wes Peters telling him that Wright was sick and in the hospital. Wright died a few days later on April 9. "Nobody expected him to die. He didn't look like ninety-one. He had a charisma, the way he wore clothes and his sense of style . . . that was the thing about Mr. Wright," noted Marshall.

"The only person I can compare Mr. Wright to is Albert Schweitzer," said Marshall, who encountered Schweitzer during his Peace Corps days in Africa. "They both had so much of the same qualities. Both had big egos and the same tremendous desire for being admired."

Did Marshall model himself after Wright? "They say you can't copy someone like Mr. Wright," responded Marshall to the question in the 1982 interview. "But having been around him so much and him being such a strong individual, you can't help but have some of it rub off."

Indeed, Marshall must have gained enormous self-confidence from this special relationship between two men separated by more than fifty years in age. "He almost never told anybody that you're great or that you're doing a wonderful job," said

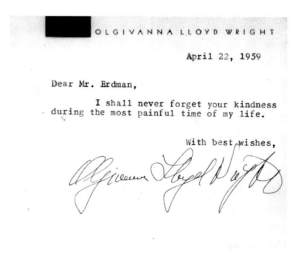

Wright's widow expresses her appreciation for Marshall's friendship.

Frank Lloyd Wright's funeral procession, April 12, 1959. Wright's home, Taliesin, is seen in the background.

Marshall. "There was a time I remember when we had a job and they [the potential client] called Mr. Wright about me and he gave a glowing recommendation, even though he chewed me out royally. This was just his way."

Marshall accompanied the horse-drawn casket in the funeral procession from Taliesin to the nearby Unity Chapel, the small Lloyd Jones chapel next to the family's graveyard. "Wes Peters told me what a terrible [financial] shape Taliesin was in. So I gave them $5,000 and I told Mrs. Wright that this was pittance for what Mr. Wright had done for me. Though it was a helluva lot of money for me at the time."

After Wright's death, Mrs. Wright would often comment to Marshall on how much her late husband loved him, much to the surprise of Marshall.

For a man who dealt with earlier losses in his life by shutting all memories out, Marshall was now learning how to grieve. Reflecting on his own feelings at the time, Marshall, still emotional years later, said simply, "I felt that I lost a great friend."

Marshall giving a Saturday morning lecture to his employees.

stepping into the spotlight

BY 1960, THE MEDICAL CLINIC BUSINESS was flourishing, and Erdman & Associates was still building houses, schools, and churches. But Marshall, according to his close associates, was restless. For the rest of his life it was characteristic that, when a period of tranquility was at hand, Marshall would shake things up. He was never satisfied and that, as much as anything, may have been central to his success.

The loss of his mentor and idol left a void in his life. Wright's death might have precipitated Marshall's next move. In the summer of 1960, Marshall surprised everyone by announcing he would be returning to the University of Illinois for the fall semester. Sure enough, in September Marshall enrolled at Urbana-Champaign as a nonresident to study architecture. Did he have hopes of emulating his mentor and achieving greatness in the field of design? Or did he simply want to fill some gaps in his earlier training?

Whatever his reason, his renewed academic pursuits lasted only one semester. Nonetheless, while in school he carried a full load of classes that included architectural design, freehand drawing, history of ancient architecture, and materials and methods of construction. He even managed to attain a respectable 2.9 grade point average this time.

Marshall thoroughly enjoyed the experience, although he admitted to friends that it was difficult to run a business and go to school full time. It was undoubtedly hard on his family as well. He would fly home from Champaign in the company plane on weekends.

He gave a speech in March 1961 to the West Side Madison Rotary Club and during his talk encouraged others to do what he had done.

"Many business and professional men would benefit by going back to college," Marshall said, "to get more humility, and to learn that universities have a great deal more to offer to you and your problems than you thought possible." A novelty at the time, continuing education in the business world would not become accepted practice for another generation.

In early 1961, it was time to really get a hand on the business. He recognized a need for addition-

Erdman architect Kurt Helin (foreground) at work in the drafting room.

al help in the accounting area. Marshall had never had a financial officer (no surprise to his creditors throughout the 1950s), a number cruncher who could help him make tough calls on the growth and direction of the business. He placed an advertisement for a chief accountant in the *Wall Street Journal,* and Richard Garland, who was living in Milwaukee, saw it and answered it.

Marshall was impressed by Garland's background in accounting for a construction firm and offered him the job. Garland accepted it, becoming chief accountant of Marshall Erdman & Associates in 1961.

"It was an opportune time to join them," Garland said. "An exciting time. The medical build-

ings were really taking off. Marshall was very excited but he said he was exhausted. When he showed me the financial statements he told me he'd been pushing and pushing and the business was turning around."

In 1961, Garland said, the financial problems that had haunted Marshall through the 1950s were still evident, but they were fading. That year the company made a $61,000 profit from sales of around $5 million, Garland said. "Marshall was very proud of that," he said. "It was all verified by Price Waterhouse."

The following year, 1962, that profit would grow to $215,000. The company kept signing more contracts as its medical facilities became known. "It [the profit] just kept growing," Garland said.

In 1960, Erdman & Associates purchased this twin-engine Aero Commander.

"Marshall couldn't believe it."

The growth was exciting, with new offices being opened, and airplanes being purchased—the trappings of success that could hardly have been imagined just a few years earlier, when creditors were still being ducked even as the Erdman name was becoming well known.

With success came more publicity, and this time the press was touting Marshall Erdman, not his association with Frank Lloyd Wright.

In February of 1960, *The Capital Times* wrote ("Two Join Erdman in Expansion," February 26, 1960): "The Erdman company began its medical building operations in the Midwest. Last year it opened a New York office to handle the medical buildings and Doctors Parks in the East. The com-

pany has built or has on its drawing boards or under construction a variety of contemporary styled medical buildings for more than 300 doctors in 22 states.

"To keep up with the expanding operations," the paper continued, "the company recently purchased a second airplane, a seven-place twin-engine Aero Commander, fully equipped for all-weather flying and with oxygen available for riders to enable the plane to reach its service ceiling of 28,000 feet. The plane cruises at 225 miles an hour and carries Erdman company officials nonstop from Madison to New York City in about 3 hours, 45 minutes."

Actually, the Aero Commander was purchased to replace the first airplane, a Piper Apache. The plane and its pilot, Bill Winkman, enabled project

NO ESTOS PALLASOS OTRA VEZ!

WELCOME TO HAVANA

Erdman architect Steve Mason often sketched humorous cartoons depicting Marshall in various situations. Marshall never seemed bothered by them.

managers and salesmen to get to jobs quickly in many small Midwestern towns where the company had work. It also occasionally took employees to more remote locations like Wyoming to go deer and elk hunting.

Marshall used his plane for both business and pleasure, including for family vacations. It also had a tendency to make news. Paul Okey remembered a time when Marshall flew down to see him in Naples, Florida, where Okey was vacationing with in-laws. "Marshall wanted me to come back to work early," said Okey, "so he just flew down to try and convince me. Then I told him about a flight we'd made to Cuba the year before, and nothing could stop him from doing the same thing." Never mind that Fidel Castro had since come into power.

A March 7, 1960, story ("Erdman, Companions Stir Excitement On Cuba Trip") in *The Capital Times* reported the ensuing escapade: "Erdman flew to Key West in his private plane to meet with a group of physicians who are planning to build an Erdman-designed medical center.

"Erdman, his pilot, William Winkman, and Roger Peterson decided to fly to Havana Saturday night for an overnight sightseeing tour.

"Advised that they must land in Cuba before sunset, the trio made the short 90-mile air hop across the Florida Straights but because of their unfamiliarity with flight instructions from the Cuba air control center, did not touch down at the Havana airport until shortly after sunset.

"The plane was surrounded by excited and bearded Cuban soldiers armed with pistols and machine guns and the trio was questioned for more than two hours before they were permitted to go to a downtown hotel.

"When they returned to the airport the next morning, they had to go through another intensive interrogation, but finally after paying a total of $75 in fees to various officials, the party was permitted to leave.

"Adding to the suspicions of the Cubans was the fact that the Erdman company plane is a Aero Commander, the same type of aircraft that had been used recently to bomb Havana."

Another story hit the newspapers that same month, also revolving around the Aero Commander. The *Wisconsin State Journal* reported in its March 26, 1960, edition ("GOP Letter Raises Question Over Governor's Free Rides") that the Republican Party was raising questions over the Democratic governor's free rides in a private plane. The governor, of course, was Gaylord Nelson, and the GOP's weekly newsletter, "FACTS," noted, "We make no accusations and do not imply any 'political payola,' but our citizens are entitled to know all the circumstances which certainly contain every factor of a possible conflict of interest in the governor's use of a private plane belonging to a wealthy builder."

Nelson brushed off the complaint as "nonsense" and said he had been a friend of Erdman's since the Second World War. The governor also assured the public that Erdman had no state government contracts during Nelson's administration and did not intend to do any business with the state.

The company eventually had two Aero Commanders flying for a short period. But in 1967 one of them crash-landed in Ohio. Miraculously, its three passengers walked away from the crash. Nonetheless, Marshall had had enough of his planes, and within a year had gotten rid of the other aircraft.

One of the company's Aero Commanders crash-landed in Ohio in 1967. No one was seriously hurt.

Part of the company growth at that time may have resulted from Marshall's reputation for integrity. A company that did what it said it would, on time and on budget; came back to fix anything that wasn't right at its own cost; and continued to call on the client to assure satisfaction for up to five years was unusual in the building business. The word did get around. Physicians had many opportunities at conferences to swap stories. Dick Garland learned early that for Marshall, doing a job right was as important as, maybe more important than, getting a lot of money for it.

Garland recalled a time after he'd just signed on, in 1961, when Marshall asked him to check on a medical clinic in Springfield, Illinois, that was having problems. Garland was still living in Milwaukee at the time. He went to Springfield to check on the problem.

"The doctor was upset with the basement floor and rightly so," Garland said. "It was a poor job."

Garland estimated the cost of repairing it at $2,100. But the doctor said, "Just give me $1,000 and I'll forget about it and live with it."

Aerial view of Erdman & Associates office and factory from 1958 shows University Avenue at lower right, the factory in the lower left, and Crestwood neighborhood in the upper left.

Garland paused. He could save the company $1,100 by agreeing. "No," he told the doctor, "we want to fix your basement." The doctor said, "That's insane." No, it was the way Marshall Erdman did business. If you did the job, you did it right. Garland said, "I'd only been with the company three or four months, but something had rubbed off."

Garland returned to Madison and explained the situation to Marshall. "He said if we gave him $1,000 he'd forget about It."

Marshall's eyes narrowed. "You didn't give it to him, did you?" Garland said no. A few days later, without any fanfare, Marshall asked Garland if he'd gotten a house yet in Madison. Garland said no, he was still having problems with the financing. Marshall, who had just finished some new homes on

Odana Road in Madison, offered one to Garland.

"The price was very low," Garland said. "But that's how he was. He could be very demanding, but if he felt you were committed to him and the company, he could be very generous."

Most of his acts of generosity were done very quietly. But one attracted public notice and gave an indication of his character. In the 1950s, Carson Gulley, a chef at UW–Madison, bought a house in the Crestwood area of Madison, and the neighborhood association held a tense meeting. Gulley was black. Marshall owned property in Crestwood, had built a number of homes in that neighborhood, and attended the meeting. He listened for a time and said if people were really so upset and wanted to leave Crestwood, Marshall would buy the houses of those who wanted to leave. There was much shuf-fling of feet and the meeting broke up. Carson Gulley moved to Crestwood.

Someone once said it is the actions of men and not their sentiments that make history. Which is another way of saying talk is cheap. Marshall Erdman did more than talk, not only in his coura-geous support of Carson Gulley, but many other times as well.

Bob O'Malley recalled a time some thirty-five years after the Crestwood episode when a local busi-nessman, a mutual friend of O'Malley's and Marshall's, had some financial setbacks and was in danger of losing his house. O'Malley mentioned it to Marshall. Marshall quietly raised the necessary funds (making the largest contribution himself) and cleared the debt, with one caveat: the man was not to know who had helped him.

The other side to his nature was perhaps better known. He could also be prickly, difficult, and hard to please. His temper could be daunting. Pity the poor employee who fell victim to his wrath for some infringement of his standards, or some poor judgment.

Said George Garner, a loyal factory supervisor for forty years: "It wasn't simple, because in those days he was like a firecracker. He had a very short fuse. If he thought it didn't go exactly his way, then he blew up. And there was no 'I'm sorry.' I mean, that did not exist. He could chew you out left and right, even though he was wrong doing it, but he would never apologize."

Garner remembered the time Marshall came into his work area and saw a newly installed telephone. "You don't need this!" he growled, and ripped it from

George Garner, an Erdman employee for forty years, at work in the factory.

the wall. Why, Garner was asked, did he stay? "I liked the guy," he said simply, with a shrug.

There must have been a lot of underlying respect. How else can one explain the many employ-ees who stayed with Marshall year after year, the intense loyalty? Like veterans, they each had old war stories to tell. Marshall also had several secretaries who worked for him for many years, who babied and pampered him, put up with his moods, made him special diet dishes, and hemmed his shorts. This was loyalty that went beyond the ordinary. Even after they retired and moved, they kept in touch.

Employees who couldn't stand up to his criti-cism left, or in some cases he fired them outright. It was often Paul Okey's job to patch up these rifts and, if he thought the employee was valuable, to mollify Marshall and rehire. A disgruntled group of former Erdman employees around the Madison area were known to use the word tyrant, among others, when describing their former boss.

He expected a lot. Paul Okey said, "If there were twenty-eight hours in a day, he'd expect you to work twenty-eight hours. If there were eight days in a week, he'd want eight days of work. You could never give him enough time."

George Garner agreed. He remembered traveling to Europe with Marshall to evaluate the first machinery that his boss was considering purchasing to launch a furniture business. "He used to come to my room at 5:00 in the morning to wake me up. The first day I put up with it. The second day I got up at 4:00 and left and went someplace and had breakfast and then took the train to wherever we were supposed to be. And about 11:00 he arrived and said, "I was looking for you all over the place. Where the hell you been?" I said, "Well, I got up early because I need peace at this time of the morning." Garner, of course, became one of Marshall's most respected and trusted confidants.

But Marshall never asked for more than he was willing to give himself. "He was there earlier than we were," said Dick Garland. "He led by example."

Then too, his insistence on absolute integrity in his business dealings struck a chord with his employees as well as with his clients. Paul Okey told about a medical building the company built for a group of physicians in Des Moines, Iowa, that started sinking Inexplicably. Okey visited right away, and he said, "It was bad; they couldn't close the doors. The whole building was twisted like a pretzel."

It turned out that the building had been constructed on a former landfill, and what's more, the head physician knew that—he'd gotten the land cheaper because of it. Nevertheless, Marshall insist-ed on fixing the problem. "He took great pride in his integrity," said Okey. "He told them he'd stand by his work."

And stand by it he did—to the tune of $35,000 to mudjack the whole building. "We had to auger holes down thirty-five feet to where all that old junk was—car bodies and such. And then pour wide spread cement footings. And we got the whole building plumb again," said Okey.

If you stuck with Marshall, if you endured the brutal hours and the occasional flashes of temper, you were rewarded. "He weeded people out," Garland said. "He found people who really wanted to work."

For them, Garland pointed out, Marshall early on established an employee profit-sharing plan. Initiated in 1959, the plan called for the company to contribute an amount of up to 15 percent of an employee's salary to his or her retirement fund each year the company posted a profit. This was at a time when 7 percent was more typical for businesses. But Marshall believed that it was important to share the company's success with his employees. What became remarkable was that Marshall paid out the full 15 percent to his employees each and every year for the rest of his life, even during the only year when the company was not profitable.

Marshall occasionally lacked what in recent days we have come to call people skills. Okey recalled supervising a job in Des Moines, Iowa, when suddenly, unannounced, Marshall showed up and began nitpicking the project. He could well have been right, but his manner so upset the crew that they began arguing among themselves.

"He got my mason contractor and my superintendent into a fistfight," Okey said. "They were rolling on the floor. Everyone walked off the job."

He also didn't mind facing off with the establishment, even when it was the American Institute of Architects (AIA). Marshall had a long-running feud with the AIA for their refusal to embrace his design-and-build concept. In a March 1961 luncheon speech at the Cuba Club restaurant in Madison (the same speech in which he encouraged executives to go back to college), Marshall lashed out at the AIA, claiming it was "hiding behind a cloak of professionalism." In fact, he said, putting the architect on a pedestal is actually harmful in the long run because it prevents him from getting out in the field and learning the practical side of building.

"Too many architects," Marshall said, "have been indoctrinated with the feeling that they are artists who should be subjected to no discipline or limitations on materials." That kind of elitism has no place in the real world, Marshall said, while emphasizing his love of good, professional architecture.

"I am the first and foremost to advocate that no building should be without design by the best architect," Marshall said, "but I don't say that every building has to be different, or that the architect should be on the outside looking in, rather than being part of a total responsibility organization." He concluded: "The concept of total responsibility architect-engineer-builder firms would get a lot more good buildings constructed."

Marshall and Nobel laureate Dr. Albert Schweitzer (left) together in Gabon, West Africa, while Marshall was working with the Peace Corps.

expanding horizons:
the peace corps years

IN 1961 MARSHALL'S LIFE TOOK YET another turn, one that would provide him with rewards that were more internal than monetary. President John Kennedy had selected Sargent Shriver to direct the nation's Peace Corps operations. Shriver, seeking leadership and know-how for the design and construction objectives of the newly formed Peace Corps, and acting on a suggestion from Marshall's friend Gaylord Nelson, at that time governor of Wisconsin, appointed Marshall as a consultant. His appointment took him to Puerto Rico in June 1961 with the task of building a transition training site that could house up to 150 Peace Corps volunteers headed for tropical climates.

The land was donated by the Puerto Rican government, "in the wildest part of Puerto Rico," Marshall told the *Milwaukee Journal* in an interview. The estimated cost for the project was $30,000, though Marshall suggested it would cost $500,000 if built in the United States.

His first idea was to use concrete pads for the tents the volunteers would live in during their training. That changed when he got to the site and thought about the damage from pouring all that concrete.

"Rather than destroy the forest," Marshall said, "we changed to wood platforms." They also decided against uprooting trees but instead scattered the tents around in the natural setting. "It saves money and it looks better, too," Marshall said. Along with sleeping quarters, Marshall said, "We're building kitchen facilities, a combination mess hall and classroom building, shower facilities, and latrines." No hot water in the shower, however, not with a mountain spring nearby.

"The whole thing is a crude set-up," Marshall said, adding that it was not supposed to be luxurious. "This is not intended to be designed as they have it at home. It's to give the volunteer a taste of what he can expect."

Marshall made a second trip to Puerto Rico to check on the site in July 1961. The first ninety-six Peace Corps volunteers, headed for what was then Tanganyika in Africa, were due September 2. Along with building their training camp, Marshall hoped to teach the volunteers two primary lessons: the less of the natural surroundings one destroys, the more beauty remains; and if you must destroy something, do it properly.

"Part of what I learned from Frank Lloyd Wright," Marshall said, "was to make the most of native materials—to build a building without destroying the site. I am using the teaching of the master."

The Puerto Rican project was a success, and less than a year later, the federal government once again asked Marshall for help. He was one of twenty-three top-ranking U.S. business leaders named to the Commerce Committee for the Alliance for Progress (COMAP). Secretary of Commerce Luther Hodges appointed Marshall to the Housing Task Force of COMAP, an initiative by President Kennedy to revitalize Latin America.

On May 9, 1962, Marshall went to Washington to meet with the President, along with other committee members, and to plot strategy. Marshall's assignment was to develop home designs that could be built at minimum expense—$2,000 to $4,000—while "maintaining some kind of human scale," Marshall said later. The first work was to be done in Venezuela, but this was changed to the Dominican Republic, where housing problems were more acute.

In June, Marshall, along with two other Housing Task Force committee members and several people from the Commerce Department, flew to the Dominican Republic. "The goal," as he would state in a letter to Sen. Hubert Humphrey (later vice president), "was to see if we could get private industry, both of the United States and the Dominican Republic, to work together to get a housing project going in the Dominican Republic."

Marshall returned from the Dominican Republic highly optimistic. He wrote Humphrey:

"Being a bit unorthodox and having more luck than brains, we ended up with what I considered a terrific proposal to get a small housing project going immediately. I found a young architect-builder through a friend of mine in Latin America who had done a great deal of research in low-cost housing and who was extremely interested in getting any housing project going in the Dominican Republic. The houses looked excellent to me and the cost of these houses would have been less than $1,000 per unit complete."

Marshall was particularly excited because they managed to find Dominican financing for half the project, and when they returned, a U.S. organization committed for the other 50 percent. "All we needed," Marshall wrote Humphrey, "was the 70 or 80 percent guarantee AID is supposedly in a position to make."

In effect, AID—the Agency for International Development—was being asked to cosign the mortgage on the project, and it dragged its heels. It would not be the first or last time Marshall Erdman became incensed at bureaucratic timidness.

"In my naive way," he wrote Humphrey, "I felt that this was as ideal a project as you can get in the Dominican Republic. First, it was designed by a Dominican architect; second, it was to be built by the Dominican people; third, it had the unqualified blessing of the Dominican government; and fourth, it was to be built in San Pedro Macoris, a port city on the southern coast of the Dominican Republic where communist agitation was great and where housing

Marshall with Peace Corps volunteers in Gabon, 1963.

needs are desperate."

Marshall ended his letter to Senator Humphrey by pleading exasperation. "I realize this would not have solved the Dominican housing problem. But this would have been more than has been done in the housing field since the new government took over. . . . After a great deal of red tape and discussion, AID refused the necessary guarantee and the project has come to a complete stop. I am sure there were probably good reasons why they turned it down but it is difficult for me to understand it."

Humphrey would remember that letter, and he would remember Marshall Erdman. "He ended up being on good terms with Hubert Humphrey," Dick Garland recalled. AID, with Humphrey paying closer attention, would be of greater assistance in the future, particularly in Tunisia.

In June and July 1962, Marshall completed the second phase of the Peace Corps training camp in Puerto Rico. It took six weeks to design and build the twenty-building camp to house more than 100 volunteers.

In fall 1962, he was asked by the Peace Corps to go to Gabon, West Africa, to help manage a school construction project. For Marshall, it would be his most ambitious and time-consuming commitment yet for the Peace Corps.

But he accepted without hesitation. He believed that if you didn't expose yourself to new ideas, new challenges, you risked complacency. Going abroad and doing good work in foreign countries probably hearkened back to his political science days and his interest in foreign service.

The status quo was never enough for Marshall, and, also, he simply enjoyed traveling. On the European trips in particular, friends, family, and associates would remark on the change that came over Marshall. Abroad he was relaxed, in unfailing good

Peace Corps volunteers and Gabonese workers in front of a school they're building.

design. There were many hurdles that needed to be overcome. Politically, the project was unpopular with the French in Gabon, who were unable to match the quality for the same price. In fact, the speed with which they were built and the apparent ease of construction astounded the Gabonese workers. As one of the AID administrators wrote, in "utility, comfort and appearance, they are superior to others previously constructed in Gabon."

Marshall was proud of the schools and took a personal interest in how they looked. He ordered plantings around the foundation of one of the early ones and was horrified when he arrived on the site

Marshall on a 1962 camping trip in northern Wisconsin with (from left) Tim, Debbie, Dan, and Rusty. Joyce bore the burden of caring for the children during Marshall's long stints in Africa with the Peace Corps.

humor. He spoke German fluently, which endeared him to the Germans. (If Marshall harbored any ill feelings toward Germans because of what the Nazis did to his father and brother, he hid them well.) He had seemingly endless curiosity and stamina, which served him well as he gathered information.

The Gabon project was a joint Peace Corps/AID initiative to design and oversee construction of thirty three-classroom schools and eighty teachers' houses. In late 1962 he met with local Gabonese and Peace Corps/AID administrators, visited sites, and made recommendations on materials. Marshall set up a training course in school construction for Peace Corps volunteers. Design for the schools was based on three premises: they had to be functional without frills, constructed of native materials at low cost, and able to be constructed by relatively unskilled labor.

Eventually some 30 schools and 100 houses were constructed in Gabon, based on Marshall's

Marshall supervises a delivery of materials from a river barge, the most reliable transportation available in Gabon.

to see the bushes and flowers being cut down by workers with machetes. He had to swallow his anger when the local school superintendent explained that snakes would nest in the plantings and be a threat to the students.

Work did not always stay on the schedule Marshall established. Letters to him in Madison from lieutenants left in charge described setbacks. There were occasional difficulties between the Peace Corps volunteers and their supervisors, who were often of a military background and didn't appreciate the fact that some of the volunteers preferred to

make friends with the natives and spend time teaching and singing rather than building. The deadline they were on was frequently brutal—schools had to be completed before the volunteers finished their tour of duty and returned home.

Sometimes, materials did not arrive, were damaged, or were of poor quality. There were always problems with trucks. Field supervisors tried to alter the Erdman design in order to cut corners, which of course irritated him. But all in all, the project was an amazing success, and Marshall received a letter of commendation from

Dr. Schweitzer giving Marshall a tour of his medical compound in Lambaréné, Gabon.

the State Department for his participation.

The project in Gabon was extended through 1965, and this obviously required Marshall to spend yet more time away from his family. Marshall spent all of March and April 1963 with the Peace Corps volunteers in Libreville, the capital of Gabon. It was his longest stint away from his family since he had been married. This seemed to present a paradox for Marshall because he was enjoying the challenge of the assignment, but the letters he wrote home indicate a husband growing more and more homesick. "It is Easter morning and I am very sad and lonely for you and the kids," Marshall wrote his wife on April 14. "I miss you all so much that I can't wait till the end of the month when I will get home. I love you all so much."

Another letter to Joyce on April 20 expressed more of his feelings. "I just reread your letter of April 10 and I am so homesick I can't wait to get home and stay there. I really did not realize how difficult I made it for you by going away for such a long period at one time. I hope I never have to do this again. . . . I can't wait to see you all and spend the weekends all of us together on the farm."

While Marshall was sympathetic to Joyce's situation with four young children to take care of alone, he was also very energized by the whole experience. "This experience in Gabon will teach me a great deal about the Peace Corps and the problems of working in underdeveloped countries," he wrote in the April 14 letter. "It is hard to imagine some of the problems until one experiences them yourself. I will have a great deal to tell you when I get home." On April 20 he wrote, "Darling I really miss you terribly and I am going to appreciate you and everything home so much more. This will have been an experience even greater than the war years for me."

It was during Marshall's Gabon experience that he had the great fortune of meeting another giant figure of the twentieth century, the famed Nobel laureate and philosopher, Dr. Albert Schweitzer. It was not surprising that Marshall recalled that Schweitzer, at nearly ninety, was the only other person he had ever met who exuded the same presence and aura as Frank Lloyd Wright.

Schweitzer left his native Germany to build a hospital in the middle of the jungle near Lambaréné, Gabon, in 1913 and had lived there ever since, providing the locals with modern medicine and health care. Respected throughout the world for his humanitarian work in Africa, Schweitzer had an interest in the Peace Corps efforts in Gabon and followed Marshall's projects closely.

Schweitzer supported Marshall's efforts to use native materials in his Peace Corps buildings. Schweitzer's own hospital was built of native woods against the wishes of the Gabonese government, who wanted a more modern-appearing structure. But the hospital was still holding up to the tropical climate fifty years later.

Marshall at a small market in Tunisia while working for the Peace Corps.

In September 1963 Marshall took a boat trip down the Ogowe River to Lambaréné and spent time with Schweitzer touring his compound. They conversed in German.

"I walked around with Mr. Schweitzer one time for about two hours, and he was showing me his buildings and he considered himself a great designer. We walked into every shack that he had built there. He developed a certain type of double roof that allowed air to circulate in between and it did seem to cool off the buildings a bit. Dr. Schweitzer was saying in every building, 'Das ist unglaublich kühl, nicht wahr?' [this is unbelievably cool, isn't

Lumberyard outside Mendustrie factory. The "M" logo on the factory was a play on Erdman's "E" logo turned on its side.

it?] And I would say 'Jawohl!'"

After Gabon came concurrent projects in the Virgin Islands and Tunisia that kept Marshall on the move throughout the 1960s. St. Thomas, in the Virgin Islands, had become a Peace Corps headquarters. In 1963, Peace Corps volunteers built two three-room schools designed by Erdman, similar to the Gabon schools, as the forerunners of what would become a much larger undertaking.

In 1964, he was invited to Tunisia. Garland said, "AID asked us to help them there. They wanted us to set up a millwork plant." Marshall went as part of a group of American businessmen on a trip sponsored by AID and the Small Business Association. Among Marshall's contributions was the concept of standardization, which apparently was an unfamiliar one in Tunisia.

"He'd come back and tell wonderful stories," Garland said. "Hundreds of stories. At the time in Tunisia they'd cut holes in walls and then build windows to fit them. Marshall said, 'Why not make the windows all the same size and when you build a house you cut the hole that size?'"

The result was a joint-venture manufacturing

Marshall explains the work they're doing in the Mendustrie factory to Hubert Humphrey.

company set up in Tunisia in 1966 to produce standardized, prefabricated windows, doors, and other building components. The company, called Mendustrie, employed about thirty Tunisians. Erdman & Associates invested $100,000 and received an AID loan of $105,000. About 15 percent of the start-up capital came from the leading architects and builders of the country.

His friend and longtime business associate Bob Kassell was involved in the Tunisian project. Marshall called him to see if he would help out and, as Kassell said, "since everything he [Marshall] had ever

touched as far as I was concerned was either exotic or at least interesting, and always an educational thing, I decided to go over there. . . ." He assisted Marshall in managing the project. "The thing about Marshall, he was not in it to get a fat federal job," said Kassel. "He spent a lot of time in the Peace Corps, did a lot of business with them, but the Peace Corps was really a charity on his part."

Tunisian President Habib Bourguiba was very interested in the work Marshall was doing in his country. Kassel recalled the time he and Marshall were dinner guests of Bourguiba at his mansion.

Bourguiba told Marshall he didn't want him to build a big factory and build big houses for the rich. "I want you to come here and teach of my people how to drive a nail, how to lay a brick, etc." This was a man after Marshall's own heart, and it was no wonder Marshall always spoke very highly of Bourguiba.

When Hubert Humphrey, on a nine-nation African swing as vice president, came through Tunisia in 1968, Mendustrie was producing high-quality doors, windows, and components, with a full stock of standardized products for immediate delivery to consumers. The first-ever millwork catalog in Tunisia had been distributed, describing the modular standard window and door units as well as installation methods. Marshall met with Humphrey to review the Mendustrie prefabrication plant, and Humphrey commended Marshall for his work.

"He was successful in Africa," recalled Edgar Tafel, the famed Wright apprentice who'd met Marshall at Wright's funeral in 1959 and worked with him on and off over the next two decades. "Word got around. St. Thomas was next."

In January 1967, Marshall embarked on one of his last and most ambitious Peace Corps projects, in St. Thomas, Virgin Islands. It was a Peace Corps training center that eventually consisted of eleven buildings: six dormitories, a kitchen and dining building for 200, a classroom building, a library and lecture hall, and quarters for the married staff.

"Marshall came to New York and showed me the plat map," Tafel said. "Everything looked fine, but then he went down there and found out the island was essentially run by a single family, and you can imagine how that was. He went through a lot,

but he got it done."

Jerry Sholts, then an eighteen-year-old carpenter with the Erdman company, called his assignment in the Virgin Islands "the greatest experience of my life." It was then that he really got to know Marshall, he said. "We had a $300,000 budget to do six buildings," said Sholts. "When we'd done six, we still had half the money left. So rather than take the money and run, Marshall said, 'We'll build six more.' And we did—or actually five. It was then I knew I wanted to work for this guy. I'd been around contractors all my life, and I saw a lot of bad ones out there. My dad was a contractor, and he had integrity—and here was a guy with twice as much!"

Sholts had been with the firm ever since, managing the construction department and becoming a senior vice president.

Back on the home front during this period, the three oldest Erdman children were approaching high school age and were demanding a lot less of their mother's attention. In September 1966, Debbie and next-door neighbor Abby Hart, Ed and Martha's daughter, went off together for a year of high school in French-speaking Switzerland. By the middle of the school year, Joyce had decided that as long as her husband was going to be away from home so much anyway, why not pack up the rest of the family and join the girls in the Alpine village of Crans-Montana in Switzerland. It worked out well. Marshall's family was closer to his work in Tunisia, and Joyce got to spend six months practicing her skiing as well as her French.

Marshall at this point in his life could truly be considered a man of the world: jetting to Switzer-

Marshall leads Humphrey on a tour of his Peace Corps work in Tunisia in 1968.

land to visit his family, down to Tunisia for the Peace Corps, back to Madison to keep an eye on the family house as well as his own company, and then occasionally down to the Virgin Islands to manage that Peace Corps project.

On-site managers for his Peace Corps work were employees of his company or friends who were recruited and willing to volunteer their time.

Said Bob Kassel, one of those recruited: "It was a fascinating project. Because of my trips down there—many with Marshall—I got to know the governor of the islands, and any number of senators and congressmen who wanted to ride the coattails of the Peace Corps.

"We all did a good job, and Marshall especially got all sorts of accolades from the government for having done what he did in the islands, giving them almost a million-dollar school for little or nothing. . . ."

At the dedication ceremony in January of 1968, Ralph Palewonsky, governor of the Virgin Islands, pointed out that the project had been originally budgeted for $500,000 but Marshall had said he could do it for $250,000, if he was allowed a free hand in the design and building.

"Mr. Erdman cut through a forest of red tape," the governor said. "He improvised and economized and practically worked a miracle in drawing this project through to the success it represents today."

Recognition for Marshall's achievements in Tunisia and the Virgin Islands was written into the

Marshall (right) and Joyce (center) admiring a school completed by the Peace Corps volunteers in the Virgin Islands.

Congressional Record, and he received national news coverage in the United States.

He was proud of his Peace Corps work and gained much satisfaction from the effort, although he didn't boast about his involvement. It was just another challenge, another void that needed filling. Along with the adventures and subsequent stories, the Peace Corps experience for Marshall was a chance to give something back.

Sounding more like the political science gradu-ate, Marshall told the *Milwaukee Journal* on November 7, 1965: "I feel that the greatest asset of the peace corps is not what we do for these other countries, but what they do for us. The ex-peace corps volunteers have learned so much, have gotten such a grasp of the world, they are bound to shape our future world policy in a good way."

"He did that work out of the goodness of his heart," Tafel said. "This is where he could help the government and make a difference for the people. It was an educational charity program, in a sense."

MARSHALL ERDMAN AND ASSOCIATES, INC.

5117 UNIVERSITY AVENUE, MADISON, WISCONSIN 238-0211 (608)

January 16, 1968

The Honorable Hubert H. Humphrey
Vice President of the United States
The Capitol
Washington, D.C.

Dear Mr. Vice President:

The visit with you to Tunisia and your inspection of our plant there will remain as the summit of my career. Your consideration has not only given me the greatest sense of accomplishment, but I believe will also encourage others in the private sector to "export" American know-how and initiative to developing countries such as Tunisia. I firmly believe American industry, properly motivated, can do a great deal for those developing countries and provide a better world for everyone at the same time.

Your personal inspiration and leadership have no equal. Ambassador Russell told me that he has never seen President Bourguiba respond so warmly and enthusiastically to anyone before. America needs this kind of leadership.

If at any time I can be of any assistance to you, no matter how small, in furthering the American way of life, there is nothing I would not do.

Mr. Vice President, I want to thank you and Mrs. Humphrey for this most inspiring experience. I will continue to work in whatever way I can to make America and the rest of the world a little bit better for all of us to live in.

With utmost admiration and respect,

Sincerely yours,

Marshall Erdman

ME:pw

DESIGN   ENGINEERING   PREFABRICATION   CONSTRUCTION

Marshall corresponds with Vice President Humphrey after meeting him in Tunisia.

Marshall watches as prefabricated medical mods are trucked from the factory. With him is Roger Hauck (left) and Fran Furry, plant manager.

nurturing the fifth child

ONE OF THE CURIOUS CONTRADICTIONS in Marshall Erdman was between his desire to expand his own horizons, conquer new vistas and take risks, while his voice urged caution for the company. This alter ego, never far from the surface, remembered lean times and worse.

His cautious, frugal nature certainly exhibited itself when it came to his own corporate offices. The building that began as a modest wooden structure on University Avenue expanded, but it expanded incrementally, in spartan attachments.

From the odd triangular windows of his second-floor office, he could look out over University Avenue and the parking lot, keeping a watchful eye over who was coming and going and whether their cars were ostentatious or in keeping with their means. He abhorred ostentation and was known to fire consultants who he thought were driving cars that were too fancy ("we must be paying them too much," he would grumble). He himself preferred Volkswagens, modest but reliable. His was always white. Joyce also drove a Volkswagen.

His executive secretary Grace Lukken, who worked with Marshall for the last eighteen years of his life, remembered the time she was in the little VW with Marshall when they ran out of gas on University Avenue. Rather than pay for someone to come help them, he had her steer the car while he pushed it several blocks to the nearest gas station.

The office building grew longer and longer, until it finally turned a corner and incorporated the building to the west of Erdman that had housed McGilligan's Upholstery. This became a large space

Grace Lukken, Marshall's secretary, at her office.

for the architectural working drawings department, the young architects and draftsmen who made the detailed drawings for construction managers to follow. Another addition behind it housed the engineers. Various departments were shuffled through the basement until they outgrew their space, and when the building was virtually bursting at the seams, Marshall would grudgingly allow another addition. Then he would hover over the construction, keeping a watchful eye out for any hint of unnecessary expense or frivolity.

Another way he saved money was to have the office staff put on all the parties and lunches for the firm. Said Lukken: "He was so proud of the fact. We didn't order in lunches. He felt we could never afford it. We didn't have a lot of big dinners unless we did it ourselves. You don't know how many times I walked into Sam's Club to pick up food. All the secretaries would be slicing ham and cheese. Of course, you didn't do this during the working day. You did it through your lunch hour or after work at night, and you got it out to the [Erdman family] farm. That was our big spot. We had great parties out there, and they were good parties because people could talk.

"But if they only knew how hard we worked to put on a dinner out there! Let's see, the last one was in '93 or so. We fed about sixty people out there—beer, wine, and food—for $2.50 a head. Now, that wasn't long ago."

It was not just over his office space and parties that he kept tight control. "Marshall in a sense did everything he could to keep the company from growing," said Roger Hauck, who joined the firm in 1969 and would eventually become president.

"He needed to have his fingers on everything."

Of course, the business would continue to expand beyond anyone's wildest imagination, but for a time, Marshall contented himself with growing in a way that was at once expansive and conservative. He bought land.

"As the company grew in the '60s," Dick Garland said, "Marshall couldn't believe it. He kept saying, 'We have to slow down.' But we had money in the bank, and bills were paid off. We didn't owe anybody anything. What we did at that time was buy land. Marshall loved to buy real estate. We bought the property off Whitney Way (next to the Beltline Highway on what was then the far west side of Madison), where the YMCA is today, in 1962 or '63. Buying land was an investment."

It was also another example, Garland believed, of Marshall's foresight. "Marshall said, 'I want to invest until it hurts.' We bought 3,000 acres in Spring Green for $285,000. We bought a farm in Middleton. We put the whole area that is now Middleton Hills together in three or four years, picking up a piece at a time." The large Spring Green parcel was just east of Wright's Taliesin. It is in Wisconsin's driftless area, among the most beautiful landscapes in the country, full of woods and wildlife, gentle fields, and sharp hills that when climbed offer unparalleled views. This was Wright country, and perhaps that persuaded Marshall to buy the land.

He purchased the land through a Dodgeville real estate agent, but there was a problem. A farmer named Virgil Crook had 600 acres in the middle and no intention of selling. Virgil's son, Howard Crook,

DRIVING MISS DAISY........ ..... PUSHING MS. GRACIE

Steve Mason documented the gas station incident.

recalled, "My parents were the only people who refused to sell their property without being allowed to keep their own house."

In the course of the negotiations, Marshall came to admire the farmer who didn't want to sell. Marshall always liked people who stood their ground, provided they knew what they were talking about, and Virgil Crook knew farming. A deal was finally cut. The Crooks would sell, but they'd get to keep their house on fifteen acres, and Virgil would manage the property for Erdman & Associates, which he did for sixteen years. His respect and admiration for Crook piqued Marshall's interest in farming.

"My dad was a very strong-minded person," Howard Crook said, "and they came to a mutual respect fairly early."

After the land was first acquired, Marshall would come out often on weekends. Sometimes Joyce would be with him, or one or two of the kids. Tim and Rusty Erdman spent two weeks at the farm one summer—"learning how to work" is the way

Howard Crook remembered Marshall putting it. Marshall loved the area, the countryside. Crook recalled that once, driving with his daughter, Debbie, near his Middleton farm, Marshall said the country reminded him of Lithuania.

Howard Crook, barely a teenager, worked the Spring Green area farm. On a farm, everyone works. "One time I was away from the house, at one of the other farms," Crook recalled. "I was maybe thirteen, and I was feeding hogs." Marshall drove up and noticed him. "How'd you get over here?" Marshall asked. Crook shrugged. "I drove that pickup." Marshall just raised his eyebrows and smiled. Said Crook, "I think he got a kick out of seeing all that work and productivity that he was essentially driving."

For their part, the Crook family got a kick out of seeing him. "There was always a question in our family's mind of why he wanted the land," Crook said. "There was the relationship with Wright, of course, and we thought that was probably a lot of it.

But now I wonder if Marshall wasn't just interested in farming.

"In the first five years he had it," Crook said, "Marshall came out quite a bit. He was very interested in it. He spent a lot of Sundays out there. As a kid I remember his showing up in his square-back Volkswagen. Sometimes he'd come in the house, but I remember him usually just standing in the yard, talking about the property, asking my dad questions. 'What are we doing here?'

"He'd want to go drive around the property," Crook continued. "Sometimes Marshall saw me and invited me to ride along. He liked to drive around the pastures, open up gates, and ask my dad what was going on. Marshall wanted a lot of cattle, so Dad went out and purchased Black Angus and Herefords. My dad was a good farmer, and he had great ideas. He worked with the University of Wisconsin on some things, and Marshall always supported that. There were disease-free hogs coming into Iowa and Nebraska, different kinds of feed mixes, and my dad wanted to try these things. Again, Marshall supported him."

It was a serious working farm, with up to 500 cattle and 120 hogs, and the grain to feed them. "It was marginally profitable," Crook said, "as farms always are, but it was more so than a lot of them. And the nice thing for us was that Marshall stood behind us. When my dad went out and bought cattle he knew he could write a check and there wouldn't be a problem. Marshall, without just handing over a blank check, had a willingness to invest and back us."

By the late '60s, Marshall's visits became more

sporadic, and Crook remembered seeing more of company officers like Dick Garland. It was time for another new venture. Marshall had his eye on another piece of property, and while the acreage was small, the idea of what to do with it was not.

It was fifteen acres in the village of Waunakee, north of Madison. On May 15, 1969, Marshall notified village officials that his company would purchase fifteen acres in Waunakee's new industrial park with an option on an additional fifteen acres. By December 1969, the total acreage had increased to forty-seven and ground had been broken on a 50,000-square-foot production building.

Eventually the facility would become home to Techline, the Erdman company's cabinetry and furniture division. But in the late '60s, all Marshall knew for certain was that he had seen things in his travels to Europe that excited him very much. They had methods of manufacturing that controlled costs but did not sacrifice quality. And if they could do it in Europe, why couldn't Marshall Erdman do it in Waunakee?

Dr. Ingo Grebe, an engineer Marshall met in Germany who later became a close friend, admired Marshall's vision and willingness to try what hadn't been tried before. In the late '60s, that vision meant bringing European manufacturing techniques to America before anyone else did. The travels he had taken during the Peace Corps years had opened his eyes to new furniture-making technology. He had seen machines that could mass produce furniture components so precisely machined that the parts were interchangeable.

"He was an interpreter of ideas and he spanned

European woodworking machinery at Waunakee factory mass produced standardized cabinetry components.

both continents," Grebe said. "Marshall just had a sense of where the industry would go in research and development, furniture, overlays, and so on. He took a chance. He was a man who had the idea that America and Germany—or Europe, for he also used Italian machinery—had to work together. He took what was good in Europe, what was new and better, back to America. He had a wide vision. He could live, or think, on two continents."

His first European-imported machinery was housed in the back of the University Avenue offices. George Garner, who was hired in 1955 to run the cabinetry operation when the company was still the Erdman-Peiss Lumber Company, said Marshall ordered the machinery before he had any place to put it. "I came back from Europe and maybe six to eight weeks later the machinery arrived. So in the

meantime I was chopping the holes into concrete for the anchors. We couldn't afford the jackhammers, so I was there with the cold chisel and bit maul making the holes.

"The machines were in the lower range of machinery at the time. But this is what we could afford, how we started out. This was just for making medical cabinetry."

In a video, taped years later, Marshall explained it this way: "It came about because we were designing and building the clinics, and we built our own laboratory cabinets. During my travels through Europe I discovered a new technology to make the cabinets. We were the first ones to bring it to the United States, in 1967 . . . and it became so efficient that we were producing all our needs in about 20 percent of the time, and we had a plant that was much too big for what we needed for our medical facilities."

When Roger Hauck arrived at the Erdman firm in 1969, his first assignment was to build the Waunakee plant, get it up and running. To his mind this was an initiation test. "Marshall liked to throw you in the water and see what happened," Hauck recalled. "The decision to build it came before I arrived. He had bought some equipment in Europe, based on his experiences building overseas. In doing that, he had discovered this equipment they used over there because they don't have a lot of wood. They needed to use every scrap.

"Marshall got so excited about doing it that way instead of the old-style cabinet shop way that he went out and bought the land in Waunakee. When I came to work for him, the land was being cleared, and the start of the foundation might have been in. I had been living in nice hotels in Europe and when I saw it I was glad I wasn't out there. Of course, a month later, Marshall told me to go out and build the factory."

It was not the first or last time Marshall would challenge a new employee in that manner. "He would test people constantly," Dick Garland said. Garland recalled a time in the 1960s, shortly after the company had bought the property adjacent to where the Erdman family's Middleton farm now stands: "We had been working hard on building a warehouse for the plant on University Avenue. A bunch of guys had been looking forward to getting off Friday and hunting deer on that Middleton land. Marshall came to them and said, 'You've got to pour concrete and get it done.' Again, it was a

test. How far would we go for him? Would we go the whole nine yards? And they always did, grumbling all the way."

One thing it accomplished, whether Marshall intended it or not, was to develop camaraderie among co-workers. "It wasn't out of a dislike for Marshall," Garland said. "It was more, 'OK, by God, let's show him and get it done!' He had an ability to galvanize people, to inspire them with his own work ethic."

Roger Hauck was ready to work, though at the outset, he had at least as many reservations about Marshall as Marshall had about him. Hauck was top executive talent, one of the most important hires, along with Garland and Robert Zweifel, that Marshall would make in the 1960s. Zweifel, a University of Illinois graduate who joined the company in 1961, was a gifted architect, designer, and engineer who rose to company vice president in 1968. His untimely death due to an aneurysm in the early 1970s was a crushing personal and professional blow to Marshall.

It was Hauck who would step into the void. He had come to the firm by a circuitous route. After graduating with an engineering degree from Ohio State University, he went on to earn an M.B.A. at Harvard in 1961. Hauck stayed in Boston and formed a market research consulting firm with two other recent grads.

One of Hauck's clients was the Schlitz Brewing Company of Milwaukee. He traveled throughout Europe checking on investment opportunities for Schlitz, and after his consulting firm disbanded, Schlitz offered Hauck a job.

Marshall describes his Sears furniture line to Gov. Patrick Lucey.

"I took it and moved to Wisconsin," he said. The Schlitz job, however, involved constant travel, and after a few years, Hauck, newly married, wanted to settle down. "My wife, Ann, had gone to school in Madison. We decided it would be fun to move to Madison." This was 1969, and an intriguing job opportunity had been mentioned to Hauck by Sheldon Lubar, who Hauck had met through Schlitz's accounting firm and who served on Erdman's board of directors. Lubar told Hauck the Erdman firm was growing and looking for management talent.

"It sounded interesting," Hauck said. "I had a clear idea of what I wanted: engineering content, an ownership position, and line responsibility, as opposed to doing studies. It sounded good, but there was a problem. I learned they had had a problem finding people who could tolerate Marshall."

Hauck actually went through tests with an industrial psychologist, "to see if I could do submarine duty, I guess," he recalled with a laugh. "At the same time, though, that was a period for me to learn about Marshall."

At an early face-to-face meeting, Hauck learned what all who had dealings with Marshall eventually found out—if he could be irascible and exasperating, he could also be ingratiating. "I liked Marshall," Hauck said. "I told him, 'You have a reputation for not being able to delegate any responsibility. I've talked to as many people about you as you have about me.' He charmed me off my feet by saying, 'You're right. It's a problem, and I'm trying to fix it.' We laughed and there was a bond there."

Hauck joined the firm as assistant to the president, Marshall, and the Waunakee plant was his first assignment. It took two years, but he got it built. "My thinking was, 'I'll stand my ground with Marshall. If it works, it works. If not, I'm out of here,'" Hauck said. "As it turned out, he liked people who stood their ground—as long as you were on solid ground. If not, you were ground into powder. But if you were, he loved to duke it out. That made him happy."

In years to come, the two would often have confrontations, frequently over the handling of employees. Marshall joked that he and Roger could always "kiss and make up," but it was evident that these blowups took a toll on Hauck.

The Waunakee plant was 90,000 square feet when first completed, though significant expansion was not far off. "It was just for the cabinets for our medical buildings," Hauck said. Which meant, among other things, that the plant was too big, with too much capacity for what Erdman needed at the time. "There was enough business to use it about three or four hours a week," Hauck said. "The machines were for mass production, and essentially we had no business."

That, however, showed a side of Marshall that Hauck admired. "It was totally inefficient, but it was an investment in the future. That's the way he was. The company could afford it. He didn't care if he could sell cabinetry at that moment. He wanted to get experience with it." It was fortunate that there was time to get acquainted with the new machines. No one could make head or tails of them when they arrived, and Marshall had to import European technicians to train his own people how to use them. It took approximately two years before they were up and running.

The new technology had quickly become a passion. "The furniture business was Marshall's first love for his last ten or fifteen years," Dick Garland said. "He liked the extra stimulus of something new, different. The medical buildings weren't enough for his appetite. I'd see him when they got in some new packages of hardware for furniture, and he'd be all aglow, opening them like a kid at Christmas. 'Look at all these things,' he'd say."

"The factory looked huge at the time over there," said George Garner, "with the few pieces of machinery that were inside. But then once it got filled up with all the new machinery, it began to look more and more like a factory."

But at first, it was a bit lonely out there in Waunakee. There was a plant, and all that great innovative machinery, but no customers. It was driving Hauck a little crazy.

"Finally, I went to a pay phone, because I didn't want to use the phone in the office, and I literally dialed the general information number in Chicago

The Erdman family home at 3408 Circle Close in Shorewood Hills, designed by next-door neighbor William Kaeser.

for Sears Roebuck. I got an operator and eventually got hold of the guy who bought cabinetry."

Sears wasn't interested, at least not then. "They bought cabinetry in Belgium," Hauck said. But a few months later, changes in currency rates made doing business with foreign markets less desirable. The man called Hauck back. "Sears became our first bread-and-butter furniture customer. Three or four million dollars within a couple of years."

It was a relationship that would continue to blossom through the '70s. At the end of the decade Marshall Erdman & Associates would earn the "Symbol of Excellence" award from two separate buying departments at Sears.

Jack Ingold, Sears's national merchandise manager, pointed out that Sears bought from more than 12,000 manufacturers nationally but gave the Symbol of Excellence award to only 5 percent of them. The yearly awards, Ingold said, were given to suppliers who demonstrated the "ability to maintain quality, ship merchandise on schedule, and keep down returns and service problems."

"We're flattered," Marshall said on receiving the award. "This was our first experience in consumer products, and when we first started doing business with Sears, we didn't know how we'd fit in, if we'd be able to compete, and if our quality would be appreciated."

Perhaps this recognition added to the confidence Marshall now felt in his own success. Hauck said that Marshall finally became convinced that to attract good people to the company, and maybe more important, to keep them, the company had to grow. If a business is static, good employees leave for better opportunities. In the end, growth made good business sense, and that, in Hauck's view, was Marshall's strength. "His business sense was unassailable," Hauck said. "That was Marshall's 'value-added.' His

The Erdmans at their farm near Middleton in 1972.
Standing left to right: Tim, Marshall, Debbie, Rusty;
kneeling: Dan, and Joyce.

principles were as valid at the end as they were at the beginning, not only the economics of the process, but taking responsibility for the finished product."

As the company prospered, there were greater demands on his time. Like many other businessmen of his era, work came first for Marshall. His family and friends always joked that the company was his fifth child. There was no question, however, that it was the one that got the most attention. Fortunately for his four biological children, his wife, Joyce, was extraordinary. She raised the kids while at the same time becoming a community leader. Some of her accomplishments, as mentioned earlier, were the first ever for a woman.

Debbie left for Middlebury College in 1968 and, as she says, "never really came back." Although the family was close and stayed in constant contact—largely through Joyce's efforts—Debbie estab-

lished a completely independent career. She finished medical school and started an obstetrics practice in Montana, where she and her husband, Andreas Luder, bought a home.

Tim, who had accompanied his father on a number of trips in the company plane in the 1950s and '60s, headed for school in Colorado a short time later. He was a child of the '60s, in rebellion against the establishment. He was interested in jazz and skiing and made friends who were seeking alternative lifestyles rather than pursuing careers. Marshall had a great deal of difficulty with what he saw as his oldest son's lack of seriousness. "Tim really got the worst of it," said Rusty. "There was a lot of friction."

Rusty got his undergraduate degree at the University of Wisconsin. He was interested in oceanography and got his Ph.D. at the Scripps Oceanographic Institute in San Diego, where he met his future wife. "I knew I didn't want to get involved in the company," he said, "but I had to resist pressure. The family was very intense. There was a lot of obstinacy. You can't have two Erdmans trying to run the same thing." He remembered a childhood of stormy battles, "things flying around the kitchen."

Rusty became computer proficient in graduate school, and from time to time Marshall would lure him back for a temporary consulting stint. One had to do with setting up a computer point-of-sale program for Techline studios and another with computer video monitoring of a large medical building being constructed in Sioux Falls, South Dakota. Architects in the Madison office could oversee

Marshall loved to spend weekends working at the family farm. The house he built is pictured behind him.

progress by logging on to a specific site. But Rusty never stayed long, eventually starting his own oceanographic monitoring business based in Miami and Italy, where his wife taught.

The child who seemed to relate best to Marshall as a parent was Dan, the youngest. Dan recalled his childhood as "great." "Papa probably saw me as his last chance to be a father and thus spent a little more time with me than he had with the others." Dan saw in his mother and father a tempestuous but loving relationship. "Sometimes after a fight Papa would stomp out and stay at the farm for a day or two. But then it was usually Papa who would apologize, kiss, and make up, and then things were lovey-dovey until the next storm. It was all part of their relationship. They respected each other and thrived on each other's strengths. They were a perfect match, in many ways. They were both doers. They loved accomplishing things, and they respected one another for it.

They didn't spend that much money. What made them happy was doing things."

Often that would involve friends, many of whom had started careers around the same time and after much hard work become successful. Gaylord Nelson became governor, a U.S. senator, and one of the country's most articulate and respected spokesmen for the environment. Another good friend, Miles McMillin, became editor of *The Capital Times* and was a regular at the Middleton farm with his wife, Elsie, and their children.

Dan observed wryly that his father seemed to dote on other people's kids more than his own. "He adored Mr. Hart's two girls, Abby and Kappo," Dan said. "He was a lot nicer to them than he was to us." He shook his head in mystification.

"On the weekends we'd go to the farm and work," Dan recalled. "Eighty acres—that's a lot of upkeep. We put in a pool and tennis court out

Marshall and Joyce on their tennis court at the farm.

Meeting House ten years earlier.

The rolling property was originally pastureland with wooded ravines. But Joyce and Marshall immediately began mowing a lawn and planting trees all over, including a large tract of white and red pines.

Early in December of 1970, Marshall called his friend Miles McMillin and suggested he come out and cut down his own Christmas tree. McMillin recalled that Marshall had laid a "siren song" on him "about the pleasures of a nostalgic return to the past when it was customary to go into the woods and bring out your own Christmas tree."

In his front-page "Hello, Wisconsin" column in *The Capital Times*, McMillin referred to Marshall as a "Madison building genius" and described his family's excitement as they anticipated "selecting a Christmas tree from the countless conifers Marshall has planted on his lovely country place."

The vision was better than the reality, at least for McMillin himself. "By the time we had gone up and down a few hills my legs felt as though they were hot irons and, at last, I flung myself onto the hillside crust and cried out for someone to bring 'that damned Erdman' to carry me out."

Although working was Marshall's favorite occupation, he was amazingly athletic. This was in spite of the fact that he had a continual battle with keeping his weight down. Though he was rail thin when he first met Joyce, success seemed to go hand in hand with weight gain for Marshall. He was an excellent dancer and ice skater, and quite a capable tennis player and skier as well.

While he constantly failed one diet after another that Joyce put in front of him, he stayed surpris-

there, but we could never play when Papa was there. He'd expect us to be working all the time." Joyce and Marshall had bought the eighty acres in Middleton in 1959 and built a second home as a retreat. Over the years it was always referred to as "the farm," though there was never any attempt to farm in the literal sense.

For the Erdman family, the farm was a constant in their lives, a place where they worked together, played together, entertained friends, and hosted company events. The farmhouse Marshall designed and built clearly reflected the influence of Frank Lloyd Wright. Built into the side of a hill, with a horizontal profile, the house's limestone walls came from the same quarry used for the Unitarian

ingly fit. He didn't smoke except for an occasional cigar or pipe. He rarely drank in spite of being in the company of friends who drank heavily, often to excess. Marshall usually went to bed right after dinner and would be up before dawn, weekdays or not.

He did take pleasure in vacation time spent with his family. He was quoted in a *Wisconsin State Journal* "Know Your Madisonian" column in the early 1960s that he enjoyed camping Up North with his family. In later years over Christmas, the Erdmans packed into the family station wagon to make the twenty-hour drive straight through to Aspen, Colorado, for their ski vacations.

McMillin also wrote with regularity about Joyce, who, particularly as the children got older, established herself as a force in Madison and indeed Wisconsin, quite apart from Marshall's business success. Most of her work had a humanitarian purpose, often involving education. Another concern was the environment. As Joe Melli, a prominent Madison attorney who served with Joyce in the Wisconsin Student Association in the 1940s and admired her over the years, said, "She knew how to move people and how to get things done." Dave Zweifel, who had worked as a reporter under McMillin at *The Capital Times* before becoming editor in the early 1980s, said much the same: "She had an uncanny knack for getting people to say yes to projects that they really wanted to get out of doing."

Zweifel continued: "Her trailblazing for the women's movement didn't come about through shrill threats or ultimatums. It came about because she showed anyone beyond any doubt that a woman was just as capable, just as intelligent, just as

Tim, Marshall, and Joyce pose for a photo during a family Christmas vacation in Aspen, Colorado, 1975.

able to lead as a man."

In the 1950s, Joyce's friend Gaylord Nelson had appointed her to the Governor's Commission on Human Rights, where she raised concerns about the treatment of Wisconsin Indians. In the 1960s, working with the UW, she helped establish the Junior Year Abroad program. In November of 1968 she wrote McMillin a letter, part of which he quoted in his *Capital Times* column:

"As I look around the countryside today," Joyce wrote, "I'm quite appalled to see that billboards seem to be proliferating at an epidemic rate. Only a year or so ago, for example, Highway 23, which I know fairly well around the Spring Green area, was actually a scenic route—very lovely indeed. Now the signs are all over and every time we drive out

The University of Wisconsin Board of Regents in 1982 with Joyce (seated center) as president.

there a few more have sprung up. So I think I'll spend some time this winter seeing if I can rally support to generate billboard control legislation."

There was precedent for Joyce's interest. Lady Bird Johnson, when her husband was president, had started a national campaign against billboards. Joyce succeeded in having them banned from the Village of Shorewood Hills. In 1973 she was elected the first woman president of that village. In 1975 Governor Patrick Lucey appointed her to the UW Board of Regents, and by the end of the decade she became the first female president of that august body as well.

As son Dan observed, each of his parents' individual successes spurred on the other. There may have been an edge there at times. "They'd have their ego battles," Ed Hart observed, but the result was accomplishment and good works. In 1971, the west branch of Madison's YMCA named Marshall Erdman its Man of the Year. "If it was not for [him]," the Y newsletter exclaimed, "we would not

have our wonderful facility." The building, which still stands, is near Whitney Way and the Beltline. "He gave impetus to the whole idea when he donated the land where our building now stands. He, more than any man, has made it possible for so many to find happiness and enjoyment in their leisure hours."

The company had hit its stride. No more early morning meetings to discuss which creditors could be stalled for a week and which needed immediate attention. There would still be missteps, but miscues at this stage were affordable.

Since the Waunakee plant was in operation just a few hours a week to make cabinets for the medical buildings, in 1971 Marshall decided to employ it to mass produce modular homes that could be sold to low-income families or to others as a second home. The exterior walls would define the entire living area while demountable interior walls would, according to chief architect Bob Zweifel, "make the whole dwelling unit adaptable to different families or the changing needs of one family." Marshall himself added: "We provide attractive room dividers which offer versatility even expensive homes don't have."

It didn't work. The modular homes never really got beyond the developmental stage. In March 1972, a trade magazine editor wrote Marshall asking whether they might want to collaborate on an article on the new homes.

Three weeks later, Marshall replied. "Our modular homes have not been successful yet," he wrote. "Although we have spent a lot of time and money on the houses, we still do not have a unit that I feel is something we can brag about."

Then Marshall mentioned that the company was trying the same approach with medical buildings: "At this moment, we are spending most of our time on modular clinics, which seem to be working out a bit better."

Modular clinics were three-dimensional "boxes," built in the factory, complete with wall covering, windows, plumbing, and electricity. They could be trucked to a site and erected on a foundation, and be fully functional in approximately three months, depending on size. They continued to be a small but important part of the medical building business from about 1971 through 1991, during which time 566 medical buildings were constructed in this way, most of them consisting of more than one "box" or "mod." A few dramatic photographs of clinics being set in place by large cranes encouraged the false conclusion on the part of the public that all Erdman clinics were created this way.

Meanwhile, the firm continued its traditional approach, which was prefabrication of individual building components. The basic unit was the exterior wall panel, fitted with windows, doors, and trim. Interior wall panels were covered with vinyl and also precut for windows and doors. The two-by-tens to connect them were cut to fit. Everything was shipped on Erdman trucks to the site where they were put together, more or less like a child's ready-to-assemble toy house. The ingenious method did save time over what would be considered traditional by other builders, where all the construction was done on site.

During those early years, buildings tended to be about 5,000 to 10,000 square feet. Then they started to grow, and a few 20,000- and 30,000-square-foot buildings showed up on the boards. The system, however, was highly adaptable and accommodated these larger buildings as well. The bigger buildings had steel frames, and Marshall saw a way to cut costs by starting his own steel shop, where the steel I-beams were cut to fit, so that they would be ready to erect and weld when they arrived on the site. Marshall was proud of the economies and efficiency of the system and couldn't see any reason to do things differently.

Bob Davis, an architect who worked for the firm for thirty-four years, remembered being in Marshall's office when he got a call from a physician who wanted his new 30,000-square-foot building to be custom built, no prefabrication. Davis said, "Marshall turned it down! I couldn't believe it! That was one of the biggest buildings we'd been asked to do! But it was his way or not at all. He even offered to help the guy find an architect."

By the time Marshall began experimenting with modular homes in 1971, the firm had built

A prefabricated medical mod is set in place on a construction site.

medical facilities in forty-two states and had regional offices in New Jersey, Dallas, and Atlanta. Revenues were more than $20 million annually. The buildings, however, were designed to accommodate single practitioners or, at the most, small group practices. But there was more change and growth on the horizon as the health care industry in the United States faced a complete upheaval.

Within fifteen years, a short period of time when talking about the vastness of the change at hand, the individual medical practitioner would be nearly extinct. The economics of health care was forcing consolidation. A whole new glossary of buzzwords was being coined to describe the changes. "Managed care"—health care driven by the insurer rather than the physician—was one. Somehow Marshall would grasp this new reality and act on it.

Even Roger Hauck, who balked at calling Marshall a visionary, was awed at Marshall's ability to do what Hauck referred to as "seizing the day."

Hauck recalled: "When I came to the company, in the late '60s, there really wasn't any organization in the company. It was more 'throw it in the air and see where it lands,' which was an asset to Marshall. He wasn't bound by any organizational thinking. That was the kind of mind he had. He was opportunistic, in the good sense of that word. He'd see an opportunity and he'd move, because he didn't have a lot of structure to worry about, who was in the way, and whose feelings might be hurt."

His approach, if disconcerting to those dependent on organizational charts, meant maximum flexibility. If an idea looked good, he'd swing people into action.

Marshall celebrates with Ann Doody (second from left), owner of Techline Studio Madison, and her employees (from left) Deborah Tracy, Leah Knox, and Mary Fiegel.

medical morphosis, and techline is born

IN SEPTEMBER 1971, BOB ZWEIFEL, VICE president in charge of architecture for the company, flew to Washington, D.C., for an unusual meeting. About a dozen people—some doctors and some, like Zweifel, experts in other areas of the medical business—sat down for a day at the behest of the U.S. Department of Health, Education, and Welfare to discuss what were being called HMOs (Health Maintenance Organizations).

A few days after the meeting, Assistant Surgeon General Harald Graning wrote Zweifel a letter thanking him for his participation. "While there are no specific funds available at this time for implementation of Health Maintenance Organizations, or for regional facilities, it is clear there is a trend in this direction," Graning wrote.

It was quite a compliment to Erdman & Associates that Zweifel was invited. Others at the meeting included a representative from Minnesota's famed Mayo Clinic, a physician from the Harvard Community Health Plan, and the program director of the Kellogg Foundation in Battle Creek, Michigan. It was heady company for Marshall Erdman &

Associates, and a testimonial to its reputation. By 1972 the company was building clinics in almost every state in the country, and to do that, it was setting up regional offices.

"You can't be an out-of-towner," Hauck said, explaining the decision to establish local offices of the Erdman firm, first in Princeton, New Jersey, then in short order in Dallas and Atlanta. "There were any number of reasons to be local," Hauck said. "Obviously you can be more responsive when there's a problem. And we couldn't afford to be shipping people back and forth. At the time, the buildings themselves were small enough that the profit margin wouldn't sustain a lot of additional expense."

Edgar Tafel, the Wright apprentice with whom Marshall had stayed in contact after Wright's 1959 funeral, was licensed as an architect throughout the East Coast, and he helped Erdman get established in the area. Marshall had ingratiated himself early with Tafel by asking if he wanted to hear what Mr. Wright had told Marshall about him. Somewhat nervously, Tafel said he'd like to hear. Marshall smiled. "He said, 'Edgar is a man with a mind of his own'"—high praise from a man who seldom gave compliments. Tafel felt, too, that Marshall respected the fact that he, Edgar, had left Taliesin and Wright's immense shadow to strike out on his own.

"I persuaded Marshall that Princeton was the place to go [for a regional office]," Tafel said. "The name, you know, has quality. People say Princeton and everyone knows where it is. So they did go over to Princeton and rented part of an old house. That was their first office."

From that outpost, Tafel occasionally accompanied Marshall on what were, in reality, sales trips. But Marshall, of course, was hardly a conventional salesman.

"I remember once going to Newport, Rhode Island," Tafel said. "We came down in the company airplane, chasing cows off the runway, landed, and went to the law firm representing these doctors who wanted to hire us. They talked price and starting dates, and then when some contractual details were being discussed, an attorney told Marshall he needn't be concerned with subcontracting since that would be handled locally."

Marshall slapped his hand on the table. "I told you from the beginning that we have total responsibility." The attorney was unbending. Marshall said, "Look, if anything goes wrong, we'll come and fix it." Still there was no concession on the part of the lawyer. Finally Marshall said, "I guess we have to leave." He turned to their pilot: "Rev up the plane." Tafel, with a laugh, recalled, "The lawyers started to panic and asked us to wait outside a minute. When we came back in, one said, 'We'll do it your way.'"

The August 1973 issue of *Systems Building*

News magazine took note of Erdman's success in an article titled "A New Concept of Building for the Medical Profession." The piece took particular note of the "total control" philosophy that Marshall, in his singular way, had communicated to the Rhode Island doctors. "Marshall's policy of total responsibility does not end with a completed building. Two corporate people make a career of calling back on previously built medical facilities looking for areas of improvement."

Bob Zweifel explained: "There is no charge for this service and it pays off in two ways. First, we learn what might be improved in subsequent buildings in terms of design and product quality. Second, doctors appreciate our continuing interest and refer us to colleagues who are interested in building their own medical office building. The net result is that over 50 percent of our new business can be traced to referrals from doctors who have previously used Erdman services."

Marshall's approach was proving its value. Those doctors who had Erdman-built offices were extremely loyal. From time to time, retired doctors and their wives on their way through Madison from Kansas or Illinois would stop at the corporate offices, "just to say hello." They were proud of their buildings. And they told their friends.

The *Systems Building News* piece mentioned the modular miniclinics that Erdman was manufacturing for small-town physicians, but Zweifel pointed out: "Our original office buildings housed two or three doctors. The trend now is to larger buildings serving 10 to 100 doctors."

It was the 1974 expansion of the Marshfield

The Marshfield Clinic addition, completed in 1975, was a breakthrough for Erdman & Associates.

Clinic that set the stage for the truly phenomenal growth that Erdman & Associates enjoyed over the next two decades.

The large addition to the highly regarded Marshfield Clinic in central Wisconsin would be an important step for Erdman. "Marshfield was a breakthrough for us," Hauck said. "It really showed what we could do with group practices."

In early 1974, Erdman began construction on the $8 million expansion that would double the size of the clinic. However, tragedy struck when Bob Zweifel, so instrumental to the company's success as an architect, designer, and engineer, died suddenly of a brain aneurysm.

Marshall was devastated. "Marshall cried for three months," Hauck said. "This was an emotional man." There were practical problems, as well. "Zweifel had most of the Marshfield expan-

sion in his head," Hauck says. "There was no real contract, the drawings weren't complete."

Hauck and others stepped into the breach, and Marshfield was a success, opening in June 1975. It was the single largest project the company had ever done.

Marshfield was indicative of the direction health care was moving, but much of it was uncharted water. Medical advances now permitted physicians to treat patients in ways not even dreamed of only a decade before, but the equipment and technology such miracles required was hugely expensive. Administrators, government regulators, and insurance adjusters looked for ways to control costs. One place to start was by getting more doctors under one roof. Someone, of course, had to design and build this next generation of facilities.

Said Hauck, "Marshfield convinced us that

multi-specialty clinics were where our future lay. Being an independent practitioner was becoming obsolete as a way to practice medicine." The demand for small facilities dropped overnight, and buildings became progressively larger, grander, even monumental. Marshall balked at monumental and insisted that buildings had to be functional, first, and make sense economically, second.

Sometimes even the client needed to be shown the light. Gaylord Nelson recalled when Erdman was hired to build the Monroe Clinic in Wisconsin. The architecture department had drawn a large glass entryway, nearly sixty feet high, and when Marshall saw it, he was enraged. It didn't fit the building, and it would inflate heating and cooling costs. But the clinic had specifically requested it, the designers told Marshall.

"You tell them," Marshall said, "they don't have enough money to pay me to do something that isn't right." He offered to redesign the entryway for no cost. The clinic agreed.

The change from smaller to larger buildings spurred hiring, as more architects, engineers, and interior designers were added to the staff. Project architects, specially trained to work in the field with clients, brought back the requirements of physician groups to be incorporated into design; construction supervisors had to oversee increasingly complex projects.

Hauck said the continued growth of the Erdman firm—and the era of extraordinary expansion in the early '80s in particular, when revenues doubled from $57 million in 1983 to $114 million in 1985—came because it was quick to perceive the sweeping changes at hand.

"We got in early," Hauck said. "Today clinics are absolutely dominant, of course. But early on we supported the group practice organizations, and we got extremely good at designing group practice facilities. Erdman had the best designers in America. Nobody knew how to design clinics the way our people designed clinics. And still do."

Interiors, in particular, are the key. "You take 200 physicians," Hauck said, "and try to work out traffic flows, interrelationships, efficient use of space. That understanding is what made our company grow. Anybody can build a medical office building with a few suites. But the clinics, the group practices, are the tough ones. Not the exteriors, but the internal function. That was the real advantage we had."

Hauck credits Marshall Erdman for a second advantage the firm enjoyed: "Control over cost. Marshall knew how to buy. He was tight when it came to business. He'd give you the shirt off his back personally. But when it came to business, he was tight." The design-and-build approach had its own economic advantages. With designers and builders in the same firm, it was easy to get feedback from the field, learn better ways to solve problems, and avoid overruns.

By the mid-1970s, the Erdman firm focused on medical facilities as its principal income source, at least as far as designing and building went. "Marshall couldn't be moved on that," Hauck said. The company wasn't, for instance, going to start building athletic stadiums. "Stick with medical buildings," Hauck recalled Marshall saying. "There was sound reasoning behind it. We could do something no one else could do, so stick with it."

In the 1970s, Erdman was in a strong bargaining position with medical clients. No one else could claim the broad experience, the thorough understanding of medical facility needs. The main competition was the local architect, the "brother-in-law" of the head surgeon, and it was hard for local architects to match the experience of a well-seasoned firm like Erdman & Associates.

Houses and schools were no longer in the mix. The firm could have continued to thrive for some decades on its medical business alone. But it was the tight-fisted business sense Hauck refers to, along with a deeply held belief in the concept of design-and-build, that got Marshall Erdman involved in a controversial project in downtown Madison, a state office building. Marshall was in his midfifties, business was booming, and there was little reason to get involved, but he had served on the State Building Commission and thought taxpayer dollars were being wasted by the conventional system of building government offices.

Of Marshall's foray into the state office business, Hauck said, "It was an attempt to justify design-and-build."

In the mid-1970s, a Wisconsin law requiring the state to build under the usual system of hiring an architect to draw up plans and having contractors bid on general construction, electrical, and mechanical work was changed. A construction union challenged the new law, but in 1976 a Dane County judge dismissed the suit. The state was free to hire what is referred to as "single point" firms, or companies that take a project through from draw-

ings to completion.

Marshall saw an opportunity to prove his point. The first state project he bid on, in 1978, was for an $8.8 million office on the corner of Webster and King Streets in downtown Madison. It was General Executive Facility 2, or GEF II, as everyone called it. Erdman lost the bid to another Madison builder, Findorff, which had teamed with a Milwaukee architect for the project.

The result, when GEF II opened in 1979, was a building that, while cost-efficient, was panned for aesthetic reasons by nearly everyone. The most offended was Whitney Gould, later architecture critic for the *Milwaukee Journal Sentinel* but then with *The Capital Times*. "Oh, God," Gould wrote, "how could this happen, right in the middle of our beautiful, rejuvenating downtown? How did we get stuck with another of these anonymous monsters. How could the state do this to us?"

According to state senator Fred Risser, who chaired the State Building Commission, the state had little choice. "We liked Erdman's design better," Risser said, "but Findorff had the lower bid. And we were advised by the attorney general that we were obligated to take the lower bid."

Risser conceded that GEF II was an aesthetic failure. "As it stands now, it looks quite ugly. It sticks up like a big matchbox. It looks terrible." University of Wisconsin campus architect Horst Lobe concurred: "Just a monster."

Marshall, for his part, agreed: "Most people who get into design-and-build don't care about aesthetics. That's one reason it hasn't gone very far."

Marshall thought his company could do better,

The plaza in front of the state of Wisconsin's GEF III, completed in 1980, in downtown Madison.

and he didn't have to wait long. State bureaucracy was accelerating at such a rate that soon bids went out for yet another office building, to be called GEF III, just a short distance from GEF II. This time, Erdman got the bid, and Whitney Gould interrupted her diatribe against GEF II long enough to observe: "Most critics of GEF II say [Erdman's] design will be both better to look at and more responsive to the site."

"We didn't do office buildings in general," said Tim Erdman, who worked on the GEF III project.

"Marshall wanted to demonstrate design-and-build as a viable method. We guaranteed a maximum price. We told them Price Waterhouse would audit us, they always do, and anything we made over a 3 percent after-tax profit we'd return to the state."

When GEF III opened in March 1980, Marshall was proud of the cost savings. The company had guaranteed the state a maximum price of $8.5 million and brought it in $350,000 under that. The state of Wisconsin received more than $250,000 back from Erdman on the completion of

GEF III. Erdman kept $100,000 to cover warranty costs. Hauck, however, felt the building was a failure: "It was cost-efficient. In order to win the bid, you had to design a cost-efficient building above all else. But these buildings last seventy-five years, and it was architecturally deficient."

Marshall partially agreed. "It was the basics of a halfway decent building," he told the *Milwaukee Journal* in 1981. But he said that while containing cost is important, especially with taxpayers paying the bill, the state was still remiss in going for rock-bottom design costs, even going so far as to run a computer analysis on cost vs. space utilization before awarding a bid. This always means that the public areas—the corridors, lobbies, and meeting rooms—get slighted. "They cannot wash their hands," Marshall said of state officials, "and say the computer will design everything. Design and public spaces are quality matters, too."

With the completion of GEF III, it was time for Marshall to turn his attention to the excess capacity at the factory. Sears' sales were dwindling as furniture trends changed, and the wood-grain laminate line that Erdman had been supplying wasn't capturing the market.

"Obviously I was so enthused that I built a plant that was much too big for our medical facilities," Marshall said. "What to do with it? I always liked to tinker with furniture, and so a friend of mine and I designed [what became] Techline."

The friend was Tom Rosengren, an architect Marshall had first met at the University of Illinois in 1961 when he went back to school.

In 1968, Rosengren had joined Skidmore,

Marshall giving Gov. Lee Dreyfus a tour of the GEF III facility.

Owings, and Merrill, a prominent Chicago architecture firm and was assigned to design housing in Chicago that would replace some that had been demolished to build a highway. Prefabricated housing would be ideal, and someone suggested Marshall Erdman to him. "I said, 'I know that guy!' So I came to Madison. He saw me as kind of the ivory tower kid from the big city, and he was the country guy with his nose in the trenches who knew how the world really worked. We hit it off. I'll tell you this—we fought like hell. I think that adversity strengthened our relationship. I respected him, but I wasn't going to roll over if I disagreed with him.

"Our relationship grew," Rosengren said. "Marshall was interested in helping lower-income people. We built one prototype in Evanston, a northern suburb of Chicago, that won a design

The Mayo Clinic's Midelfort Clinic in Eau Claire, Wisconsin, was completed in 1995. Marshall called it his company's finest building.

award in 1971. But that was a frustrating time. I was going to design these houses and Marshall was going to manufacture them. But we couldn't get over the stigma that there was something inherently inferior about prefab. And there were union problems with doing the manufacturing outside of Chicago. After three years of arguing and prototypes, we gave up.

"But meanwhile I had made countless trips to Madison to see Marshall. There were days when he could be an S.O.B. But he knew he didn't have all the answers. He knew that I was with a major firm in Chicago. He felt he could learn something from me.

"I told him I thought he could sell some of the cabinetry he manufactured outside of just using it in his own medical facilities. And the thing that kind of got him rolling is that I had designed a house for myself in Old Town in Chicago. I was set to move in and I called the cabinetry guy up and asked how it was going. He said he hadn't started. That's how those custom guys are. I was moving in in two weeks. I called Marshall and I said I was in real trouble. I needed fifty cabinets—for the kitchen and baths and other places—and I asked if he could make them. I would come up with my own truck to pick them up. Finally, after I pleaded and begged, he agreed to do it. At which point I said, 'I don't like any of your colors. I want them all white.' He said, 'Oh my God, you're an idealist. A purist.' But he did it. They shut down their line and did it. I made my deadline.

"I told Marshall to come down and take a look. He came and saw the cabinets in my house and said, 'They're beautiful!' I said, 'Marshall, if you can make these cabinets in white, I can sell them.' He said, 'Let's do it.' That was the beginning of Tech-line. This was 1975.

"My wife, who is an architect, sold them out of our home for the first few years, and later, I was looking to get out of the corporate thing, and my house in Chicago became the first Techline Studio. That was 1979."

In a video taped years later, after the furniture division was well established and successful, Marshall talked about one of his basic philosophies of business. It is uncomplicated and deeply felt:

"If I like something well enough, and I'm honest with myself, I feel there are enough fools like me who will like it as well. So we have tried to do the best we know how without listening to market studies or what the clients want. We don't try to be fashionable, we try to be good. There is such a thing as good basic design—have a standard design of high quality, mass produced. I tell people they can have Techline in any color they like as long as it's white. We spend very little money on advertising. We get word of mouth and publicity that amounts to free advertising, because we're a little bit different and people are curious."

Marshall mentioned that his foray into the furniture business happened "without planning," and this is probably true. While a number of people thought he was a visionary, Roger Hauck, who spent twenty-five years at his side, thinks a different engine was driving his success.

"Marshall never saw the company ten or twenty years down the line," Hauck said. "If anything, maybe he saw it tomorrow. He is painted as a visionary, but he was not. Where he was absolutely brilliant, in my mind, was in seizing the day. He was also sound fundamentally. His expressed business principles were absolutely first-rate. That's how he kept people, in spite of all the other stuff. But as far as a vision, he did everything he could to keep the company from growing."

His longtime executive secretary, Grace Lukken, remembered her initiation into the company in 1978, and the early days of Techline. Marshall was looking for a new secretary, and he knew the type of person he wanted. "We were introduced by friends, and we hit it off. I think it was because of the fact that I grew up in a farm setting. He asked me to come in to the office. Of course, the first time I met him, the shorts, bow ties, knee socks, sport coat—we had a good visit, but I wasn't the least bit interested in working for the man. Then I heard his reputation—'Six months to a year and a half, and you are out of there . . .'

"But I checked out the firm, and it was a great company to come to." In typical fashion, Marshall wore her down. "I hadn't been working; I had been home for twenty years. Can you imagine what it would be like to come in and work for Marshall? You really gave your life up when you worked for him because Saturdays and Sundays meant nothing. How many times I drove him to Chicago early, early Sunday morning to a trade show at Mc-Cormick Place! Trade shows. Kitchens, baths—for Techline. Because that was his hobby. He said, 'If you see one thing today, one thing, then this trip is worth it."

"Sometimes we were there for twelve hours, and for one little thing. But he was so right. He was a genius, I really think he was. . . . He was willing to try something new. He always used to say, 'You know, I'm not always right, but let's do this.' And, he was always right. He really was."

Once Techline had been designed to Marshall's satisfaction, and enough inventory had been manufactured, he needed to introduce it to the market and make it profitable. In the early 1980s, Marshall became aware of the semiannual International Furniture Market in High Point, North Carolina. At hundreds of showrooms in this southern town, major furniture manufacturers introduce their new product lines to buyers from all the important retail outlets in the country, and some from abroad.

techline ®

furniture, cabinetry, office and closet systems

Techline was Marshall's introduction to the furniture business.

This venerable trade exposition was just what Marshall was looking for. He traveled down to High Point, became friendly with the people in charge, and leased a permanent showroom in an attractively remodeled old furniture factory building. Thereafter, for about eight days every April and October, Techline would be displayed with as much flair as the big names, the Henredons and Bakers, Natuzzi leather, and Knoll fabrics.

A full team of Erdman/Techline representatives geared up for the show. Furniture designers created new product adaptations—perhaps a different desk or drawer, maybe a new color. Techline started out as an antique white laminate, and that was always Marshall's preference. He did allow his sales representatives to urge him into several other colors—a bright white, two grays, a black, and eventually a wood grain. But

Marshall's instincts had been correct. The antique white Techline was always the top seller.

A showroom designer accompanied the furniture to High Point and chose from the vast array of accessories to create appealing furniture vignettes. Sales coordinators from the factory staffed the showroom, meeting with independent salespeople and retailers. And Marshall always came. It was a big party for him. He loved the ambience, the swarm of buyers, the excitement, the hoopla, the amazing variety of arts and artifacts, expensive goods, and cheap schlock. Most of all, he loved talking to people about Techline.

In a lunchtime talk he gave to employees in 1991, Marshall described why he liked his new business so much. He remembered the first time he took Dan to the International Furniture Market. His youngest son by then had a degree in art history and a master's in architecture, and Marshall was eager to get him involved in the company.

"I don't know how many of you have been to High Point," Marshall said. "It is the most dog-eat-dog business there is in furniture. Everybody comes, and everybody is trying to knock off, copy, steal, do anything, promise anything, just so you can make a sale. And Dan went around and people were trying to sell him this and that, and there were a lot of hucksters there . . . and in the evening he said to me, 'Do you really like this? Why are we in this furniture business? I mean, we make a living selling medical buildings and building them.' And it

A promotional photo of Techline furniture taken at the Erdman family farm.

dawned on me. I said, 'You know, the reason I'm in it is because it's so easy to excel. If you just tell the truth in the furniture business, you're miles ahead of anybody else.'

"And it's so true. I mean, if you promise something, promise them what is real. If it's good, tell them it's good; if it's bad, tell them that, too. If you're going to deliver it tomorrow, tell them. If you're not, be honest and tell them when you will. It's so easy, and it pays off. I go to High Point not to sell furniture," said Marshall. "I go there for just a lift, a boost, an ego trip. I would say that 80 to 90 percent of the people we deal with love Techline because they can

rely on us." And, of course, Techline lived up to Marshall's boasting. It was well designed and well constructed, sturdy and reliable, and so precisely machined that replacement parts would fit perfectly.

Another way to sell Techline was through architect-owned Techline Studios, where the full range of Techline's cabinetry capabilities could be demonstrated. These studios provided design and installation services for homeowners looking for sleek home offices, kitchens, bedroom wall units, and closets. The concept was ingenious, and Marshall was delighted with it. Tom Rosengren's first studio in the 1970s was the prototype for those that came after.

The German Wemhoner laminating press at the Waunakee factory was the first of its kind in the United States.

The studios proliferated in the '90s, and eventually there were more than sixty, located in all major cities of the United States. They accounted for an ever-increasing proportion of sales. Marshall was exacting in his standards and made sure the studios maintained high quality in service and appearance. He loved to drop in to visit whenever he was in a studio location, often to the discomfiture of the owners.

During the 1980s and 1990s, much of Marshall's energy and enthusiasm was poured into Techline, and he spared no expense in improving the product, ordering new machinery, and expanding the factory. He was tremendously proud of his factory, and almost any visitor to his office in Madison found him- or herself being whisked away to Waunakee for a tour of the Erdman factory. Long lines of green machines shrieked and roared, laminating high-quality particleboard, sending it off by conveyor rollers to be sliced, turned, edged, and drilled. The machines were computer-controlled, set for size, quantity, and item. Huge flexible silver tubes vacuumed dust.

Conveyors in the packaging department coaxed pieces along to be cleaned and packaged in sturdy boxes and picked up and stacked in inventory by front loaders. It was a turmoil of mostly automated activity—a far cry from the first lonely days in Waunakee.

"He would show up at the Waunakee plant, I would say, at least three to four times a week," said

George Garner. And he would always come looking for me and ask how things were going and, of course, it was never good enough. You should always push for more. It was always 115 percent. I told him, 'Marshall, there is only 100 percent, not 115 percent.'

"When I told him I was going to retire—1993, I think it was—and he came out and he wanted to talk to me. He came and gave me a hug and had tears in his eyes and he said, 'You know, I don't want you to leave. Promise you'll stay.' I said, 'No Marshall, it's too late. I'm going to retire, and you better find somebody to take over.'

"By that time, or for a number of years before, he had complete confidence in what I was doing. If I wanted to buy something and I said, 'Look, we need this, we need to make a change,' he would say, 'You go ahead and get what you need.'"

New options for Techline, new furnishings for his showroom—he even sprang for advertising in national shelter publications. He insisted on creating the ads in-house to cut costs, but he didn't balk at the high placement costs at *Metropolitan Home*, *Home* magazine, and other glossy media. He paid for promotional videos and fancy brochures. His tight grip on the purse strings could loosen when he felt the necessity or the passion.

Up Reach, was a massive 3,000-pound metal sculpture Marshall constructed and placed in front of his offices.

builder as artist and public servant

IN 1982, MARSHALL RECEIVED AN appointment that ensured his continued attention to public spaces in the state of Wisconsin. Gov. Lee Dreyfus appointed him as the citizen member of the State Building Commission.

Marshall's appointment was not without controversy. His firm had just finished GEF III, a major state building project, and had actually returned money to the state once the project was done. But Marshall insisted there was no conflict of interest, and Dreyfus agreed, saying he wanted someone with Marshall's vast experience and that having done business with the state should not be seen as a detriment. "The only way you can avoid that type of thing is to put a virtue on ignorance and inexperience," Dreyfus said.

Dreyfus was in his last year as governor, but his eventual successor, Tony Earl, would retain Marshall as the citizen member of the Building Commission for several years. Marshall and Joyce were personally friendly with Earl. Gaylord Nelson hosted an early fund-raiser for Earl at the Erdman farm.

The 1980s were to be a decade when Marshall

Erdman became more active in public life. His involvement in politics was through fund-raisers for those candidates he supported, such as Madison Mayor Joe Sensenbrenner and U.S. Senate candidate Ed Garvey in the mid-1980s. But he was immersed in public projects, beginning the decade on the Building Commission and ending it by participating in two other highly visible commissions: to restore

Marshall, seated next to Gov. Tony Earl, at a State Building Commission meeting at the Wisconsin state capitol.

Gaylord Nelson, left, remained a close friend of Joyce and Marshall throughout their lives.

Taliesin and to bring about Madison's Monona Terrace Convention Center.

In his participation in public events, of course, Marshall was following in the very large footsteps of his wife, Joyce. After completing her terms as first female president of the Village of Shorewood Hills and first woman president of the UW Board of Regents, she was appointed to the University Hospital Board of Trustees and was president of *The Capital Times* Kids Fund for thirteen years.

Significantly, Joyce also helped many other local organizations, donating money, or, more important, her time and expertise. She helped launch the Kanopy Dance Group, assisted the Madison Art Center in its infancy, was involved with the Attic Angels and the Alliance for Children and Youth, and served on the state Department of Transportation Rustic Roads board and on the Ice Age Trail project. She also involved herself in the Erdman & Associates corporate contributions program, serving on a committee

made up of several company officers, including Hauck and Garland, to help determine which local organizations should receive support.

One of Joyce's most significant contributions, in hindsight, may have come in late 1985, when she successfully lobbied for Jane Coleman, wife of former Erdman company employee and board member Reed Coleman, for the job of executive director of the Madison Community Foundation. Joyce interviewed Jane and later called her "bright and assertive." Coleman got the position and subsequently turned the community foundation from a passive organization with assets of about $1 million to a highly visible and respected community charitable force. The foundation had assets of $40 million to support its annual grants program by the time Coleman retired a decade later.

Joyce had always been active, of course, but there may have been even more reason for it in the 1980s. It was not an easy time for the Erdmans in their private life. The kids were grown and on their own. Marshall's moodiness had become increasingly mercurial. Some of Joyce's difficulties were recorded in her diaries, which she kept faithfully, or in letters to her children. She knew her husband was battling an increasingly volatile manic depression, and she tried to understand, but it was rough.

In the office, too, he would fly into a rage over seemingly unimportant items: a coat thrown carelessly over a chair, a car parked backward in the parking lot. Employees learned to tread with soft footsteps, but Joyce bore the brunt of his illness.

At the depths of his depression, Marshall could not even get out of bed to go to work. At one point

Joyce with family and friends as they hike from bottom of Grand Canyon. From left: Dan, Miles (Cricket) McMillin, and Mary and Tim Erdman.

he stayed in bed for more than two weeks, despondent and barely talking. Joan Burke, who became a friend and one of Marshall's most trusted financial advisers, remembers Marshall coming into her office at the bank one day, and she feared he was suicidal. "He cried in my office," she said. "He said he was so depressed he couldn't shake it—he saw no reason to go on."

Joyce finally got Marshall to see a psychiatrist at the University Hospital, who prescribed anti-depressants that miraculously brought back his joie de vivre. Always an individual looking for the best deal, Marshall sent Grace Lukken out to find the cheapest place to get his pills. "He had me go all over town to find the cheapest pharmacy to fill his prescription. I tell you, I did things for that man no

other secretary would be asked to do!"

For years Marshall and Joyce had gone their separate ways in the mornings, perhaps as a way of avoiding conflict. Marshall would rise early and breakfast with his neighbors, the Harts. Lukken describes his usual routine during the '80s.

"I'd be in at six in the morning. Marshall was over at the Harts making his coffee at that time. He would call me. A lot of times, Ed wasn't even out of bed when he'd call. Of course, when Martha was living, she was always up early and she was making bread, or doing something early in the morning. Maybe sewing on Marshall's button.

"So he would call. And then, I could transfer him any place. If he wanted to talk to somebody out of the office, or if Ed and Marshall had a big fight,

Marshall was here at 6:30 in the morning. I always knew, when he came up the steps. . . . I'd say, 'What happened?'" Lukken became a loyal confidante during these difficult times.

"He'd come up to his office, go through his mail. He'd take his phone calls. He would wander around the office, but not a lot, because he knew if he saw things he didn't like, he'd blow off."

There were many good times as well. Daughter Debbie had a home and a busy medical practice in Livingston, Montana, and Marshall and Joyce had Christmas there with their children. Ed Hart and his wife came along and it was, by all accounts, a pleasant time. Joyce told everyone she was determined to cut down on all her civic commitments. She was hoping to step down from the UW School of Business's Board of Visitors as well as from the Wisconsin Academy of Science, Arts, and Letters, and the Wisconsin Clinical Cancer Advisory Board. "But the going is slow and difficult," she wrote.

How successful was she? A short time after this pronouncement, Joyce joined the board of directors of the Ice Age Trail. The first meeting was at Terry Kohler's house in Sheboygan, a beautiful 1939 home by a Frank Lloyd Wright student. They spent two hours on what Joyce later called "aimless" socializing and followed that with an hour of slides before getting down to business. If she was to stay on the board, that would have to change, she reflected.

Grace Lukken, who handled much of Marshall's personal finances, said, "Joyce was a wonderful person to work with. . . . I tell you, behind every man is a good woman, and she was there. She was super."

Marshall was more involved in civic ventures as well. He was a logical choice for certain high-level public activities as head of a very successful firm. In 1983, *Engineering News-Record*, an industry trade magazine, had reported that the Erdman firm was now among the 300 largest construction firms in the United States, and the largest in Madison, with a contract volume of $56 million in 1982.

In June of 1984, Gov. Earl asked Marshall to accompany him on a trade delegation to China. In China with Earl, perhaps drawing on his years of experience with the Peace Corps, Marshall announced an agreement to design furniture and train a team of furniture workers in Wisconsin for a furniture factory in China's Heilungjiang province. The Erdman firm would then purchase the Chinese furniture components for assembly in Wisconsin. However, as is frequently the case with such cross-cultural endeavors, the details were difficult to arrange and little came of this project.

But anyone who knew Marshall also knew that setting him loose in the halls of government with its attendant bureaucracy, putting him on the Building Commission, for instance, was to invite some vocal criticism of the status quo. Knowing Lee Dreyfus, that might be why he appointed Marshall. But even Dreyfus appeared shocked in September of 1982 when Marshall decreed, in response to a reporter's question, that the architects of a new prison in Portage should keep drawing even after environmental concerns led to a state court of appeals injunction against the prison plans.

In the fall of 1984 Marshall once again shook things up upon receiving state plans for a remodeling project at the UW's School of Family Resources and Consumer Sciences. The proposed price tag: $550,000. Marshall's take: "I could do everything they need for $250,000."

Marshall fumed about a $90,000 darkroom in the proposal with a door he called the "cream of the crop" and suggested further that an expensive venting system could be replaced by a large fan. The commission's spending recommendation on the project had in fact been doubled by the legislature's Joint Finance Committee.

"Someone from the department is related to someone on the Finance Committee," Marshall said. He didn't quite have his facts right, but he was close. Milwaukee state senator Gary George, a powerful member of Joint Finance, also served on the School of Family Resources advisory committee, and George's wife had been a student lecturer at the school.

The senator angrily defended the cost. "The school has been passed over, at least in part, because of a relative disregard for the professional careers of women represented in the school," George said.

If George was adding a little pork to the school's budget in the form of an expensive remodeling project, it would hardly be a first in the state budget annals. But Marshall was incensed. Certainly he got peoples' attention. As he became successful, and by the 1980s Marshall was by any measure financially comfortable, he seemed to take both responsibility and pleasure in challenging assumptions and provoking responses.

"I want to fire people up!" That's what Marshall told *The Capital Times* for a 1990s article on a new sculpture he had commissioned to stand in front of

Marshall with crew that designed, manufactured, and installed the sculpture Up Reach in front of the Erdman offices. Clockwise from bottom left: Marshall, artist Bo von Hohenlohe, Erdman factory employees Paul Marx, Phil Breunig, Bill Grulke, and art program manager Ellen Johnson.

the corporate offices on University Avenue.

Marshall hired California artist Bo von Hohenlohe to design what was eventually called *Up Reach*, a massive, 3,000-pound metalwork that the artist said was inspired by the prophesied retreat of South American Indians before the conquistadors. In the shape of a large curved Y, or slingshot, the piece is painted bright red and blue. As with many contemporary art installations, it took a little getting used to for some people, which, Marshall pointed out, was his intent. "I've always felt that the eye, like the mind, should be educated," he said.

Also in the Erdman tradition, the sculpture was cost-efficient. Rather than go through a dealer, Marshall contracted directly with the artist and had his own Waunakee metal shop carry out the structural design and construction of the piece. Estimated final cost: $20,000.

"I was sort of hoping that people wouldn't like it immediately," Marshall said. "I wanted it as a symbol, a statue which I hope will be controversial, so that people will put up sculptures beside their own buildings rather than ugly signs." His comments were an echo of his support for the state Percent for Art program that state senator Fred Risser had introduced. The bill required each new state building over a certain budget to spend $2/10$ of 1 percent of its budget on art. Marshall was instrumental in championing this program through the Building Commission, and he participated in several of the sculptural review committees.

Visual aesthetics were much on Marshall's mind, and he grumbled about how disappointed he had been when visiting Erdman clinics around the country by the doctors' apparent lack of interest in making the walls of the clinic anything but walls. From these loose thoughts came an entirely new department for the company. The Erdman Art Department would bring an enthusiastic response from the press and ultimately from clients and, moreover, would remain a passion with Marshall for the rest of his life.

His close friend Ed Hart never shared the passion, but he saw it in Marshall. "He always felt the doctors were not decorating their offices correctly,"

Hart said. And then with a laugh Hart recalled his friend embracing modern art. "Marshall, for some reason, liked abstract art," Hart said. "It was so bad, some of it, well, maybe it was good art from an abstract point of view. In Marshall's house he had something that was just a round black circle with a red dot in the middle of it. I said, 'What the hell is that? A target?' Marshall said, 'That is something that brightens my day every time I look at it.'"

In typical Marshall fashion, he soon had the genesis of a plan and had picked out a person he believed could make it work. His candidate was a woman named Ellen Frautschi (now Ellen Johnson) whom the Erdmans had known since the late 1960s, when she and her then husband, Jerry Frautschi, moved to Shorewood Hills.

Ellen Johnson first met the Erdmans at a dinner party one New Year's Eve at a home in Shorewood Hills. Marshall and Joyce had just returned from Europe. "I remember Joyce standing in the living room of the house where the party was," Johnson said. "She had on a black velvet pants suit and looked elegant and lovely. She was actually the closer friend of mine, of the two, in the beginning. She was a mentor and an example for a lot of us. She was continually encouraging us to go further with our education."

They began to do some traveling together, with Johnson going along on a number of University of Wisconsin trips that Joyce made after she joined the Board of Regents. There were trips to Greece and Egypt, and then they scheduled one to Russia, which Marshall professed not to fathom. Why would anyone go to Russia? In the end, he went along. "And he was terrible the whole time," Johnson said. Years later, after Marshall's death, she would wonder if it wasn't the proximity to Lithuania and some buried memories that had made him so uncomfortable in Russia.

By the early 1980s, Johnson had divorced Jerry Frautschi and was raising her children while working at the University Hospital. On the days of his psychiatric appointments, Marshall would stop by Johnson's office to chat. "I had an inside office," she recalled, "and had always been interested in art and collected art. So since I didn't have a window, I brought some things from home." Nothing very remarkable in that. What else would you do with empty walls? But Marshall was impressed. "When he came in for treatments he would stop and see me, and he just thought it was wonderful that I had art in my office."

Still, it's a long way from admiring some wall hangings in a friend's office to beginning a new department in your company. How did Marshall get the idea to go into the corporate art business? Johnson has a theory that like so much else in Marshall's life, it may have been the influence of Frank Lloyd Wright.

"I'm sure the idea for the art department was influenced at least in part by his exposure to Wright," Johnson said. "Wright bought a lot of Japanese prints and he would sell them to people who bought his homes.

"[Marshall] got the idea to bring art into the company and provide it to clients, which would then control the way the interiors of his buildings looked. It was a logical step. Everything he thought the build-ings needed he eventually brought into the company to be produced or provided. Why not art?"

Marshall would come back fuming from a trip to visit a clinic. "I just hate the crap they have in there!" he'd shout. "Angora kitty cats!" He was talking himself into a new idea, and he was talking Johnson into it as well. "He didn't have it worked out in his head how to do it, which was unusual," Johnson said. "On most things he was already there before he started something. He was so bright, so creative, and had so much energy to back it up."

Early in 1982, Marshall mentioned his art program idea, and the notion of Ellen Johnson running it, to his wife, Joyce. "He talked lots of things over with her," Johnson said. "I'm not sure people realize that. She was a great confidante of his. Many people saw their relationship as adversarial. It was complicated, but he relied on her often."

That spring, Johnson and the Erdmans took a trip to Chicago. Marshall had arranged for an art consultant to show them around. They toured galleries, they talked, they visited museums. But at the end of the day, Johnson was nervous. She knew the pitch was coming. "I liked art and collected art, but did I really have a strong background in this? No."

In the end, it was Joyce who convinced her. "She said a couple of things that, at the time, sort of went past me," Johnson said. But Joyce knew who could work with Marshall and who could not. She said to Johnson, "You've traveled enough with Marshall, and know him well enough, that you could stand up to him. Marshall's problem is that he bowls people over and then he's not interested in them anymore. I think you'll be able to draw the

Marshall beside an original painting by Keith Haring in Erdman office gallery.

UNCOMMON SENSE—THE LIFE OF MARSHALL ERDMAN

line when he gets too difficult."

Johnson didn't know that Marshall had hired personal friends in the past, sometimes with disastrous results. In this instance, however, Joyce's instincts were right.

Marshall said to Johnson, "What would it take to get you to come?" Johnson, newly divorced, thought of her kids and her house payment and said the answer was easy: "Money." Marshall asked what her salary was. She told him. "I'll double it," he said. What could Johnson say? "I decided I might as well take a leap and try."

First, Marshall said, Johnson should talk with people in the company, some of the top executives. He suggested Roger Hauck and Reed Coleman, the latter still a member of the Erdman board. Marshall told the men, "Give her the negatives."

Hauck, company president, had serious early reservations. "He thought it would be risky for me," Johnson recalled. "Roger was trying to be honest." He eventually came around. "In terms of making people comfortable in their environment," he said years later, "it's the most important thing we do. It's a logical extension of our design philosophy."

On Johnson's first day of work, it was Hauck, not Marshall, who showed her around. She had never been inside the University Avenue offices, and they did not impress her.

"I thought, 'My God, this is an architectural firm? What do people think when they come in?'" It was spartan, even to the point of a broken window that had been patched over with cardboard. Hauck shrugged. "Marshall won't let me fix it."

Certainly there was no apparent interest in art.

"There were three pictures in the entire office," Johnson said. "I thought architects knew all about art and appreciated it. It was just another example of all that I didn't know."

Showing Johnson around that first day, Hauck said, "You probably won't have a lot of business for a while, so why don't you fix up this place around here?"

Johnson recalled the infancy of the art program: "We didn't have any inventory. We had to figure out where to buy art, because in effect we were going to be a gallery. We had to be able to buy art wholesale. We couldn't just go into a gallery and say, 'We'll take three of those.' The first thing we had to do was figure out where to buy the art."

Johnson spent much of her first year just creating a structure for the art program. "It was hard to break into the business," she recalled. "No one in Madison would really help us. They saw us as competition. So we decided to buy no local artists, which put them at ease a bit, and the other rule was we wouldn't buy artists who were related to anyone at the company or were employees themselves. And we'd have to buy prints.

"They were building a hundred clinics and office buildings a year, all over the country," she said. "We knew we had to use multiples or graphics. No way could we buy originals."

While Johnson was forging her art department from scratch, learning on the job and slowly finding her way, she found she had one hole card—the ultimate hole card. "I had to figure out a system, and there were no models for this kind of thing. But I had tremendous power, energy, and support behind me."

She was referring, of course, to Marshall. "He

backed me and he backed the program. He wanted it that much. If anyone gave us trouble and he got wind of it, he'd mow them down, so it became a sacred cow at the company. Marshall never really did lose interest in it. I went with him to the last building he visited before he died. It was in Eau Claire, the Midelfort Clinic. He walked up and down those corridors and he said, 'We've done it. We not only know how to build them now, we know how to do the interiors.'"

And that was part of the attraction for Marshall. Putting art on the clinics' walls was the final affirmation of the concept of design-and-build, the idea Marshall had embraced early and argued for throughout his career—the "total responsibility" approach, as he liked to call it.

When the *Wisconsin State Journal* took note of the art program in early 1987, with a lengthy piece and color picture of Marshall standing beside a Francois Boisrond acrylic hanging in the University Avenue headquarters, both Marshall and Hauck stressed design-and-build: "Our firm is extremely vertically integrated," Hauck said. "It gives us flexibility and efficiency." Marshall went a step further: "We are the only firm that carries the design and build concept to what I consider its true limits." There seems little doubt that in offering art to his company's clients, he was hearkening back to Frank Lloyd Wright's insistence on total design control.

The art department was the final culmination of Marshall's gradual strategies toward that "total responsibility" goal. At the Waunakee factory, cabinets and doors for the medical buildings were manufactured, and steel beams and decorative railings for the larger buildings were fabricated in the "steel shop." This capability not only assured a timely supply but also permitted control of cost and quality. A fleet of giant trucks with the Erdman logo delivered components to building sites on time for the Erdman construction superintendents to meet their schedules.

An interior design department in the Madison offices designed the look and feel of clinic interiors—specified carpeting, furniture, plants, and other elements. They were well versed in the products that would work well and would hold up under the constant traffic of a medical interior. A chair department at the factory assembled components for comfortable office and waiting room chairs.

Another interesting—and very useful—addition was the signage department, established to create all the interior and many of the exterior signs that the clinics would need. Once again, the ability to produce these signs in-house assured maximum control of quality and schedule.

Not long after the art department was initiated, Marshall saw a need for help with communications. At first he probably didn't have a fully developed plan for this area. He knew he was poor with words, and although he was masterful at his own public relations, perhaps he thought it would be useful to have some help. At a fund-raising party at the UW chancellor's house, he met Alice D'Alessio, who was working for WHA-Television. "What do you do?" he asked her. She said, "I'm a writer." "Oh," he said, "I need a writer!"

Several months of sporadic conversations took place, and in August of 1985, D'Alessio was hired

The lobby of the Dean Clinic on Fish Hatchery Road in Madison, completed in 1989, displays a fiber wall hanging by local artist Joyce Carey.

with responsibility for all interior and exterior communications. Her first project was to produce a video for marketing Techline.

Eventually the position came to include the quarterly employee newsletter, "Connections;" a quarterly marketing piece, "New Dimensions;" company annual reports; Marshall's speeches and occasionally drafts of letters; brochures for the art department; press packets and publicity for Techline; and advertisements internally for both Techline and the medical buildings, as well as purchasing ad space in national media. High-gloss "project sheets" on individual medical buildings were produced as sales tools, as were a series of informational textbooks, *How to*

Design and Build Ambulatory Healthcare Facilities, that were provided free to clients and proved to be extremely popular. Marshall was joining the marketing age, somewhat reluctantly. Marketing, like developer and human resources were among the terms he balked at, at least when applied to his business.

In the first annual report she did for the firm, D'Alessio made the mistake of referring to Marshall Erdman as a "full-service developer." The morning after the reports were delivered from the printer, he came up the steps breathing fire. "Alice," he roared, "how could you do this to me?" All copies of the new report went to the landfill, and a new version was printed without the word "developer."

The increase in print production necessitated hiring a graphic designer and photographer, as well as installing computer and darkroom capabilities, and so the total responsibility grew. Like a many-tentacled sea creature, Marshall's long arms reached out and assimilated every capability his company needed. He always truly believed, "We can do it better ourselves." Outsourcing was not in his vocabulary—nor in his budget!

Meanwhile, the art department was having the most dramatic visual effect. At its inception, Roger Hauck wrote in a letter to employees, "We hope this new [art] program will enhance the interiors of our clinics, for works of art in this kind of setting serve a double purpose: they not only enrich the lives of physicians, patients, employees, and visitors, but are also an important contribution to the cultural community."

How was it going to work? Hauck spelled out some specifics: "Our hope is to allocate a portion of the building costs for art and to write this into our initial contracts. We would like to have as much independence as possible in the selection of art work. In order to encourage this, we will exchange any art that the owner wishes to return after it has been installed in a medical building for a year. A frame shop will be built at our Madison office to provide quality framing at a reasonable price for our clients. More information on this program will be available in the near future."

Ellen Johnson recalled, "We said, 'For a dollar a square foot, you can buy our art program.'" Where did that figure come from? "We pulled it out of the air," she said. (Within a few years, the price went up to $1.50 a square foot.) "Marshall had said, 'What should we charge for this?' The first clinic we were doing was one in Colorado. I said, 'How big is the building?' He said, 'It's 60,000 square feet.' So I said, 'Let's charge $60,000.'"

"We couldn't sell it at straight cost," Johnson said. "We would have run into problems buying it after a time because the art world controls pricing in a certain way."

Johnson was getting a crash course in the ways of that insular world. She was traveling as often as once a week to Chicago and New York, where a friend, a transplanted Madison man who worked in the business, was showing her around, introducing her to a number of print publishers. "Before long we established a reputation for buying large amounts and for paying our bills once a month. That got the art world interested. Most artists leave their work in a gallery on consignment. Sometimes the artist is paid right away after a sale and sometimes people forget to pay them."

During the first year Johnson accumulated frequent-flyer miles, learned the business, and really didn't put any art in clinics. She worked instead on the corporate collection in the Erdman headquarters in Madison. Not all the company employees were enthusiastic about the contemporary prints Johnson chose for the home office. Said Lukken, "That art program—I thought he was crazy. I always told him my kids did better [art] in grade school. My refrigerator was full of better things than what we had hanging here. 'Keep looking at them,' he says, 'keep looking at them and you'll find something.' We thought he was absolutely nuts."

Many of Johnson's trips were to accumulate inventory. "The dollar was so strong," she recalled, "that we traveled abroad and bought graphics in large multiples. We put seventy-five or eighty different images in a clinic. Plus we started a poster program for the clinics' exam rooms. They might have up to 100 exam rooms that run along the exterior of the building, and we decided to put a poster in every exam room so people sitting in there would have something to look at."

Marshall would also often accompany Johnson to clinics to sell the art program. Talking to the doctors, Marshall would make an offer that was hard to turn down. He'd tell clinics, "We'll pick your art, frame it, ship it, install it. You live with it for a year, and if you want to return it, we'll take it and give you back your money."

Though in the end few pieces were returned, there was resistance. "A lot of clinics felt they should be supporting their local galleries," Johnson said. "A lot of doctors' wives thought they should be doing the selecting." Marshall wouldn't have it. The reason the program was started in the first place was because the clinics had proved incapable of handling their interiors, at least to the satisfaction of Marshall Erdman. The acceptance of the idea, both inside and outside the company, grew with time. Maybe because it was a good idea, one whose time had come.

"The most amazing thing was that after we had three or four buildings done," Johnson said, "those quickly became the buildings that all the salesmen would take their potential clients to see, because they looked so good."

Company president Roger Hauck with Marshall. Hauck guided the business during a period of tremendous growth in the 1980s and early '90s.

After Johnson hired her first framer, the art department landed a huge contract, a dollar a square foot for a 125,000-square-foot clinic in Apple Hill, Pennsylvania.

"Then Marshall had to build us a real art department. We were spilling out of the basement." And with the growth, Johnson said, "the art world began to open up to me. The word of mouth started: 'Gee, she just came out and bought eighty prints.' Then my phone began to ring a lot."

The need for a "real art department" spurred Marshall's next real estate venture. Just to the east of the Erdman headquarters, the 7UP Bottling Plant became vacant in 1985 and available for purchase. The deal was soon signed. Designers drew up plans according to Marshall's directions, and the brick building became Building Number Two, more than doubling the size of the home office. It became the new home for a spacious art department, with lots of storage and framing space, interior design, signage, graphics, and, to the rear, space for the offices and the growing number of architect and sales cubicles that made up the highly productive Midwest Division. The new building also had a gigantic central gallery that was ideal for art displays and public functions as well as a generous meeting room for the annual managers meetings or lunchtime brown bags.

The firm now had offices in Hartford, Connecticut; Washington, D.C.; Denver; Atlanta; Dallas; and Madison. In the '90s it added a California office. The managers meetings were a time for division managers to come together with corporate officers to hear how the firm was doing, what the forecasts were—and what their responsibilities were.

Marshall kept in close touch with his thriving medical building business, but he permitted Roger Hauck to do the day-to-day managing while he attended to the things that interested him most. When he was not roaming his factory or touting Techline, Marshall was caught up in the enthusiasm for his new art program. Just as, with the advent of Techline, he used to tear open the big brown boxes that arrived carrying furniture components, now it was art that consumed him. He would find a reason to wander over to the art department, which made Johnson popular with other managers. She said, "It occupied Marshall and kept him out of their way!"

Johnson recalled: "He made daily inspections of the art department. I'd never worked in private business, so I just assumed that that's what the CEO of a company did. Walk around and check on everyone every day. He would see the United Parcel man come in with tubes, and he'd come over and want to see what I'd bought. He'd want to know what it cost, what my discounts were. 'You're still not buying it well enough,' he'd say, and it would make me furious. But you know, he was right. I wasn't buying it for as low as I could have, but I didn't know it at the time."

If the Erdman foray into art needed some kind of final, outside blessing to signal its success, that arrived in a big way early in 1988 when the University of Wisconsin's Elvehjem Museum of Art decided to showcase seventy-two prints from Erdman's University Avenue headquarters in an exhibit at the museum. They had come quite a way from the time six years before when Johnson walked into the office for the first time and found just three pictures hanging in the entire building.

The show at the Elvehjem was the idea of the museum's director, Russell Panczenko. "What interested me was, first, the incredibly high quality of the art," Panczenko said. "And second, the notion of corporate collecting. Corporations are now the patrons of the twentieth century. They have replaced the great families of the fifteenth and sixteenth centuries."

Panczenko noted the quality of the artists, a virtual who's who of modern and contemporary art: Andy Warhol, Joan Miro, Frank Stella, Christo, and many others. He also gave a nod to the matting and framing done by Erdman "Their facilities are better than ours."

Perhaps what might have pleased Marshall most of all was that Panczenko said how marvelous it was that a businessperson such as Marshall Erdman had taken art out of museums and put it back into the workplace and home, back into the

Marshall with some members of his board of directors and management team. From left: Dick Garland, Bill Madden, Joyce, Ed Jenkins, Sheldon Lubar, Roger Hauck, Jack Pelisek, Reed Coleman, and Gordon Derzon.

mainstream of daily life.

With the advent of the Elvehjem show, the last of the doubting employees jumped on the art bandwagon. To hang the exhibit, the museum removed all the art from Erdman halls and offices, leaving the building as plain and stark as it had been before the existence of the art department. Said Lukken, "We couldn't stand it until they put it back. What a difference! The place was empty. Marshall said, 'Now do you see what I mean?' Well, there are still some things that I'd rather not see on walls, but he was so right."

Years earlier, Marshall had said, "What we need to do today is get the artist out of his ivory tower and into the world of everyday living."

He was as good as his word.

Joyce prepares for a long bike ride, her passion in later years.

troubles, triumphs, and tragedy

IN THE SUMMER OF 1988 PAUL OKEY retired. He had been with Marshall Erdman & Associates for nearly four decades, virtually from the beginning of Erdman's business. Okey established the company's quality control program, and to administer it, he traveled 100,000 miles a year to visit every clinic Erdman built. His careful, tireless scrutiny would be missed.

His departure also left an important gap in employee relations. For many years Okey had been the quiet peacemaker who soothed and rehired after Marshall's ill-advised outbursts. Changes in employment protection, affirmative action, and antiharassment had been added to federal and Wisconsin law in the previous years, and suddenly even Marshall was going to have to sit up and take notice. It took a couple of lawsuits for him to realize that he would have to temper his hiring/firing approach and even permit a human resources department.

One lawsuit was by a salesman who thought he had been wrongfully discharged. But the one that hurt Marshall deeply was that of a woman he had hired to head his signage department. He was fond of her ("She was like my own daughter. I gave her special treatment"), but when she drew up a plan for her new department that was more spacious than he thought she needed, it set off the fireworks. He roared at her in front of her coworkers and accused her of trying to build an empire. She walked out and would not return, though both Hauck and Marshall pleaded with her to reconsider. A lawsuit claiming sexual harassment followed and dragged on in its convoluted legal meanderings for years. Marshall grieved, but he had to bow to the new workplace reality.

Okey's retirement also coincided with a number of projects that captured Marshall Erdman's attention and, like Okey's leaving, brought both a flood of memories and a realization of the passing years, of time growing short.

There were intimations of mortality, no question. In April of 1988 Marshall had heard from the Social Security Administration that he was eligible for Social Security benefits. Well, he was and he wasn't, the letter explained. "Based on your estimate of earnings

Marshall with financial advisor Joan Burke.

for 1988, no benefits are payable while you continue to work. However, you will be due some benefits if your yearly earnings are less than $28,332. . . . If these changes occur, please notify any Social Security office promptly."

The changes didn't occur, but Marshall and Joyce were thinking about what would happen with their children and with the company once they were gone. Actually, most of the thinking was done by Joyce. Marshall would not hear of giving up control of the company, or even of planning about eventually giving it up. He was unable and unwilling to face the fact that he was mortal. It was fortunate that Joyce took the initiative for the long-term planning. She was insistent that Tim should eventually take over leadership of the company, and to that end she engineered his return to Madison from the Denver office where he had been division manager. Because

Roger Hauck had anticipated heading the company at Marshall's retirement, this turn of events precipitated his resignation. Dan, meanwhile, was being groomed to take over Techline and the Waunakee factory.

Joan Burke saw how Marshall struggled with planning for the future. "He was very concerned about leaving too much money for his children," said Burke, who started right out of high school at the old Madison Bank and Trust where Marshall was on the board of directors. "Marshall had taken relatively little money out of the company until the 1980s when it became a Sub-S Corporation and by law was forced to distribute earnings to the stockholders. That's when his personal wealth really increased."

In September 1989, the family met at length in Madison with an attorney, Dick Pitzner, who specialized in estate planning. Debbie arrived first, the night of September 7, and the next day met with Pitzner. Joyce later wrote in her diary that the meeting was "very successful," saying Debbie "understood the general aims, asked thoughtful penetrating questions and became a part of the endeavor to help maintain the company and what it stands for."

Dan arrived a couple of days later and was joined at the family farm by Tim and his fiancée, Mary, whom he had met in the Erdman company art department. They had another long meeting with the attorney, which Joyce again called "successful." Dan flew home to San Francisco, and Joyce took Tim and Mary to dinner at L'Etoile, Madison's best restaurant located on the Capitol Square. It was raining but the night was buoyant. Tim and Mary told Joyce they were planning to get married in three weeks, on September 30. That was the scheduled date for their housewarming in Telluride, where Tim had been building a vacation home. The wedding was to be a secret until then.

The next day, September 12, Joyce gave Tim something for Mary. It was her mother's engagement ring. They were touched, and Joyce was delighted "that it is to be used so appropriately." Tim and Mary felt it meant something tangible and lasting.

The following week, when Marshall left for Europe and the Milan furniture fair, Joyce was able to enjoy another of her passions—biking. She and a group of friends—Weston Wood, Henry Hart, John McNelly, and Lydie Hudson—embarked on what Joyce called "a serious bicycle expedition." She later called the trip "wonderful. A glorious day to be alive and in the countryside with friends." They biked through western Dane County, ate lunch at a good restaurant in Mazomanie, and circled the far side of Highway 14. When Joyce got back home to the house on Circle Close, she was amazed to see the odometer read seventy-two miles, the most she had ever done. She was tired, she wrote, but not exhausted.

Marshall returned from Europe in time for a special social gathering at the residence of UW chancellor Donna Shalala, who had become a friend of the Erdmans. She had visited their farm in Middleton, and now they were assisting her in buying property of her own in the area. The party Shalala hosted was for the Dalai Lama. What made it even more exciting was that His Holiness had just received the Nobel Peace Prize. There were 150 guests. Joyce would remember the Dalai Lama as "an impressively humble human being. He had a firm handshake and

Joyce (kneeling left) and her biking friends.

words for many of us individually."

A few weeks earlier there had been a fancy dinner at Taliesin, Wright's old home. Indeed the Spring Green area was still very much a part of the Erdmans' lives. This dinner, in early September of '89, was a tuxedo and long dress affair. After dinner, Effie Casey, wife of Taliesin architect Tom Casey, conducted the music, "beautifully as usual," Joyce said. The Erdmans sat at the head table with Richard Carney, managing trustee of the Frank Lloyd Wright Foundation. It could not have been otherwise. Financially and emotionally, Marshall continued to be very much involved with Taliesin.

In June 1988, Gov. Tommy Thompson had appointed a twenty-eight-member group called the Governor's Commission on Taliesin. He chose Marshall Erdman to chair it. There was some irony in that, which Marshall appreciated.

Said Tom Casey, "Marshall pointed out that for years he'd been trying to get Democratic governors, many of whom were his friends, to come out and see the help Taliesin needed. And when one finally did, it was a Republican governor whom he didn't know personally." They did, of course, get to know one another, and they developed a strong mutual respect.

Once again, Marshall's appointment, just like his Building Commission appointment a decade earlier, was not without controversy. This time the controversy was over the fact that Erdman owned some 3,000 acres of property adjacent to Taliesin. Wouldn't Erdman stand to benefit if the commission he would be chairing recommended major renovations to Taliesin?

Again, there was an irony at work. Marshall Erdman had been trying to give away most of his Spring Green property for many years. In the middle 1970s, a friend of Marshall's, Phil Lewis, a landscape architecture professor who ran the university's Environmental Awareness Center, approached Marshall. Lewis had a fascination with the driftless area, a rugged area of southwestern Wisconsin that had not been flattened and strewn with boulders by receding glaciers. Marshall's property was in the driftless area, and Lewis, worried that developers from Chicago or Minneapolis would see the scenic land as a development opportunity, made a suggestion to Marshall. The property, he said, would be ideal for university programs that would study how the land could best be developed while preserving its natural resources. Would Marshall consider donating it to the UW?

He first made an offer to the University of Wisconsin in October 1984. The UW could have 2,500 acres if it would simply maintain the property. The other 500 would be kept for recreational use (mainly hunting) by Erdman company employees. Marshall, not renowned for his patience, was not

pleased that the UW did not immediately embrace the offer. When the controversy over his chairing the Taliesin commission subsequently arose, he told the university, in February 1990, to make a decision: "It's dragged out long enough," Marshall said.

The land meant a lot to him. The Erdman company purchased the property in 1962, and Marshall and his family, along with many Erdman employees, had enjoyed it for years. Marshall admitted that one reason he bought it was because Frank Lloyd Wright, until his death in 1959, had been urging him to do it. "He was worried that the property near Taliesin would just become chopped up and become a Wisconsin Dells development," Marshall said.

There were essentially two problems that the university had with his gift. Harry Peterson, an assistant to UW Chancellor Donna Shalala, said that while the UW appreciated the offer, it would cost the school "hundreds of thousands of dollars" to take it over and assume operating and maintenance responsibility. Another caveat was that Marshall was insisting the UW agree never to sell the land in the future. What good was donating it, Marshall reasoned, if the UW turned around a few years later and sold it to a developer for a theme park? Local school and county officials in the area were also opposed to the donation. UW–Madison, as a state agency, would be largely exempt from paying property taxes on the land. It was a significant amount of revenue to a small community. Erdman paid more than $40,000 in taxes on the land in 1989.

Finally, in March 1990, Marshall threw up his hands. He had set a March 1 deadline for UW officials to make a decision on the land. As that dead-line approached, he agreed to extend it to April 15. But when the company board of directors met in early March, they changed their minds, and the UW was notified that the offer was being with-drawn. There didn't seem to be hard feelings. "We were appreciative of the fact that the offer was made," Peterson said. "We really had not conclud-ed yet what we could do with the property."

In 1988, when he was appointed by Thompson to head the Taliesin Preservation Commission, Marshall dismissed the idea of a conflict of interest, and to anyone who knew him, he was telling the truth. Driving up the price of real estate did not motivate Marshall Erdman at this stage of the game. He said he would "swear on a stack of Bibles" that he had no development plans for the area and indeed was actively trying to keep that from happening. Apparently his assurance mollified the critics.

The commission met through the summer of 1988 with a goal of getting Thompson a final report and recommendations by November. Marshall had Alice D'Alessio attend the meetings with him and draft the final report. In March 1989, the commission's proposal was made public. Among the recommendations in the report: spend-ing $14.7 million to restore Taliesin, with another $1 million spent on furnishings and decorative arts; construction of a $3.9 million visitor center nearby capable of handling 200,000 visitors a year, along with a $400,000 tram system to carry visi-tors around the property; and finally, a variety of educational and fund-raising programs designed to preserve and further Wright's legacy.

Marshall and Gov. Tommy Thompson examine a model at the Frank Lloyd Wright Visitor Center near Taliesin.

On March 20, Thompson pronounced himself pleased with the commission's work. "Clearly Taliesin is a great Wisconsin treasure," the governor said, "and I look forward to working with the Frank Lloyd Wright Foundation and the Taliesin Fellowship to advance the commission's recommendations."

Marshall, in his letter to Thompson introduc-ing the commission's report, said any financial investment in Taliesin by the state would be returned many times over. "I have no question in my mind that this is the best investment the state could make both economically and culturally," Marshall wrote.

Marshall with Ed Hart's daughters Abby (left) and Kappo.

Around the same time as he headed the Taliesin commission, Marshall was asked to serve on another Wright-related commission. The purpose of this one was to see if, at long last, a convention center could be built on Monona Terrace in Madison, based on a Wright design first conceived in 1938 and tinkered with for the next two decades.

It was actually a meeting of the Taliesin commission that proved the catalyst for generating the most serious talks yet about a Wright design on Lake Monona. During a drive to Spring Green, Jim Carley, a prominent Madison developer on the commission, recalled some recent newspaper stories in *The Capital Times*. In them, Jerry Nestingen, wife of the late mayor Ivan Nestingen, had lamented the fact that a 1988 plan for a Law Park convention facility had ignored the fact that Wright had a 1959 plan that could be utilized.

Carley, at the Taliesin meeting, asked Taliesin architect Charles Montooth if he might lend him a set of Wright's 1959 plans. Montooth agreed and returned shortly with a twenty-pound roll of plans based on Wright's '59 design but actually finished by Taliesin architects in 1960 after Wright's death.

Leaving Taliesin with the roll of plans under his arms, Carley ran into Marshall.

"What are those?" Marshall asked.

Carley told him, explaining that he was curious as to whether they might be adapted for a convention center. Marshall scoffed, "It will never work."

But he was intrigued enough to be part of a twelve-person group that made an unpublicized trip to Taliesin in June of 1989 to hear architect Tony Puttnam explain how he thought the plan could be adapted and a Wright center built on Lake Monona. An unstated purpose of the trip was to see if the mix of a dozen city leaders from business and government could get along, work together, and develop the beginnings of a chemistry they would need to pull off a project of this scope. Besides Marshall, the group included mayor Paul Soglin, newspaper publishers and editors, Carley, TV executive George Nelson, and Thompson administrator Jim Klauser.

As Marshall warmed to the idea, he made significant financial contributions and used his considerable contacts and influence to help make Monona Terrace a reality. The center opened to a great deal of acclaim and worldwide publicity in 1997.

If Marshall was somewhat involved in the Monona Terrace project, he had another in mind that would be his alone. His swan song, as he would call it, would be Middleton Hills.

But before Middleton Hills would be built, or even announced as an idea to the public, Marshall would endure a shocking and devastating loss.

Marshall and Joyce had bought a home in 1985 in Carefree, Arizona, a desert foothills community of about 1,500 located north of Scottsdale. It was a decidedly upper-class community whose residents included well-known Hollywood personalities and sports stars.

Joyce and Marshall were staying there on February 11, 1992. As she liked to do, Joyce got up early to bike two miles into Carefree to pick up the morning newspaper. A little after 7:00 a.m., according to a Maricopa County sheriff's deputy, Joyce Erdman's front wheel locked and she was thrown over the handlebar. She hadn't worn a helmet.

Paramedics arrived at 7:35 and found her bleeding but coherent. On the way to the hospital, her vital signs deteriorated rapidly. A fire department spokesman said, "She had an intercranial arterial bleed, which basically means she was bleeding inside her skull."

Marshall was notified of the accident by the police and immediately drove down to Scottsdale Memorial Hospital where his wife was in intensive care. The four children were all reached by phone. There was nothing that could be done. Joyce Erdman was pronounced dead at the hospital at 12:02 p.m. She was sixty-seven.

Bob O'Malley, the Erdmans' old banking friend who had a place of his own in Fountain Hills, Arizona, heard the news in a call from Madison. He quickly called Marshall to offer his sympathy. "He was just devastated," O'Malley recalled. "It was just an unbelievable thing."

In Madison, the reaction was similar—shock and disbelief. She was a woman full of life and vigor, who in her sixties had taken several bike trips in France, hiked to the bottom of the Grand Canyon, and backpacked in Montana, accompanied by her children and friends. Marshall was supportive of these activities but always declined to participate.

She was a woman who had been a leader and a role model for many. For her fund-raising efforts on behalf of the UW School of Business she had just recently accepted the Dean's Award at a dinner at the Concourse Hotel. And suddenly she was gone.

Her funeral was held at the Unitarian Meeting House she had watched her husband build some forty years before, and mourners spilled over into halls and the lobby. Donna Shalala, UW–Madison Chancellor, said, "Joyce was a leader who cared deeply about her university and her community. She was a remarkable woman. She is irreplaceable."

Madison mayor Paul Soglin concurred. "When I saw her coming, I would really look forward to seeing what she had in mind this week," Soglin said. "She had this way of saying her ideas without imposing them on you."

State senator Fred Risser said, "She was a wonderful woman and she loved life. She's the type of citizen all people can be proud of."

Fellow UW Board of Regents member Herbert Grover fondly remembered serving with her. "She got right in there and mixed it up," Grover said.

Finally, UW System President Katharine Lyall said, "Joyce will be missed as a friend of the UW System, and personally, I will miss her."

If there was anything at all beyond grief to come from Joyce's tragic accident, it might have been the impetus it provided for Marshall to get a little closer to his children. The youngest, Dan, said, "That was when I got close with my dad."

Debbie, who had not only loved but also greatly respected her mother ("she was stronger than my father, and the one everybody loved"), reflected on her parents' marriage. "She was the love of his life," Debbie said. "It was a stormy marriage, but what marriage isn't? They were two strong-willed people, and sometimes Papa would try to treat Mother like an employee and she wouldn't put up with it."

She recalled that her father, who never much cared for being by himself, was miserable after Joyce's death. He took to dropping in on friends unannounced. He cried easily. Joan Burke remembered him telling her, "We didn't have a perfect marriage, but I always thought we would be together forever. . . . You don't always realize what you have until you lose it."

And he asked Debbie to travel with him, trips she came to treasure, for the time together helped break down some barriers.

"He was so unhappy," Debbie recalled. "I went to some of the furniture fairs in Europe with him. I really did get to know him and love him after my mother died. If my father had died first, we would have never gotten to know him."

As part of their estate planning, Joyce had been pushing Marshall to take out a $10 million joint life insurance policy with Northwestern Mutual Life Insurance Company for the children to help them pay for the enormous inheritance tax that was inevitable.

Not a person to throw around money lightly, Marshall thought it was too expensive, but Joyce was convinced it was the right thing to do. Marshall, who had already been diagnosed with the prostate cancer that would eventually take his life, was uninsurable. But because it was a "second to die" policy, Northwestern Mutual figured they had a good bet because Joyce was in excellent physical condition. Joyce finally got her husband to agree to the insurance, the papers were signed, and the policy went into effect February 10, 1992. . . . Joyce would die the next day. The story has been life insurance salesperson lore in Madison ever since.

Marshall, in an effort to ease his pain and faced with his own inevitable demise, began focusing more on philanthropic interests. He worked with University of Wisconsin School of Business Dean Andrew Policano and Professor Urban Wemmerlov to establish a new graduate program in the School of Business that would combine disciplines in both business and engineering. He donated $2 million to the UW business school to endow what became known as the Joyce Erdman Center for Manufacturing and Technology Management (MTM). The goal of the program was to produce graduates with better skills to enhance American industrial competitiveness worldwide. He also made a significant charitable pledge to the Madison Art Center, where Joyce had served as board president.

Ed Hart and Marshall, after both lost their wives, often visited Marshall's daughter Debbie in Montana.

Aerial view of the Middleton Hills residential development under construction in 2002, about 50 percent complete. Lake Mendota is seen in the upper right.

CHAPTER 14

swan song

IF ANYTHING WAS GOING TO PULL Marshall out of the abyss, besides time with his children, it was a business venture that he could embrace with his customary passion for a new project. Friends and colleagues had seen it before with his immersion in the prefabricated homes, the introduction of Techline, and then again with the art program to enhance the medical buildings.

His new venture, which must have been percolating in his mind for years, was for an innovative development on 153 acres of land that he owned in Middleton. He liked to say that when he had bought it thirty years before, the family would picnic there and pick wild strawberries. It was beautiful, high, rolling land overlooking the western end of Lake Mendota, with a panoramic view of the university and the state capitol in the distance. He knew he wanted to do something special with this land. He just wasn't sure what. Over the years, he had solicited plans from various people, including one for a kind of "company town" where employees would live in the homes.

His first serious attempt at developing his Middleton property came as a result of a proposed joint venture between Erdman & Associates and the

architectural firm of Skidmore, Owings, and Merrill (SOM) of Chicago in 1971. Marshall knew Tom Rosengren from their company and became friends with its general manager, Bruce Graham. SOM had an interest in providing quality housing at an affordable price. Marshall had a new factory in Waunakee that was just starting to experiment in prefabricated modular housing units.

The initial phase of the plan was to build sixty-eight owner-occupied townhouses "organized in efficient clusters with little or no alteration of the existing terrain or vegetation." Open space would be organized to provide a "sequential link between all clusters and the amenities such as the school, shopping, and recreational spaces." The partnership called for Erdman to provide the land and construction of the modular units, and SOM to provide capital, design, and engineering.

A general development plan was drafted titled "Middleton Hills Planned Community Development" that called for the sale of townhouses to begin in 1972. The project, however, got bogged down in efforts to rezone the land, and within a year Marshall had lost his enthusiasm and had moved on to other projects.

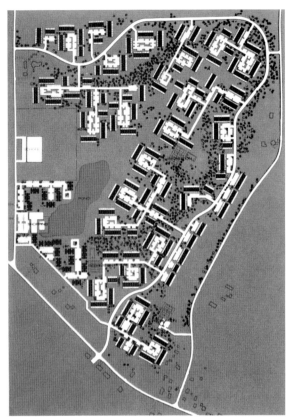

A 1972 plan of Middleton Hills, a collaboration between Erdman & Associates and Chicago architecture firm SOM. Century Avenue runs diagonally along lower left.

It was nearly twenty years later when a new idea began to crystallize in Marshall's mind. Dan Ramsey, mayor of the city of Middleton, was now encouraging Marshall to develop his 153 acres. Middleton had grown around three sides of the property, and the city wanted the additional tax revenue a development would bring.

Marshall had read an article in an architectural magazine about a Miami-based architectural firm called DPZ that was designing and building a new kind of community that they were calling "New Urbanism." A local attorney, Susan King, who was familiar with Andres Duany of the Miami firm, encouraged Marshall to explore the possibilities of a

TND (traditional neighborhood development).

In a 1996 article in *Land Lines*, William Fulton wrote, "The New Urbanism has captured the imagination of the American public like no urban planning movement in decades." This article, written sometime after the one that captured Marshall's attention, credits the New Urbanists with seeking to redefine the nature of the American metropolis by reintroducing traditional notions of neighborhood design and fitting those ideas into a variety of urban and suburban settings.

It continues, "The New Urbanism began as a reaction to conventional suburban planning as it has been practiced in the United States since the 1940s. New Urbanists view the decentralized, auto-oriented suburb as a recipe for disaster . . . creating ever-increasing congestion on roads, lack of meaningful civic life, loss of open space, limited opportunities for children and others without cars, and a general discontent among suburbanites."

The article went on to say that the New Urbanism owed much to the City Beautiful and Garden City movements of the early twentieth century and mentioned the widely publicized new town of Seaside, Florida, as the first example. Although various planning and design principles were associated with New Urbanism, most definitions included the following ideas:

- walkable neighborhoods oriented around the five-minute walk
- primary orientation around public transit systems
- greater integration of different types of land use at the neighborhood level
- smaller lots, larger green spaces, narrow streets

Andres Duany and Marshall at design charrette for Middleton Hills.

DPZ's husband-and-wife team of Andres Duany and Elizabeth Plater-Zyberk had designed Seaside and were involved in a number of other similar projects. Duany and Plater-Zyberk had drawn raves for their designs from Florida to Washington, D.C.

Marshall contacted Duany and after a number of conversations, invited him to Madison to make a presentation to Middleton officials and residents at the Middleton Public Library in July 1993. About sixty residents and Middleton officials attended.

Duany could not have imagined that the unusual man who picked him up that day at the Dane County Airport would become a close friend and influence on his life.

"He picked me up at the airport and he was wearing these Bermuda shorts," Duany recalled. "But I remember thinking right away that this was a fabulous guy. We got along perfectly. He was very charming."

There were going to be some setbacks along the road to what would become Middleton Hills, par-

Andres Duany's 1995 master plan for Middleton Hills.

beat. "It's only conceptual today," city council member Dave Egan said. "I think it's headed in the right direction."

Liz Erpenbach, a council member whose son-in-law, Russ Feingold, had recently been elected to the United States Senate, was enthusiastic. "It reminded me of my old neighborhood [in Minneapolis]," Erpenbach said. "We had alleys and we could walk to church and walk to the store and walk to school."

One Middleton resident was skeptical. Bill Liebl told *The Capital Times* he thought Marshall and Duany had put on "a pretty good sales job. Whether or not it's practical remains to be seen."

For his part, Duany was excited about the site's potential. "You have to admit it was full of possibilities," Duany said. "Virtually anything would have worked well there. You have the great long views, the rolling landscape. It was a wonderful property."

Madison has a reputation for contentiousness when it comes to new or innovative proposals. Middleton is close enough to share some of Madison's eccentricities, and it was unlikely that the development could be launched without some controversy. By February 1994, the Middleton Public Works Committee was insisting that the project, now known as Middleton Hills, not proceed until some significant changes were made in Duany's design. In addition, 100 Middleton residents had signed a petition in opposition, saying they were worried about traffic and urging that the land be used as a park.

Some of the complaints that were raised during planning sessions were those that are common to most New Urbanist communities: the traditional neighborhoods that the New Urbanists hope to replicate are

ticularly when it came to changing the existing zoning regulations having to do with variances, setbacks, street widths, et cetera, but that first meeting in July of '93 went well.

Marshall told the group about how he envisioned an old-fashioned neighborhood community that would integrate all kinds of development: residential, retail, offices, churches, and schools. Walking would be the primary mode of transportation within the neighborhood. Marshall added that he would not proceed unless both Middleton residents and elected officials were firmly on board.

Marshall then introduced Duany, who gave a slide presentation. The mood in the room was up-

characterized by compactness, small scale, and diversity of building types. But increasingly, the economic and lifestyle demands of urban and even suburban life seem to require facilities on a massive scale.

Transportation was perhaps the most contentious single aspect of the New Urbanism, which is often "sold" to public officials based on its supposed transportation benefits. Reduced dependence on the automobile, increased transit use, shorter trips, and a more flexible hierarchy of streets make common sense, but getting people to give up their dependence on the automobile has proved daunting.

The city's problem with Middleton Hills, however, was largely the proposed width of the streets in the neighborhood. Duany's streets as designed were twenty-six feet wide, which he argued would slow down traffic and actually create a safer neighborhood. This measurement went against the city codes. Middleton required thirty-two feet for any new development, and local officials such as fire chiefs and traffic engineers who establish these codes were loath to alter them.

Public Works Chairwoman Julie Brunette was curt when asked about the city's stance by a reporter. "We're looking at the nuts and bolts and how to get the plows and the garbage trucks up there long after Mr. Erdman and Mr. Duany have moved on to their next visionary project," she said. Marshall on his part argued that having streets wide enough for two fire trucks to pass one another, leaving space on either side for parked cars, was excessive.

Marshall was angered, frustrated, and more than a little hurt by the reaction he was getting from some. He told Marc Eisen of *Isthmus,* "This will be my

swan song. I believe in it. Don't make too much of this, but I want this to be my contribution to the community. I want to do something worthwhile." When he wasn't getting the type of response he expected, he told his friends he'd just drop the whole thing if Middleton didn't welcome the project.

Meanwhile, Duany helped soothe Marshall. He had told Marshall to expect this type of community reaction. "It was identical to what we run across everywhere," Duany said. "But one of the things Marshall was sure about was that he would not compromise. That was unusual. He wanted to do it right or not at all, and he made that very clear. He was not interested in doing anything less than perfect. He didn't have to do it as a business."

Marshall's banking friend, Bob O'Malley, recalled a conversation with Marshall in which Marshall said, "I don't want to lose more than $10 million on this." O'Malley smiled. "He was willing to take a risk to prove a point."

Amid the controversy, Duany found much to admire in Marshall Erdman, the man.

"I got to know him quite well," Duany said. "He was never anything but marvelous. He was absolutely supportive of creativity, which is a rare talent. Being creative is one thing, but being really supportive of creativity is another, and that was a particular ability he had. It's something that I try to do in my office, support creativity."

Duany recalled later being surprised at the impact Marshall had made on him. "He had the ability to connect with people on a level other than just business. He wasn't just one of my favorite clients in life. He was one of my favorite people in life."

Groundbreaking for Middleton Hills, August 12, 1995—the same date as the Unitarian Meeting House forty-six years earlier. Left to right: project manager Jim Zeigler, Middleton City Planner Eileen Kelly, Marshall, Middleton Mayor Dan Ramsey, Dane County Executive Rick Phelps, and Tim Erdman.

Middleton Hills was important to Marshall on at least two levels: he wanted it to be a model that other land planners would follow, revolutionizing the development of new communities. And, as he stated more than once, "I want to be loved for it." The recognition from others for this farsighted project was an essential element in his gratification. He wasn't going to be denied his swan song.

Marshall negotiated with Middleton officials, he lobbied and cajoled, and by August 1994 he thought he had won over the doubters. The Middleton Plan Commission gave a unanimous thumbs-up to Middleton Hills, but then, on August 16, the city council, which had to give final approval, decided to table a vote that had been set. There were more petitions from area residents and lingering concerns about street widths and safety, about alleys as potential sites for crime and drug dealing.

Finally, on September 6 the city council voted unanimously to approve the Middleton Hills development. A compromise had been reached on the streets issue. "I'm delighted," Marshall told reporters after the council vote. "We'll be working on drawings immediately. I hope this will be as much of a success as I'd hoped it would be."

About that time, Marshall's personal life also took a turn. Dorothy Ballantyne—Dotty to her friends—a vice president of CUNA Mutual Funds in Madison, had been introduced to Marshall at a party in 1993. "I thought he looked kind of interesting," Ballantyne recalled. "But he didn't really pay much attention to me, and I suppose I didn't pay much attention to him."

Still, Marshall called and asked her to dinner not long after that party. Another time, they took a drive to Spring Green. "But I was traveling a lot in my job, and he was busy with Middleton Hills."

In spring 1994, Ballantyne said, something

View across wetlands in Middleton Hills.

clicked, and they started seeing one another much more frequently. They began to travel together. That winter, '94 into '95, Ballantyne would go to Arizona with Marshall seven times. She was getting to know him as a complex and extraordinary man. "His curiosity and will played a big part in his success," she said. "He was determined and principled, and it wasn't anything he plotted out, it was who he was. He was a very integrated person."

Together they went to Germany and Italy for woodworking shows. In the United States there were trips to Washington, San Antonio, and New Orleans. They were spending more and more time together. Dotty quit her job in May 1995.

In June, they married, at the Erdman farm. The ceremony was small and brief, performed by the Rev. Max Gaebler, of the Unitarian Fellowship. Attending

were Ed Hart, Grace and Ralph Lukken, Fred Miller, Ellen Johnson, Marshall's sons Tim and Dan, Tim's wife Mary, Dan's friend Deborah Tracy, and Dotty's close friend Shelley Hamel and her husband, David. Marshall's daughter Debbie was not there, and he had a painful telephone conversation with her the morning of the wedding, which Debbie was against. She had, after all, idolized Joyce.

All the Erdman children at first viewed their father's whirlwind romance with a bit of a skeptical eye. Yet it could not compare to his lightning quick courtship of their mother years earlier. Before long it was obvious to everyone, and eventually even to Debbie, that Marshall and Dotty were truly in love and very happy together. Dan spoke of the situation at his father's memorial service: "Then Dotty came to the rescue. We were granted backup status to being on call for Papa's need for constant attention and subject of his critical eye. But much more importantly, Papa found the companionship and love he had lost."

For his part, Marshall was delighted. "He had a new wife and he was enjoying himself," Hart said. "The day after they got married they went to Alaska. They got back and went to Europe. They were traveling all over the place."

Dotty recalled, "Once I was in Marshall's office and I saw a blurb he had done in *Madison Magazine* where he said he wanted to go to Alaska." When Marshall walked in the room she said, "Marshall, I didn't know you wanted to go to Alaska." Ballantyne hates the cold, and Alaska was way down on her list of places to see, but here she had found something Marshall hadn't done. "There wasn't very much of that," she said later. "He was very excited to see Alaska, and we had a wonderful trip."

In June 1995, Andres Duany was back in Madison. In February, the Middleton Plan Commission had approved the preliminary plat for Middleton Hills, with the first of the planned 438 homes set to begin construction in the fall. Duany had come to town not only to check on Middleton Hills but to deliver the keynote address at a land use symposium at the State Historical Society of Wisconsin.

Duany gave a feisty speech, questioning why Middleton Hills had faced such scrutiny while other sprawling subdivisions had been instantly green lighted. Some people thought his comments bordered on insulting, as when he described Wisconsinites as "Joe Six-Packs." He even attacked environmentalists, pointing out that the average

eagle or turtle in the United States has better living conditions than the man in a big city who faces a one-hour commute back and forth daily to work. He also went after Madison planners for allowing the massive American Family building on the city's east side. "Can it be you've permitted an insurance company to build a palace the size of Versailles?"

As Duany himself said, he could be "undiplomatic" because Middleton Hills was off the ground. Roads and sewers were going in.

In August, Erdman & Associates held a groundbreaking at one of the highest points of the property. It was a breezy, sunny day, and the lake sparkled off in the distance, stretching to the familiar Madison skyline. Marshall and his son Tim were joined by Middleton Mayor Dan Ramsey and Dane County Executive Rick Phelps, along with various Middleton Hills planners and designers. Marshall gave a short speech emphasizing his hope that the project would become a model for others to follow, but he seemed tired. The event was captured for the newspapers and on video by Wisconsin Public Television. Although the first homes did not start construction that fall, they did the following spring, when work on a general store also commenced. Marshall Erdman would not see it.

He and Dotty had gone to Montana for three weeks following their Alaska trip, and Marshall had seemed to be doing fine. He told Dotty, "You know, this is the longest time I've ever taken off work." He was really enjoying it. They bought a Montana ranch, which Ed Hart described as "a quarter mile of frontage on the Yellowstone River, about twenty minutes from Debbie's place," and Marshall talked about spending even more time away from the office.

It was on a trip to Montana that Marshall first opened up to Dotty about his childhood. "I tried like crazy," Dotty said, "to learn about his past. He'd say he couldn't remember." Then, one day in Montana, Marshall started talking about his brother. The brother who didn't make it out of Lithuania, who was supposed to have come to America, whose place Marshall took. The next day he said, "Last night I found myself singing the Lithuanian national anthem."

Mortality may have been crowding him. "When I first met Marshall," Dotty said, "he told me he had prostate cancer. He said that the fall before Joyce died, he was operated on for prostate cancer and it had spread, but he said it hadn't gone to the bone. Everything I knew about it was that you could live quite a while. He always talked about ten or fifteen years."

The doctors watched him closely from then on. In May 1995, Dotty had gone to a medical appointment with Marshall. The doctor came in with X-rays that showed the cancer had spread to the bone. "I nearly fainted," Dotty said.

While he had disclosed his illness to her, Marshall didn't like talking about health issues. "He might not have wanted to know" exactly what was happening to him, Dotty surmises. "He didn't want to live as an invalid. His biggest fear was that I would have to take care of him." That, at least, didn't happen.

In August, a blood test showed Marshall's blood values were not good. He went to the Mayo Clinic, but the diagnosis was the same. "It looked

Marshall with his second wife, Dotty Ballantyne.

like there wasn't much time," Dotty said.

They decided to go back out to Montana in September. Marshall was doing pretty well. "It was a week of intense activity," Dotty said. His son Rusty flew in, as did Ed Hart and Fred Miller.

One afternoon, Hart recalled, the three of them, Hart, Miller, and Marshall, were sitting on the porch of Marshall's new ranch, enjoying the fall splendor and chatting. At one point Marshall excused himself to go to the bathroom.

"He didn't come back," Hart said. He and Miller went looking. Marshall was lying on his bed, sleeping. He had taken a pain pill, and it had put him out.

The next day he seemed better. They went for a long hike, Dotty recalled. "That evening we hosted a huge dinner party. It was wonderful."

Hart agreed, "Everything seemed fine."

The next day Hart and Miller flew back to Madison. "A day or so after that he just collapsed," Hart said. "They brought him home on a medical plane with a doctor and nurse and they put him in

University Hospital."

Within three days, on September 17, Marshall Erdman was dead. He was twelve days short of his seventy-third birthday.

As he had throughout his entire life, Marshall had lived life to the fullest, right up to the end. "It was very sudden," Dotty said. "He lived, really lived. Until the absolute last."

Marshall's death was major news in Madison and beyond. Both Madison papers ran front-page headlines and stories. His obituary and photograph appeared in *The New York Times*.

The *Wisconsin State Journal*'s headline read, "A Builder of Madison Dies." The story noted his many accomplishments and added: "Although he became a very wealthy man, Erdman never became pretentious or snobbish. He was a friendly person who laughed easily and who maintained loyal, life-long friendships."

The Capital Times' headline said, "Erdman's Legacy Lauded," and the subhead referred to him as a "visionary builder."

Gaylord Nelson was heartsick at the news of the death of one of his closest friends in the world. "He was extra special," Nelson said from Washington. "There was nobody like him in his integrity, and in his commitment to his profession."

Marc Eisen, editor of the Madison weekly *Isthmus,* was probably the journalist who most appreciated Marshall's accomplishments and style. In a personal appreciation published in the paper, Eisen said Marshall "pretty much cut his own path through life." Eisen duly noted Erdman's many business successes but also fondly remembered the time Marshall

had rescued him from a furious Pleasant Rowland, the woman behind the Pleasant Company doll empire. Rowland, a close friend and supporter of Marshall, had spied Eisen taking notes at a Middleton Hills planning session when she thought he had no business to do so. Marshall jumped in front of Rowland and told her Eisen was a good and honest reporter. He later mentioned to Eisen how much he respected the strong-minded Rowland but added, "And people say I'm tough to work for!"

Eisen had written extensively of Middleton Hills and knew the bond that had formed between Marshall and Andres Duany. On Marshall's death, Eisen thought to call Duany, who had been deeply affected by the news.

Duany was typically thoughtful and forthcoming, recalling his friend. "He had a very straightforward relationship with people," Duany said. "Very unpretentious. I saw him interact with employees of all types, and it seemed as if there was no hierarchy. It was personal. He was 'Marshall' to everybody."

"He had been honed, I think, by Frank Lloyd Wright to take risks for the sake of design," Duany continued. "One of the things we have to appreciate is that he really created a supportive atmosphere for planning Middleton Hills. He created an atmosphere during the charrette [an intensive three-day design session held at the Erdman offices during which designers and interested parties all collaborated] where the creativity was really at a high point. It was as if it were internal to our own office instead of, as often happens, an adversarial relationship with the marketing people, the bankers, and overseers.

"It's funny," Duany concluded. "I was going to

Marshall shows off big fish he caught on Alaska trip with Dotty.

call Marshall up and spend a couple of days with him just discussing business. I thought the kind of advice he could give wouldn't be available anywhere else. The exact opposite of the Harvard Business School. It had everything to do with human interaction and very little to do with abstract business procedures. You know, Marshall was one of the people I wanted to be like. He is one of the few people I wanted to be like."

Estate planning after the death of Joyce had fallen on the shoulders of Joan Burke, whom Marshall had asked to be the personal representative for his estate in 1994. The IRS places a huge premium on the value of voting control stock. With Marshall holding voting control, there was considerable financial motivation to relinquish it before his death. But this was not an easy step to take for a man who had created everything he had from the ground up. Burke recalled him saying that he was not going to turn over control of the company "so the kids can put me in a nursing home."

But eventually Marshall came to accept his own mortality and, with the help of Burke and the lawyers at Michael Best and Friedrich, a plan was worked out to give up eventual control through the creation of a charitable trust. The cancer, however, was progressing faster than anyone expected, and it became apparent that there would not be enough time for this strategy. A decision was made shortly before he and Dotty went out to Montana in September. Marshall called Burke and asked her to meet him at the farm.

"I went out there and fixed him breakfast. I asked him to be honest with himself—did he think there

was enough time for the charitable trust? And he finally said, 'Let's go ahead and gift the shares to the kids.' It was a very emotional thing for both of us."

Tim Erdman was now running the company. His relationship with his father had never been easy; perhaps they were too much alike. "He knew the boys were doing fine," Gaylord Nelson said of Marshall's parenting. "But he wasn't about to say that. I told him, 'God, Marshall, Tim is just like you, he has all your good characteristics, the perfectionism, and so on. That's a wonderful young man.' He appreciated hearing that, but he wasn't going to say, 'Well, you know, he's turned out fine.' He just wasn't going to say that."

In a 1998 interview with *Madison Magazine*, Tim said, "It took me 40 years to understand my father's operating philosophy. He seemed so contradictory, and yet his strength was his consistency."

Tim continued, "When I got back to Madison six years ago, people weren't exactly glad to see me. I was a fly in the ointment of a lot of people's succession plans. But I'm not worried about making my mark. That will come with time. My grandfather once told me never to lose my enthusiasm. For me, that's not a problem."

In a more recent interview, by his own admission Tim felt challenged to fill the large shoes of his father. "I always thought I had inherited my father's ability to judge people, to make decisions. But I've made some mistakes over the years. And Marshall, of course, is always there. In any situation, I have to ask, 'What would Marshall have done?' I don't want to. But it is an integral part of me. It's a distraction. I always tell myself it was easier for Marshall. He didn't have to constantly wonder what his father would have done."

The children, of course, were still learning things about their father. Debbie recalled sitting with the family the day Marshall died. "He died about 8:00 a.m.," she said. "About 10:00, we were just sitting around and we got this call from David Levitan." Debbie took the call, and Levitan said, "I'm a cousin of your father's." She immediately thought it was a crank call. "No way," she said. "We don't have any cousins."

But, of course, they did, and Debbie and Dan, particularly Debbie, would spend much time in the next months learning as much as possible about their father's early life and extended family. It was like unraveling a double mystery—the secret life itself, and the reason for his silence. They found themselves speculating about the reason for his secrecy, but the early life itself has gradually unfolded, in fascinating ways.

That November, David Levitan's brother, Max Levitan, wrote Debbie a letter, following up on a phone call his wife, Beth, had made.

"Genetically, we were third cousins," Max wrote. "That is, on the borderline of where consanguinity fades in significance into randomness. Our respective maternal grandmothers were first cousins. Our families were much closer than indicated by the degree of relationship because our roots were in the same village, Tverai, in Lithuania."

Max went on to detail the story of Marshall's youth, his coming to Chicago, the break that came when Marshall and Joyce made the decision to follow her parents' suggestion and deny his Jewish ancestry. "Your father's early life was horrendous," Levitan wrote, "and this was undoubtedly a factor in the long silence. And considering what he went through, we salute him for having been able not just to survive, but to excel."

Later, the Erdman children would meet the Levitans and other members of the family they never knew they had. Debbie would journey to Lithuania with Dotty and learn still more. It was, as she said, a final gift.

On September 21, 1995, four days after his death, a standing-room-only crowd packed the memorial service for Marshall Erdman at the First Unitarian Meeting House—the building that had launched his career and that, just three years earlier, had been the site for Joyce Erdman's memorial service. The audience was a mix of dignitaries and business associates, employees, friends, and neighbors, including former governors, Nelson and Earl, Madison Mayor Paul Soglin, Wisconsin's first lady Sue Ann Thompson, Wright apprentice Edgar Tafel, and Wisconsin Supreme Court Justice Roland Day.

"He was so marvelously consistent yet, never predictable," spoke the youngest Erdman son, Dan. "He was always correcting us and telling us how to do things the right way. The most frustrating thing was nine times out of ten he would be right."

Gaylord Nelson also spoke, recalling Marshall's antipathy for lawyers. He got a large laugh with the story of how Frank Lloyd Wright, on being introduced by Marshall to Nelson and told Nelson was a state senator, said, "Marshall, do we really need one?"

Max Gaebler, who had just performed Marshall's marriage in June, presided over his funeral in

September. He read poetry at the service, including Dylan Thomas's "And Death Shall Have No Dominion." Pianist Howard Karp and a string quartet of UW faculty played a movement from Schubert's "Trout" quintet, one of Marshall's favorites. Soprano Wendy Rowe sang "Rusalka's Song to the Moon" by Dvorak. The Rev. Michael Schuler, pastor of the Unitarian Society, gave a closing prayer.

In the days and months after his death, there were letters and phone calls to the family from dignitaries and business leaders, and ordinary people as well—most with a story to tell of how Marshall Erdman touched their lives. Perhaps they met him only once, but they remembered.

The family received a letter from Bob Schlicht, president of M&I Bank of Madison, shortly after Marshall's death telling his story:

"In 1987 I was fortunate enough to be assigned the account relationship with Marshall Erdman & Associates. It was fascinating for me as a banker to see a company that was so large and successful, but really treated its employees like a small company.

From a banking perspective, I have not seen or dealt with anyone in my years of banking more successful in the business world than your dad.

"When I personally was going through some difficult times, I'd often stop Marshall and ask his opinion about certain things. He had a unique way of giving advice and telling you straight up what the situation was. . . . Your dad had a profound influence on my career and life and I will never forget him."

Nor will many others who crossed paths with Marshall Erdman. He arrived in his adopted country as a boy with little but an uncompromising belief in himself and his own sense of how to do things.

The thousands of medical buildings, homes, and other structures he built, the business he nurtured into a giant with hundreds of employees, all stand as tangible evidence of his work. Yet his greatest legacy may be how he lived, his style and vitality, and his impact on those whose lives he touched. It all seemed so simple to him. "Just use a little common sense" he often exhorted those around him. Clearly, though, there was nothing common about this man.

West Madison/Hilldale neighborhood. University Avenue is on the left.

The following is a list of all known structures built by Marshall Erdman in the Madison area. Company records of the building projects were destroyed in a warehouse fire in 1965, making it difficult to create a completely accurate list. Many of Erdman's U-Form-IT prefab houses were built by other contractors, but are included in this list. If you recognize any errors or omissions, please send them to Dan Erdman, 1721 Hickory Drive, Madison, WI 53705.

Midvale/Near West Side

YEAR BUILT	ADDRESS	ORIGINAL OWNER/OCCUPANT	ARCHITECT/MODEL
1947	509 N. Meadow Lane	Elsie Fansler	(First Erdman House)
1947	505 N. Meadow Lane	Paul & June Hennie	
1947	221 N. Meadow Lane	Marvin & Helen Olson	
1948	5 S. Midvale Blvd.	Philip & Margaret Derse	
1948	9 S. Midvale Blvd.	George & Keiko Kido	
1948	13 S. Midvale Blvd.	Keith & Joan Roberts	
1948	17 S. Midvale Blvd.	John & Elizabeth Weaver	
1948	2810 Arbor Drive	Fred & Vi Miller	
1949	40 Glenway	Joseph & Ann Mire	
1949	36 Glenway	Paul & Elizabeth Settlage	
1949	2805 Sylvan Ave.	John & Josephine Jenkins	
1949	106 Vaughn Court	Harry & Katherine Lichter	
1949	4341 Bagley Parkway	John & Frances Newhouse	
1950	110 Vaughn Court	Bryant & Ruth Kearl	
1950	118 Vaughn Court	Charles & Judith Heidelberger	Herb Fritz
1950	814 Ottawa Trail	Wilbur & Edith Harris	
1950	210 S. Owen Drive	Robert & Frances Ozanne	Herb Fritz
1950	4052 Cherokee Drive	Lloyd & Esther Frank	Herb Fritz
1950	509 N. Franklin Ave.	Minnie Anderson Apartments (4 Units)	
1950	31 Bagley Court	Santos & Olga Zingale	Herb Fritz
1950	507 N. Franklin Ave.	Fitzpatrick-Thompson Apartments (4 Units)	
1950	533 Gatley Terrace	Alvin & Marjorie LePage	
1951	602 Hilltop Drive	Oswald & Jane Anderson	
1951	505 N. Franklin Ave.	Fitzpatrick-Thompson Apartments (4 Units)	
1951	307 S. Owen Drive	Everett & Elenore Melvin	
1951	2802 Ridge Road	Russell & Virginia Dymond	
1951	2811 Ridge Road	Wilbur & Marjorie Dudley	Herb Fritz
1951	2737 Lynn Terrace	Erdman Apartments (4 Units)	
1951	2725 Lynn Terrace	Cooper Apartments (4 Units)	
1951	2828 Sylvan Ave.	Edwin & Phyllis Young	Herb Fritz
1951	626 Gatley Terrace	Robert & Ruth Drayton	

Midvale/Near West Side *(continued)*

YEAR BUILT	ADDRESS	ORIGINAL OWNER/OCCUPANT	ARCHITECT/MODEL
1951	301 Palomino Lane	Elizabeth Ritzmann Apartments (3 Units)	
1952	310 Palomino Lane	Reuschlein Apartments (4 Units)	
1953	314 Palomino Lane	Hart-Jamieson Apartments (4 Units)	
1953	402 Palomino Lane	Hart-Jamieson Apartments (4 Units)	
1953	2815 Ridge Road	Claude & Marion Hungerford	
1954	317 Eugenia Ave.	Hart-Jamieson Apartments (4 Units)	
1954	502 Hilton Drive	John Murray	
1954	4334 Upland Drive	Bill Hinkley	
1954	4909 Eyre Lane	Oscar & Jean Johnson	
1954	441 Hilton Drive	Eugene & Dorothy Kobey	
1954	435 Hilton Drive	Emil & Betty Finner	
1955	444 Hilton Drive	Jean & Ethel Werderitsch	
1955	1001 Tumalo Trail	Phillip & Helen Drotning	"C-4"
1955	4141 Nakoma Road	Clifford & Elizabeth Reuschlein	
1955	5010 Milward Drive	Frank Granner	
1956	3718 Zwerg Drive	John & Lois McComb	"F-1"
1956	3714 Zwerg Drive	Laurie Carlson	
1956	5 Kewaunee Court	Seymour & Frances Crepea	
1957	3515 W. Beltline Highway	Arnold & Lora Jackson	FLW Prefab I Model
1958	434 Rushmore Lane	D.A. & Frances Caul	
1958	430 Rushmore Lane	Kenneth & Beverly Sachtjen	
1958	433 Rushmore Lane	Reinhoed & Patricia Zempel	
1958	429 Rushmore Lane	Franz & Elfriede Vitovec	
1958	5049 La Crosse Lane	Sturges & Marilyn Bailey	"Faircrest"
1959	4409 Waite Lane	William & Wanda Doudna	"Faircrest"
1959	110 Marinette Trail	Walter & Mary Ellen Rudin	FLW Prefab II Model (Parade House)
1959	5 Ashland Court	Harold & Elizabeth Linden	"G"
1959	4705 LaFayette	Roy & Doris Mita	"G"
1959	4814 Tokay Blvd.	Edward & Mary Hommel	"Greymount"
1959	5113 Pepin Place	Fred & Mary Bloodgood	"Shannon"
1959	5110 Pepin Place	David & Lillian Aide	"Shannon"
1960	457 Hilltop Drive	Wallace & Mary Heins	"Sherman"
1960	466 S. Segoe	Theodore & Margarete Hamerow	"D"
1961	5101 Odana Road	Zigurds & Maija Zile	"Shannon"
1961	5034 Odana Road	George & Marian Wise	
1961	5030 Odana Road	William & Dolores Edwards	
1961	5026 Odana Road	Richard & Ramaa Crawford	
1961	5022 Odana Road	Ole & Vivian Stalheim	
1961	5018 Odana Road	Marilyn Huinas	
1961	5014 Odana Road	Dennis & Ruth Behrendt	
1961	5010 Odana Road	John & Dorothy Mark	
1961	5006 Odana Road	Hans & Martine den Daas	
1961	5002 Odana Road	Richard & Betty Garland	
1964	1515 Vilas Ave.	Edith Frank	(Last Erdman House)

Shorewood Hills/Indian Hills/Spring Harbor

YEAR BUILT	ADDRESS	ORIGINAL OWNER/OCCUPANT	ARCHITECT/MODEL
1947	910 Cornell Court	Marshall & Joyce Erdman	
1947	914 Cornell Court	Theodore & Dorothy Lively	
1948	3140 Oxford Road	Delmar & Alice Karlen	
1948	906 Cornell Court	Robert & Erma Arthur	
1948	902 Cornell Court	John & Janet Berger	
1948	1015 University Bay Drive	Robert & Katherine Burris	
1949	1210 Bowdoin Road	David & Ellsworth Mack	
1950	1504 Sumac Drive	Larry & Geraldine Fitzpatrick	Doris Mohs
1950	1003 Oak Way	Vera & Sam Schwid	Herb Fritz
1951	3539 Topping Road	Charles & Fern Thompson	
1951	957 University Bay Drive	Margaret & C. Leonard Huskins	Herb Fritz (Demolished)
1951	3420 Sunset Drive	Jane & E. Weston Wood	Herb Fritz
1951	3408 Circle Close	Marshall & Joyce Erdman	William Kaeser
1951	1138 Minocqua Crescent	Axel & Julia Dahlgren	
1953	5030 Flambeau Road	Edwin & Anna Wideen	
1954	3404 Tallyho Lane	Stanley & Alice Dresen	
1954	3538 Topping Road	Samuel & Ernestine Chechik	
1954	3329 Tallyho Lane	Urban & Gayle Richgels	"A-4"
1954	3502 Tallyho Lane	Wilma & H.A. Wiggers	"B"
1954	5129 Flambeau Road	Joseph & Lorraine Capossela	
1954	3508 Tallyho Lane	Robin & Marjorie Riley	
1954	3409 Tallyho Lane	Don & Jane Irwin	
1954	3405 Tallyho Lane	Edmond & Mae Dimond	
1954	5117 Flambeau Road	Kermit & Frances Berger	(Parade House)
1954	5125 Flambeau Road	Edwin & Edith Hartung	
1955	3532 Tallyho Lane	Gunards & Irene Hans	
1955	3526 Tallyho Lane	Alfred & Brigitte Evans	
1956	5121 Flambeau Road	William & Elizabeth Lister	
1956	3518 Tallyho Lane	James & Jean Potter	
1956	5118 Lake Mendota Drive	Robert & Celest Regenberg	
1956	2704 Harvard Drive	Rolf & Mary Olsen	
1956	2708 Harvard Drive	Anne Strong	
1956	2714 Harvard Drive	Hans & Marion Ruhig	
1959	1714 Hickory Drive	Wesley & Pheobe Winch	"D"
1959	3554 Tallyho Lane	Emily Chervenik	"Shannon"
1960	5013 Lake Mendota Drive	Stephen & Helen Willoughby	"Shannon"
1963	1805 Baker Ave.	Maurice & Frances Webb	

Crestwood/Middleton

YEAR BUILT	ADDRESS	ORIGINAL OWNER/OCCUPANT	ARCHITECT/MODEL
1949	5741 Elder Place	Robert & Martha Lewis	
1952	5729 Elder Place	John & Mary Diehl	
1953	5742 Forsythia Place	Ronald & Mildred Anderson	"A-1"
1953	5738 Forsythia Place	Michael & Dorothy Sorge	
1953	5734 Forsythia Place	Julian & Dorothy Sund	
1953	5746 Forsythia Place	Allen & Joyce Moran	"B-1"
1954	5615 Crestwood Place	Clarence & Janet Docken	"B-5"
1954	5750 Forsythia Place	Clayton & Ella Frye	"A-1"

Crestwood/Middleton *(continued)*

YEAR BUILT	ADDRESS	ORIGINAL OWNER/OCCUPANT	ARCHITECT/MODEL
1954	5626 Crestwood Place	Knight & Dorothy Webster	
1954	5620 Crestwood Place	Earl & Eugenia Loyster	
1954	5618 Crestwood Place	Leroy & Lois Chambers	"B-2"
1954	212 Bordner Drive	Norman & Mary Michie	
1954	5608 Crestwood Place	Dean & Faye Frey	"B-2"
1954	5611 Crestwood Place	Royal & Marilyn Gibson	
1954	6415 Lakeview Blvd.	Henry Ramisch Apartments (4 Units)	
1954	2021 Lakeview Ave.	Henry Ramisch Apartments (4 Units)	
1954	6406 Lakeview Blvd.	Vance & Jean Setterholm	
1954	6402 Lakeview Blvd.	Herbert & Nan Simonson	
1954	6314 Lakeview Blvd.	James & Audrey Abrahamson	
1954	6302 Lakeview Blvd.	Llewellyn & Jane Roberts	
1954	118 Alden Drive	Jack & Patty Glassen	
1955	6310 Lakeview Blvd.	Wilson & Conchera Hannan	
1955	5701 Cedar Place	Carson & Beatrice Gulley	
1955	5710 Arbor Vitae Place	Thomas & Eva Laufer	"C-4"
1955	5814 Anchorage Ave.	Wallace & Dorothy Lemon	"G"
1955	5627 Crestwood Place	Gaylord & Carrie Lee Nelson	"C-4"
1955	220 Bordner Drive	Jerome & Rosemary Foy	
1955	5623 Crestwood Place	Robert Retherford	
1955	5758 Forsythia Place	Helene & Hugh Lovell	
1955	233 Bordner Drive	Robert & Carol Burns	"D"
1956	217 Bordner Drive	Howard & Loretta Larsen	
1956	2 Wakeman	Robert & Marjorie Wiggen	
1956	1500 Capital Ave.	David & Adele Carley	"C-4"
1956	200 Bordner Drive	Gary & Ruthanne Nathanson	
1956	1508 Capital Ave.	Henry & Martha Okagaki	"F-4"
1956	1505 Capital Ave.	James Schmeltzer	"F-1"
1956	5702 Old Sauk Road	Takeru Higuchi	
1956	5917 Old Middleton Road	Roger & Myrtle Fieldhouse	
1956	1509 Capital Ave.	Jack & Elizabeth Steinberg	"G-1"
1956	6219 Countryside Lane	Leon & Edith Isaksen	
1956	10 N. Rock Road	Eugene & Patricia King	
1956	14 N. Rock Road	Carl & Lila Carlson	
1956	1504 Capital Ave.	Perry & Jane Moss	"G"
1956	5817 Anchorage Ave.	Eugene & Mary Van Tamelen	First FLW Prefab I Model
1957	5809 Anchorage Ave.	Thomas & Rita Rausch	"F"
1957	5810 Anchorage Ave.	Herman & Charlotte Von Elba	"G"
1957	5806 Anchorage Ave.	Elmer & Nancy Meyer	"D"
1957	5818 Anchorage Ave.	Howard & Virginia Koop	"C"
1957	5806 Cable Ave.	Richard & Patricia Boelke	"C"
1958	1725 Heim Ave.	Quinton & Dorothy Kolb	"Faircrest"
1958	1709 Heim Ave.	Edmund & Edna O'Gara	"G"
1958	9 Veblen Place	Steve & Alice Varesi	
1958	17 Veblen Place	Robert & Martha Lewis	
1959	5705 Forsythia Place	Mrs. Lee B. Zeldin	"Fairmount"
1959	1 Veblen Place	Leslie & Barbara Fishel	"Faircrest"
1959	1406 West Skyline Drive	Charles & Elizabeth Curtis	"C"

Crestwood/Middleton *(continued)*

YEAR BUILT	ADDRESS	ORIGINAL OWNER/OCCUPANT	ARCHITECT/MODEL
1959	21 Veblen Place	John & Frances Kane	"D"
1959	5702 Anchorage Ave.	Bernard & Florence Waldman	"Shannon"
1960	5 Veblen Place	Silas & Betsy Johnson	"Jackson"
1961	13 Veblen Place	Norris & Alice Tibbetts	
1961	5910 Old Middleton Road	Phyllis Duckwitz	
1962	5905 Old Middleton Road	Thomas Conway	
1963	6801 Forest Glade Court	Raymond & Joyce Gloeckler	

Hammersley Road Area (South of Beltline)

YEAR BUILT	ADDRESS	ORIGINAL OWNER/OCCUPANT	ARCHITECT/MODEL
1951	5117 Loruth Terrace	William & Antoinette Wright	
1951	5118 Loruth Terrace	William & Mary Henthorn	
1951	1205 Loruth Terrace	James & Betty Motr	
1951	5105 Loruth Terrace	Glen & Joyce Clark	
1951	5113 Loruth Terrace		(Street Address Has Since Changed)
1951	5129 Loruth Terrace		(Street Address Has Since Changed)
1951	5426 Whitcombe Drive	Wallace & Helen Wilson	
1951	5513 Dorsett Drive	Harry & Mary Stroebe	
1951	4413 Boulder Terrace	Richard & Edith Meulenberg	(Model House)
1951	5505 Dorsett Drive	Neil & Jeanette Woodington	
1953	5505 Tolman Terrace	Paul & Nancy Okey	
1953	5609 Hammersley Road	Paul & Lilly Degne	
1954	5146 Loruth Terrace	James Lahey	"B-5"
1954	5901 Hammersley Road	Fred Hayden	
1954	5801 Hammersley Road	Frank & Jean Vaugh	
1954	5606 Barton Road	Louis & Eunice Bethke	
1954	5709 Tolman Terrace	Harvey & Louise Smith	
1954	5728 Dorset Drive	John & Loraine Desmond	
1956	5305 Raymond Road	Walter & Betty Hariu	
1956	5513 Raymond Road	Sherman & Martha Vinograd	"F" (Parade House)
1956	5313 Russet Road	Robert & Marie Mitchell	
1956	5310 Hammersley	Fred & Marianne Meixner	
1956	2109 Aspen	Lloyd & Marilyn Gleason	"Faircrest"
1958	5717 Crabapple Lane	Carl & Mary Kleinheinz	"A"
1960	5617 Hempstad Road	Dean & Greta Beck	(*Better Homes & Gardens* Model)
1961	5306 Barton Road	Peter & Pat Chinetti	
1961	5102 Dorsett Drive	Gordon & Carol Van Keuren	"Sherman"
1961	5205 Whitcombe Drive	James & Elaine Martin	"E"
1961	1702 S. Whitney Way	Earl & Lillian Marquardt	
1963	910 Hampshire Place	Marvin & Barbara Ebel	"Faircrest"
1964	5402 Tolman Terrace	Robert & Marva Graff	"Faircrest"
1964	5406 Tolman Terrace	Lloyd & Helen Rahm	

East Side/Monona

YEAR BUILT	ADDRESS	ORIGINAL OWNER/OCCUPANT	ARCHITECT/MODEL
1950	1949 E. Washington Ave.	Albert & Mildred Ness (2-Flat Apartment)	Edward Tough
1950	4213 Drexel Ave.	Charlene Whitcomb	
1951	5309 Tonyawatha Trail	Robert & Verna Doyle	
1953	34 Fuller Drive	Charles & Bess Anderes	
1953	6105 Bridge Road	George Young	
1953	3329 Quincy Ave.	Lloyd & Jean Lueptow	
1954	505 Moygara St.	Roland & Edith Diehl	"B-5"
1954	1649 Sunfield	Arthur & Charlene Kaltenberg	
1956	1908 Sherman Ave.	Collins & Bonnie Ferris	
1956	4706 Winnequah Road	William P. Lentz	
1956	5021 Spaanem Ave.	Vincent Brabender	
1956	6110 Winnequah Road	Phillip T. Drotning	
1956	6112 Winnequah Road	Phillip T. Drotning	
1958	5437 Esther Beach Road	Arnold & Irene Offerdahl	"D"
1958	5421 Esther Beach Road	Charles & Blanche Cornwell	"D"
1958-1959	Sherman Village	(100 Houses)	Harry Brody, Developer
	Delaware Blvd: 4722, 4718, 4714, 1201, 1205, 1209, 1213, 1217, 1221, 1225, 1301, 1302, 1305, 1306, 1309, 1310, 1313, 1317, 1314, 1318, 1401, 1402, 1405, 1406, 1409, 1410, 1413, 1414, 1417, 1418, 1421, 1422, 1426		
	Montana Circle: 1, 2, 3, 4, 5, 6, 7, 8		
	Wyoming Way: 1401, 1405, 1409, 1413, 1417		
	Monica Lane: 1102, 1106, 1110, 1114, 1118, 1122, 1126, 1202, 1206, 1210, 1214, 1218, 1222, 1226, 1230, 1234, 1301, 1302, 1305, 1306, 1309, 1310, 1313, 1314, 1317, 1320, 1321, 1325, 1328, 1329, 1332		
	Northland Drive: 1105, 1109, 1110, 1113, 1114, 1117, 1118, 1121, 1122, 1125, 1126, 1129, 1130, 1133, 1134, 1137, 1138		
	Mandrake Road: 4701, 4705, 4707, 4713, 4717, 4721		
1958	5429 Esther Beach Road	Russell & Joan Colvin	"B"
1959	5801 Winnequah Road	Jack Watts	"G"
1960	201 Acewood Blvd.	Donald & Joanne Brinkmeier	
1960	209 Crystal Lane	Donald & Anita Karnitz	
1960	105 Cameo Lane	John & Lucille Kotch	
1960	113 Cameo Lane	A. H. & Virginia Poggensee	
1960	125 Cameo Lane	Ralph & Martha Johnston	

Medical/Commercial

YEAR BUILT	ADDRESS	ORIGINAL OWNER/OCCUPANT	ARCHITECT/MODEL
1949	5117 University Ave.	Erdman & Associates Office and Factory	William Kaeser
1950	3320 University Ave.	Town & Country Furniture Store	(Demolished)
1950	5001 University Ave.	Fitzpatrick Lumber Co. Warehouse	William Kaeser
1950	702 Ruskin St.	Wheeler Transfer & Storage (Koschke Transfer)	Weiler & Strang
1950	3322 University Ave.	Avenue Cleaners	(Demolished)
1950	831 University Ave.	Choles Flower Shop	(Demolished)
1950	Monona Drive	Morningside Sanitarium	(Demolished)
1951	1 Gifford Pinochet Drive	Forest Products Testing Lab (Addition)	
1951	603 State Street	Brat House (State Street Brats)	
1952	Olbrich Park Shelter	City of Madison	(Demolished)
1952	Truax Air Force Base	Administration Building	(Demolished)
1953	Charmany Farms	University of Wisconsin	(Demolished)
1954	3414 Monroe St.	Heathcote & Moore, D.D.S. (Neckerman Agency) (First Medical Building)	
1954	1200 E. Washington Ave.	Risberg Shell Gas Station (Roadway Transmission)	
1954	5117 University Ave.	Erdman & Associates Factory	William Kaeser (Demolished)
1954	7549 Graber Road	Graber Office Building (Addition)	
1954	341 State St.	Lindsey's Shell Service Station	(Demolished)
1954	2047 Winnebago	WKOW Radio Station (Addition)	
1955	2701 Marshall Court, Doctors Park	Jacobs, D.D.S.	William Kaeser
1955	2705 Marshall Court, Doctors Park	Walker D.D.S., Washburn, M.D., Roisum, M.D.	William Kaeser
1955	2710 Marshall Court, Doctors Park	Schultz, M.D.	William Kaeser
1954	901 W. Beltline Highway	Howard Johnson's Restaurant	(Demolished)
1955	802 W. Washington Ave.	Avenue 66 Service Station	(Demolished)
1956	317 S. Park St.	Phil's Super Service Station	(Demolished)
1956	Waunakee	Marquis, M.D.	
1956	2713, 2715 Marshall Court, Doctors Park	Dieter, M.D., Greene, M.D., Norby, M.D.	
1956	411 W. Main St.	Murphy, Gavin, Stolper & Desmond (Wisconsin Division of Probation)	
1956	1300 S. Midvale Blvd.	Brookwood Shopping Center	Robert Brooks, Developer
1957	2716 Marshall Court, Doctors Park	Madison Radiation Betatron Center	(Demolished)
1957	2707, 2709, 2711 Marshall Court, Doctors Park	Liebl, M.D., Keepman, M.D., Kammer, D.D.S.	
1957	200 Eagle Heights Drive	UW Married Student Housing (9 Prefab Buildings/100 Apartments)	
1957	2700 Marshall Court, Doctors Park	Prescription Pharmacy	William Kaeser
1964	5510 Medical Circle	Westgate Dental Associates	
1965	5534 Medical Circle	Madison Psychiatric Assoc.	
1966	670 S. Whitney Way	Westgate Bank	
1967	5530 Medical Circle	Gaarder & Miller, M.D.	
1967	2727 Marshall Court, Doctors Park	Psychiatric Group, Inc.	
1967	2725 Marshall Court, Doctors Park	Carey, D.D.S., Peterson, D.D.S.	
1969	5714 Odana Road	Odana Medical Center	
1969	890 Wingra Drive	Dental Health Clinic	
1970	5520 Medical Circle	Periodontics Limited	
1970	2704 Marshall Court	Bone & Joint Surgery Associates	
1972	Waunakee	Karls, D.D.S., Labella, D.D.S.	
1974	Sun Prairie	Dean Medical Center	
1979	125 S. Webster	GEF III (State of Wisconsin)	
1979	Waunakee	Waunakee Community Medical Center	
1983	814 Atlas Ave.	Group Health Cooperative	
1985	7601 Murphy Drive	Group Health Cooperative	

YEAR BUILT	ADDRESS	ORIGINAL OWNER/OCCUPANT	ARCHITECT/MODEL
1985	1 S. Park St.	Group Health Cooperative	
1985	1025 Regent St.	Davis-Duehr Eye Clinic	
1986	49 Walbridge	Dental Health Associates of Madison	
1986	1106 John Nolen Drive	Turville Bay MRI Facility	
1986	1102 John Nolen Drive	Southern Wisconsin Radiotherapy Center	
1987	1313 Fish Hatchery Road	Dean Medical Center	
1992	202 S. Gammon Road	Dean Medical Center	
1992	890 Wingra Drive	Wingra Building Group	
1993	4030 E. Towne Blvd.	Dean Medical Center	
1995	610 N. Whitney Way	PSC Building (State of Wisconsin)	
2000	752 N. High Point Road	Dean West Clinic	
2003	4301 E. Buckeye Road	Dean East Clinic	

School/Church

YEAR BUILT	ADDRESS	ORIGINAL OWNER/OCCUPANT	ARCHITECT/MODEL
1950	900 University Bay Drive	Unitarian Meeting House	Frank Lloyd Wright
1952	McFarland	McFarland School	
1953	100 Nichols Road	Nichols Elementary School	
1954	Monona	Monona School	
1954	401 S. Owen Drive	Queen of Peace	Weiler & Strang
1956	3910 Mineral Point Road	Bethany Methodist Church	
1957	Highway 23, Spring Green	Wyoming Valley School	Frank Lloyd Wright
1958	6200 Monona Drive	Faith Baptist Church	Herb Fritz (First Prefab Church)
1959	4801 Waukesha St.	Velma Hamilton (Van Hise) School (Addition)	
1960	120 S. Rosa Road	Glenn Stephens Elementary School	(Last General Contracting Job)
1961	McKenna & Nichols roads	Monona Methodist Church	
1963	6101 University Ave.	Asbury Methodist Church Parsonage	
1976	Waunakee	Waunakee Junior High School (Addition)	

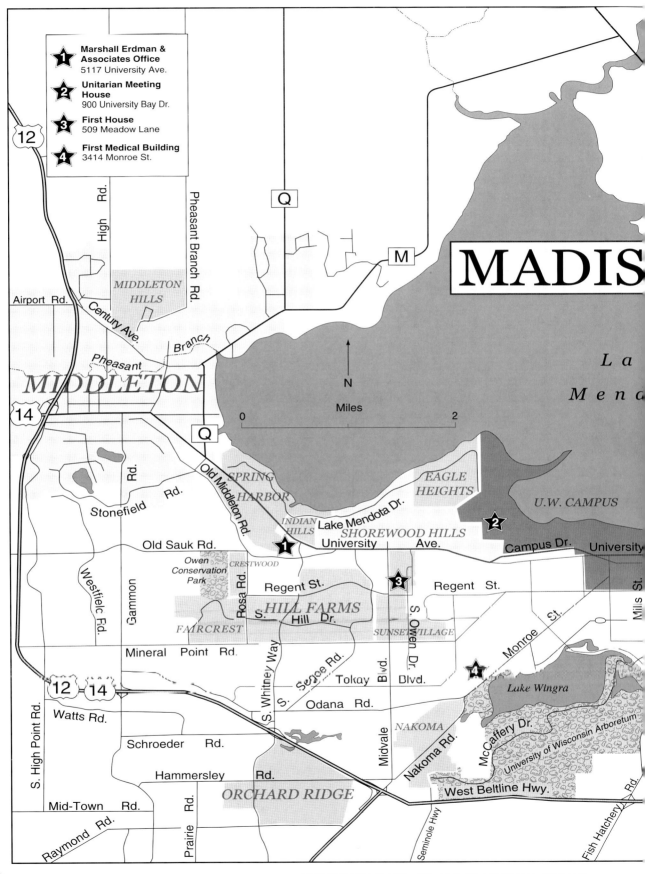

★1	**Marshall Erdman & Associates Office** 5117 University Ave.
★2	**Unitarian Meeting House** 900 University Bay Dr.
★3	**First House** 509 Meadow Lane
★4	**First Medical Building** 3414 Monroe St.

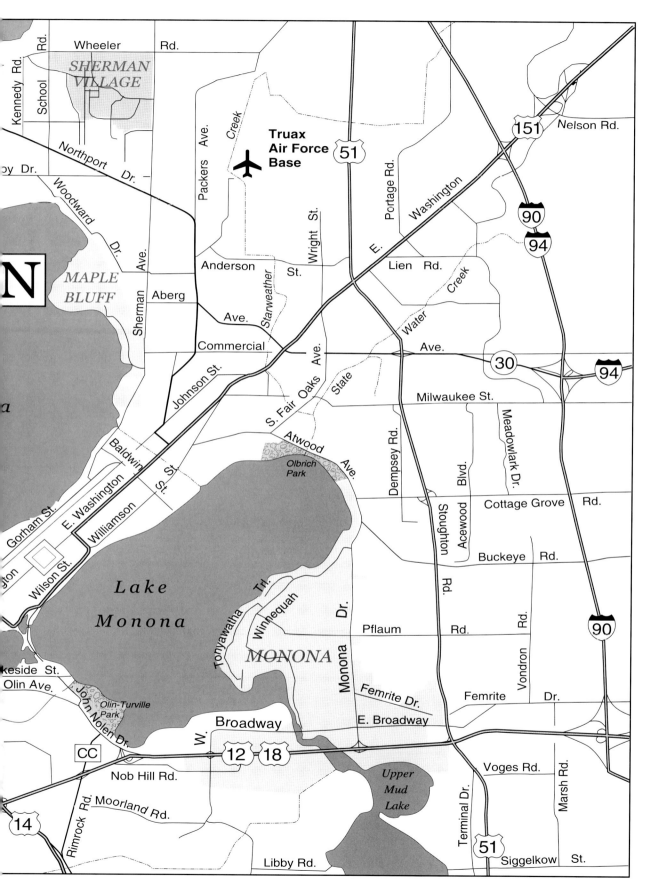

From 1953 to 1964, Erdman & Associates had more than one dozen prefab house models it built, in addition to the Frank Lloyd Wright models. Each one had numerous variations and options. Following are some of the Erdman models.

Faircrest

Fairhill

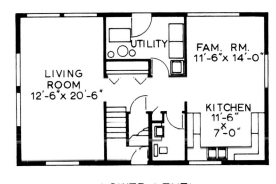

LOWER LEVEL

Greymount

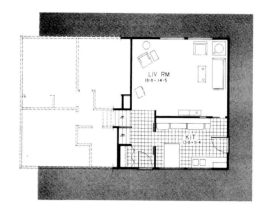

Jackson

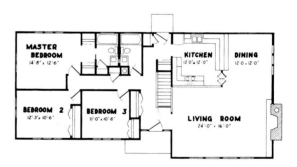

Shannon

Model A

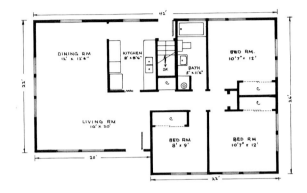

Model B

Model D

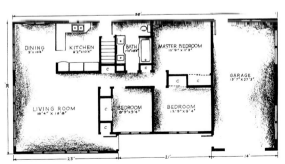

Model E

Model F

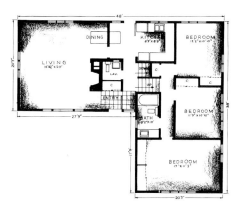

Model G

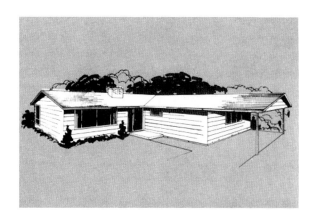

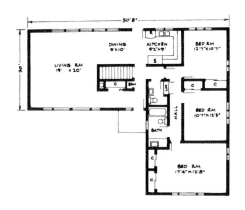

All photos and illustrations courtesy of Dan Erdman, except:

Cover and Page x: Photo by Brent Nicastro; Page 9: Courtesy *Wisconsin State Journal*, photo by Scott Seid; Page 12: Map by UW–Madison Cartographic Laboratory; Page 36: Courtesy the *Badger* yearbook, UW–Madison; Page 37: Courtesy the *Badger* yearbook, UW–Madison; Page 48: Photo by Ezra Stoller, ©Esto; Page 60: Courtesy Wisconsin Historical Society, WHi (N48) 5413, photo by John Newhouse; Page 61: Courtesy Frank Lloyd Wright Foundation, 5031.003, photo by Marilyn Hammes; Page 62: Courtesy Wisconsin Historical Society, WHi (x3) 46577, photo by John Newhouse; Page 66: Courtesy *Milwaukee Sentinel*, October 7, 1951, ©2003 Journal Sentinel Inc., reproduced with permission; Page 68: Courtesy Frank Lloyd Wright Foundation, 6820.003, photo by Michael A. Vaccaro; Page 70: Courtesy Wisconsin Historical Society, William Kaeser Collection, WHi-5075; Page 76: Courtesy *Life*; Page 87: Courtesy *House & Home*; Page 88: Courtesy *Milwaukee Journal*, March 23, 1958, photo by Donald Nusbaum, ©2003 Journal Sentinel Inc., reproduced with permission; Page 92: Courtesy Wisconsin Historical Society, WHi-5072, photo by William Wollin; Page 94: Courtesy *Wisconsin State Journal*; Page 95: Courtesy Wisconsin Historical Society, WHi-5069, photo by William Wollin; Page 99: Courtesy Wisconsin Historical Society, WHi-5071, photo by William Wollin; Pages 102-103: Courtesy Wisconsin Historical Society, *Milwaukee Journal* Collection, WHi-3146; Page 110: Courtesy Wisconsin Historical Society, WHi-5070, photo by William Wollin; Page 168: Courtesy *Wisconsin State Journal*; Page 181: Courtesy *The Capital Times*; Page 187: Photo by Skot Weidemann; Page 189: Photo by Brent Nicastro; Page 202: Courtesy Wisconsin Historical Society, WHi-5078, photo by John Newhouse; Page 212-213: Map by UW–Madison Cartographic Laboratory; Back cover of dust jacket: Photo by Zane Williams.